Behavioral Economics for Tourism

Perspectives on Business and Policy in the Travel Industry

Perspectives on Behavioral Economics and the Economics of Behavior

Behavioral Economics for Tourism

Perspectives on Business and Policy in the Travel Industry

Milena S. Nikolova
Founder and CEO, BehaviorSMART

Expert in Behavior-Smart Thinking in the Travel Industry

Series Editor

Morris Altman

ELSEVIER

ACADEMIC PRESS
An imprint of Elsevier

Academic Press is an imprint of Elsevier
125 London Wall, London EC2Y 5AS, United Kingdom
525 B Street, Suite 1650, San Diego, CA 92101, United States
50 Hampshire Street, 5th Floor, Cambridge, MA 02139, United States
The Boulevard, Langford Lane, Kidlington, Oxford OX5 1GB, United Kingdom

British Library Cataloguing-in-Publication Data
A catalogue record for this book is available from the British Library

Library of Congress Cataloging-in-Publication Data
A catalog record for this book is available from the Library of Congress

ISBN: 978-0-12-813808-3

For Information on all Academic Press publications
visit our website at https://www.elsevier.com/books-and-journals

Publisher: Candice Janco
Acquisitions Editor: Scott J. Bentley
Editorial Project Manager: Lindsay C. Lawrence
Production Project Manager: Maria Bernard
Cover Designer: Victoria Pearson

Typeset by MPS Limited, Chennai, India

Contents

About the author

Milena S. Nikolova is a researcher and expert in tourism. She received her PhD from The George Washington University School of Business and her MS in Psychology from the Sofia University in Bulgaria. She has 15 years of combined experience as academic educator and researcher at The George Washington University School of Business and the Department of Business at the American University in Bulgaria. Her profile combines academic background with practitioner experience as global expert who has worked with tourism businesses and institutions across four continents. Her research and professional interests focus on traveler psychology and behavioral tactics for tourism business and policy. She is a frequent speaker at tourism industry events on these topics. Currently, she is actively engaged in piloting innovation programs applying behavioral solutions for sustainability and market success for travel destinations.

Acknowledgments

This book is a key milestone in my professional journey shaped by many people who have supported and inspired me, as well as expanded my horizons. I cannot forget the assistance extended by the many colleagues and friends but I begin by recognizing the monumental support (and patience) of my family. My parents, Kamelia and Stefan, are the very foundation of who I am today both personally and professionally; and I do not have enough words to thank them for all their care, leading to the completion of this book and I am very sure that their support will continue in the future too. My husband Metodi and our three children Martina, Stefania, and Boyan will probably never forget the writing of this book. They patiently accepted the months, weeks, and days that I spent with the laptop, constantly ensuring them that "I am almost done." I am grateful that they remained supportive and helped me to successfully complete this project. Another important member of my family and my source of endless support is my sister Gergana who, in addition to being my closest person, is a colleague and my safe zone for crazy professional ideas that I would not share with anyone else.

There are many colleagues who have been the source of knowledge and insights that have influenced the way I see the dynamics in the global travel ecosystem, and the ways in which human behavior explains them. I would like to mention some of them. The two people from whom I have learned the most about tourism are Hannah Messerli and Iain Christie. Hannah and I have occasionally collaborated on different professional projects since 2004, when we first met. Over the years, she remained a mentor and one of my biggest supporters in key moments of my career. She has taught me a great deal about tourism and economic development. Iain Christie is the first person I ever heard to talk about the need to involve sociologists in the planning and management of tourism because of the importance of the human factor. At the end of his active career as a leading tourism expert at the World Bank, He began teaching at the George Washington University School of Business where I was working on my PhD. He was my professor in Tourism Planning during the second year of my program but I actually learned from him much more later when I co-taught Tourism Planning and Tourism Economics with him. The wealth of field stories, examples, and professional discussions that he shared while we prepared lectures and designed assignments, are the best school I could ever hope for. Throughout the years of working in economic development, I have worked with a lot of colleagues who kept enriching my knowledge and my thinking about how to make sustainable tourism development work well.

In the most recent years, I had the opportunity to interact and work with many successful entrepreneurs, destination professionals, and industry leaders. Working with the Adventure Travel Trade Association shifted my focus from big picture tourism development projects and immersed me in the daily realities of tourism businesses and tourism destinations. I gained much better understanding of the challenges of making tourism work well on the level of the individual service provider or the local destination management organization. Again two people from the industry community stand out as a source of knowledge and insights that I feel have enriched my own perspectives are Shannon Stowell and Christopher Doyle. Shannon is one of the most inspiring industry leaders I have collaborated with. His soft way of sharing thoughts and opinions about complicated challenges in our industry made every dialog we have had exceptional. Chris and his ability to see important dynamics that will be shaping or disrupting the tourism industry in the future are extraordinary. The many crazy discussions we have had about the different paths that are possible for our sector after today's crises have pushed my thinking and inspired my own imagination.

Without mentioning specific names, I want to recognize few of my fantastic friends and colleagues from the industry who have been a dream audience at the sessions and talks that I have delivered on behavioral economics. It was one of them who told me after one of my lectures that she foresees me as an author of a book on this topic. This was the first time the idea of writing was planted in my mind.

I want to acknowledge two more colleagues who helped me to believe in the value of the behavior-smart thinking for our industry realities. Åsa Stanaway from Västmanland Tourism was the first tourism board professional who approached me with interest in experimenting with behavioral approaches on destination level. The project that is described at the end of this book was the very first demonstration of the practical power of behavioral thinking. The second person who supported my beliefs that behavioral economic can bring great value to industry realities was the experienced sustainable tourism professional Bård Jervan.

In conclusion, I express my deepest gratitude to the people who helped to make this book a reality. One of the most talented students I have had is Darya Yanitskaya, an illustrator who helped to visualize some of the concepts and ideas throughout the text. I thank the Elsevier team and especially the two editors who worked with me on this project—Katerina Zaliva and Lindsay Lawrence. Bearing with my numerous delays, the guidance, the support, and the extraordinary patience that the two of them provided throughout this project is amazing. I owe the fact that this book is a reality to them just as much as all others mentioned in this section.

Milena S. Nikolova

Introduction: Behavioral economics: the economics of every day

Why this book?

Tourism is one of the largest industries of the global economy. It contributes 10% to the global GDP and is responsible for one in every 10 jobs around the world. Currently more than 1.2 billion people embark on an international trip each year, and their number is expected to approach 2 billion by year 2030 (WTTC, 2017). In many countries, tourism is the leading economic sector generating the main share of exports and employment.

In addition to being a driver of economic growth, tourism can be vehicle for enhancing social benefits and sustainable management of natural and cultural assets. Countries that host more visitors are able to collect more taxes and reinvest them in the betterment of infrastructure and public services that improve the quality of the living for local residents. The promotion of nature-based experiences and cultural attractions generates funds for their maintenance and proper preservation. Better-traveled people are also generally more knowledgeable and tolerant to different cultures and lifestyles (Gustafson, 2009). Communities hosting tourist experiences retain more pride in their heritage and are more likely to preserve and pass on traditions to the next generations (Besculides, Lee, & Mccormick, 2002). Thus tourism is also seen as having power to promote peace and intercultural tolerance (Becken & Carmignani, 2016; Farmaki, 2017).

With its scale, however, tourism also holds potential for causing significant harm. The growing presence of tourists at many popular destinations has overwhelmed residents, triggering antitourist movements. *Overtourism* is becoming a widely used term to describe tourism growth that goes beyond what an area can handle without distortion of its everyday life or its familiar setting. Increased numbers of arrivals means more planes, trains, or cruise ships, which produces more environmental and noise pollution. The simultaneous presence of large numbers of people in towns or around attractions means a larger footprint and limited ability to mindfully enjoy the surroundings. Destinations seeing growing tourist flows have experienced crises with increasing amounts of waste that overwhelm collection systems and cause pollution. Tourism has also been associated with increased levels of crime and with deteriorated quality of community life (Dyer, Gursoy, Sharma, & Carter, 2007). Places that have experienced a tourism gold rush have also seen more businesses that violate local regulations or development plans to expand quickly (Peterson & McCarthy, 1990) and benefit from immediate profits.

There is no need to continue the list of benefits or harms to make the point that tourism produces powerful impacts that need to be managed in ways that stimulate the positive and suppress the negative. This book offers a way of thinking that aims at doing precisely that. By linking contemporary thinking about the travel industry with insights from the relatively young knowledge field of behavioral economics, it offers enhanced analyses of some of the main challenges and leads to potentially more effective solutions.

Why tourism needs behavioral economics thinking

Three short stories discussed later illustrate how taking a behavioral perspective provides a richer and more realistic explanation to the phenomena associated with typical challenges in the tourism industry.

Story 1: The traveler

John and Mary are busy professionals in their mid-50s and are residents of a metropolis in a well-developed country. Well educated and with successful careers, the couple enjoys a solid income and a comfortable life. Travel is part of their lifestyle and a favorite way of spending time off work with close friends. They regularly go on weekend trips, and once or twice a year, they take a 7- to 10-day journey to a different country to explore new cultures and landscapes. How do they choose their next destination? John and Mary are adventurous and willing to discover new places but are considerably conservative in terms of safety. Their rule of thumb is to choose places that someone in their social circle has visited recently and recommends as safe. Last year Mary came across an article in Outdoors magazine on the cultural and natural wealth of the Balkans region. It prompted her to suggest that they plan their next holiday there, but the couple eventually gave up the idea, as nobody they knew had travel experience in this part of Europe.

John and Mary represent the typical active travelers who are eager explorers and willing spenders. With passion for travel and a high disposable income, they are the dream visitors for many countries promoting tourism. Given the importance that John and Mary place on safety, one would think that their consideration of this factor would be systematic and reliable. As the story shows, however, their decisions about what countries to visit or avoid are quite biased and therefore limited. They are influenced by information that is immediately accessible (availability bias) and by the safety of following the choices made by others (social conformity). In purely objective terms, easily available information and the experience of single individuals are not reliable measures of a destination's safety. Moreover with little effort John and Mary can access objective safety indices that rank countries on the basis of reliable data, but they simply do not do it.

This example illustrates how a behavioral lens offers deeper understanding of the decision-making journey travelers make and explains why some countries struggle with overcoming bad reputations despite the lack of objective justifications. It also identifies the potential errors that people are likely to make when assessing the risk of undertaking a trip to another country. In fact objective safety indices frequently rank Balkan countries as much safer than the Unites States, United Kingdom, or Belgium, but that has less impact on traveler perceptions than individual stories and even immediately accessible information. In such context a behavioral perspective can help destination managers understand the real source of their image problems and lead them to tactics that bring risk perceptions of travelers closer to objective realities. It can also help agencies responsible for traveler safety identify likely errors in traveler judgment and apply tools that minimize or offset them.

Story 2: The government official

Mr. Smith celebrated his fifth year as head of the tourism promotion agency. During his years in office, the sector has been enjoying steady growth, but the new minister expressed a desire to see more impressive numbers next year. To fulfill this expectation, Mr. Smith has sketched out a plan that can boost the number of international arrivals for next year. He negotiated with the two biggest tour operators responsible for arrivals from the leading source markets that they will be subsidized with direct payments for each foreign arrival in the next season. Subsidies, he knows, will motivate the tour operators to promote shorter-term packages in the destination but to more people, thus boosting arrival numbers. Given the secure profit generated from the direct payments, the tour operators will be motivated to cut their margins and lower prices to draw larger numbers of value-oriented tourists who choose their holiday destination mainly on the basis of low price.

The story with Mr. Smith is a simple illustration of several failures that fuel some of the biggest challenges of tourism policy today. The dominant failure is the overwhelming use of arrival numbers as the main indicator measuring a country's tourism sector health. In reality the number of tourists entering a country does not reveal much about the economic performance of the sector without accounting for length of stay and spending. Focusing on arrivals alone means equalizing the impact of a visitor from a neighboring country crossing the border by car to enjoy a picnic (bringing their own food) in the mountains and returning home after that, and a tourist who arrives by plane for a 10-day trip around the country visiting different places and spending on local attractions and services. By choosing to focus on arrivals alone, Mr. Smith encourages the type of growth that has led to overtourism in many places. It also prompts him to extend incentives that not only distort competition but also decrease the economic impact of the sector by attracting more price sensitive visitors who use the country's tourism assets but spend less (if anything) in the local economy.

Applying a behavioral lens to this story helps us to understand that politics often tempt tourism policy makers to perceive and manage tourism growth by short-term measurements rather than by meeting more meaningful, long-term objectives. This makes the choice of success indicators critical, as they essentially shape the incentives and barriers that explain the behavior of market players. Incentivizing growth in pure arrival numbers encourages policy makers to resort to tools such as subsidies that distort market dynamics and suppress positive impacts. In many cases, subsidies are collected by foreign operators and airlines that then report profits in other countries.

Thanks to subsidies, travel industry agencies are ready to cut margins and lower prices to stimulate sales, thereby practically stealing market share from unsubsidized competitors. Bringing many low-spending tourists involves high opportunity costs, because capacities are unavailable for other visitors who are likely to stay and spend more. Lower spending also translates to lower profits and lower taxes collected by government, which means that on one hand Mr. Smith is spending public funds on subsidies and on the other is pushing potential tax revenues down, which places government at a double loss.

A behavioral point of view explains why it is natural for Mr. Smith to pursue the actions he does and to be motivated by the short-term need to impress his minister rather than the long-term need to achieve sustainable growth in the tourism sector (hyperbolic discounting). In such cases behavioral thinking can help to provide additional insights into tourism policy and development failures. Understanding incentives and barriers that influence the choices of policy makers and behaviors of market players is critical for policy design that can help eliminate or minimize some of the institutional challenges the tourism sectors faces.

Story 3: The tourism business

Mrs. Jones is the owner of a family hotel in a small mountain resort. Most of her guests are attracted by snow sports in the area and visit during the winter. The shrinking winter season and uneven snowfall in the last several years has motivated her to plan some improvements that will make her hotel attractive for guests during the warmer months too. She was hoping that she would be able to execute her plans this summer, but the exceptionally warm winter made the past season less profitable. Mrs. Jones is convinced that the upcoming winter will be much colder with more snow, which will translate into more guests and more profit so she can reinvest in improvements. She has considered taking out a loan but does not qualify for one. Because hotels pay taxes on the basis of reported nights spent by guests, Mrs. Jones has found it practical to save from taxes by underreporting the number of guests she receives. As a result, formal records show her business to be much less profitable and less reliable as loan candidate.

The story with Mrs. Jones is an illustration of the errors and inefficient choices made by many businesses in the tourism industry. Some of these are linked to missed opportunities for better profitability, but others, such as misreporting numbers, are linked to issues with major implications, such as distorted statistics measuring sector performance.

The business decisions of Mrs. Jones are influenced by typical biases. On one hand, she relies on a better upcoming season, despite the fact that the overall trend is one of shorter winters. Her expectation that a better season will follow a poor one is not supported by scientific evidence but serves as grounds for her preference to wait with making investments that are likely to have extended her profitable season (optimism bias and representativeness bias). Mrs. Jones is also unable to benefit from a loan due to erroneous focus on avoiding taxes by underreporting the number of guests she receives. In reality reporting correctly and paying taxes is likely to enable her to benefit from a favorable loan that will help her grow her profits by much more than she is saving by hiding taxes (mental accounting). This story also explains why the design of tourism data collection systems is so important and should be developed alongside behavioral considerations as well. Collecting arrival or nights spent numbers from hoteliers while using them for tax purposes at the same time creates incentives for misreporting. This is why in many countries' official statistics do not reflect actual volumes and growth dynamics, making it hard to assess impacts and design working policies.

These three simple stories illustrate just some of the additional insights and new dimensions that behavioral economics can offer in tourism. A behavioral outlook to some of the biggest challenges and opportunities in the travel industry can help us understand the challenges and unfold the power for good of this important global sector. This book supports the idea that behavioral thinking is not only beneficial but also will be needed more in tourism. As this text reveals later, some long-term socioeconomic trends are shaping an environment in which insights from behavioral economics will become more relevant.

How this book is organized

This book takes readers on a journey revealing the complexities of today's travel sector analyzed through a behavioral lens. Chapter 1, Primer on Behavioral Economics, offers an introduction to behavioral economics summarizing some of the key concepts and philosophies that characterize this know area of knowledge. A set of 10 short case studies presents examples for effective application of behavior-smart thinking to business, policy, and social solutions. Chapter 2, Tourism and Traditional Thinking, introduces the principles and assumptions that have shaped traditional thinking in tourism. It offers behavioral insights on why the sector is faced with some of the big challenges today. Chapter 3, Tourism of the (Near) Future: Growing, Faster, On-The-Go, builds on the traditional perspectives and discusses how some of the major socioeconomic trends reshaping the future of travel are making behavior-smart thinking more needed and relevant. Chapter 4, Behavior-Smart Thinking for Destinations, and Chapter 5, Behavior-Smart Thinking for Tourism Companies, offer a deep dive into the application of behavioral economics in day-to-day operations of destinations and individual operators. The final chapter offers a set of 10 stories that demonstrate how behavior-smart thinking can work in tourism and can help optimize both sustainability and commercial operations.

References

Becken, S., & Carmignani, F. (2016). Does tourism lead to peace? *Annals of Tourism Research*, *61*, 63–79. Available from https://doi.org/10.1016/j.annals.2016.09.002.

Besculides, A., Lee, M. E., & Mccormick, P. J. (2002). Residents' perceptions of the cultural benefits of tourism. *Annals of Tourism Research*, *29*(2), 303–319. Retrieved from <www.elsevier.com/locate/atoures>.

Dyer, P., Gursoy, D., Sharma, B., & Carter, J. (2007). Structural modeling of resident perceptions of tourism and associated development on the Sunshine Coast, Australia. *Tourism Management*, *28*, 409–422. Available from https://doi.org/10.1016/j.tourman.2006.04.002.

Farmaki, A. (2017). The tourism and peace nexus. *Tourism Management*, *59*, 528–540. Available from https://doi.org/10.1016/j.tourman.2016.09.012.

Gustafson, P. (2009). More cosmopolitan, no less local: The orientations of international travellers. *European Societies*, *11*(1), 25–47. Available from https://doi.org/10.1080/14616690802209689.

Peterson, C. A., & McCarthy, C. (1990). Greece tackles overbuilding in tourist areas. *Environmental Conservation*, *17*(2), 166–168. Retrieved from <https://www.cabdirect.org/cabdirect/abstract/19901883524>.

WTTC. (2017).*Travel & amp; Tourism Economic Impact 2017 World*. Retrieved from <https://www.wttc.org/-/media/files/reports/economic-impact-research/regions-2017/world2017.pdf>.

Chapter 1

Primer on behavioral economics

I view behavioral economics to be economics that is based on realistic assumptions and descriptions of human behavior. It is just economics with more explanatory power because the models are a better fit with the data.

Richard Thaler (2017), Nobel Prize Laureate.

Chapter Outline

Brief overview

So… what is behavioral economics?

Behavioral economics is a relatively new field that offers a psychological lens to explain decisions and behaviors people engage in across different socioeconomic contexts. By marrying insights from psychology with knowledge in economics, law, political science, and business, behavioral economics has enabled deeper understanding of why, in many different situations, people make choices that are not most beneficial and are even harmful. The fact that people often deviate from choosing the best available option and

Behavioral Economics for Tourism. DOI: https://doi.org/10.1016/B978-0-12-813808-3.00001-0

engage in seemingly irrational behavior contradicts assumptions at the core of contemporary economic arrangements, legal systems, policy design principles and even business models, most of which have been informed by traditional economic thinking.

At the core of traditional (prebehavioral) economic thinking is the belief that we, as decision makers, seek to make optimal choices that will yield the most benefits on the basis of full rationality, selfishness, and tastes that remain stable over time (Kahneman, 2011, p. 269). Part of this assumption is that every time one faces a choice, they identify all the information they can access, analyze it rigorously, and select the best option. This assumption has been considered applicable to various contexts: consumer context, when people make decisions about whether to pay more for certain brands or select generic products; traveler context, when one decides on their next holiday destination and how much they are willing to spend; political context, when citizens decide which candidates to support; social context, when people make decisions about whether to contribute to charitable organizations or spend on nicer accessories; legal context, when jury members decide on fair punishments for a criminal offences, etc. In many ways, the systems in our society are constructed around the assumption that across all these contexts, the decision maker is seeking to make the impartially optimal choice or the one that would seem like the *common sense* choice.

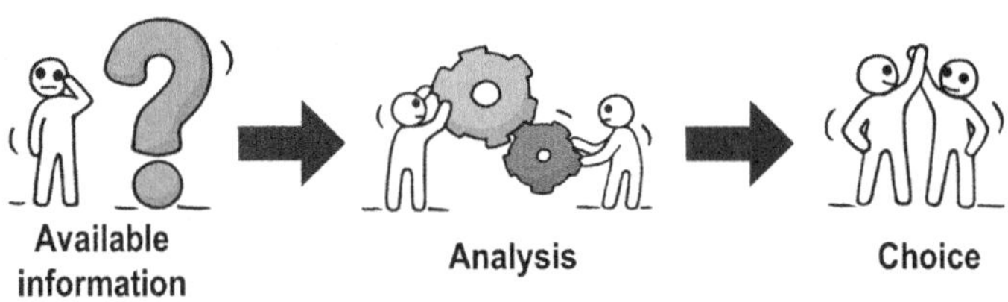

How our decisions contradict the norms for common sense

This section illustrates three fundamental domains that demonstrate the mismatch between behavioral principles and systems design in contemporary society.

Money and the financial system

One of the domains where behavioral economics has made most progress in pointing at failures of traditional (prebehavioral) economic thinking is the area of finance. Popular illustrations on the topic are the grave consequences of grounding retirement saving systems on the assumption that people are able and willing "to calculate how much they are going to earn over the rest of their lifetime, figure out how much they will need when they retire, and then save up enough to enjoy a comfortable retirement without sacrificing too much while they are still working" (Thaler & Sunstein, 2009, p. 113).

Because in reality, people are more focused on current wants (O'Donoghue & Rabin, 1999) and poor at forecasting future needs or imagining the future (Hershfield, 2011; Hershfield et al., 2011), and they under-save or do not save at all for their retirement years. This creates a complicated social problem, associated with low levels of happiness and high social cost. Behavioral sciences have helped generate a realistic analysis of the problem, guiding us to understand the mechanisms that lead people to make retirement and saving choices that seem unwise and are in fact harmful. This has served as solid ground for the development of a contemporary model for retirement policy, which has been executed successfully (see cases at the end of this chapter).

People also make money-related errors on much smaller but frequent scale. Dan Ariely has devoted his most recent book to irrationalities associated with money (Ariely, 2017), outlining many everyday situations in which people deviate from *common sense*. Treating one and the same price in different ways depending on its context is a simple example. As he discusses in context of the low-price strategy of JCPenney, consumers respond differently if the price tag of a shirt states "$20.00" or if it states "$20.00, down from $25.00" with the second option being more appealing. An explanation for this is the power of relativity, which demonstrates that in many situations, consumers have a hard time judging whether a price is relevant and good on its own, so they look for a comparison that will give them an indication. Using mark-downs is an effective way to provide immediate reference and focus consumer evaluation of the price around a gain. These are only two illustrations of the types of money-related choices behavioral economists seek to understand to reveal the misalignment of business and policy models.

Health and the safety system

A series of studies on the leading causes of death in the United States reveals a shocking trend: A disturbingly high share of deaths can be attributed to bad decisions. The analysis of Keeney (2008) demonstrates that a disproportionately high share of deaths (45%) can be traced to poor decisions made by the deceased that either directly lead to or facilitated the end of their life. Given that Keeney's study was published in 2008, this rate has probably increased further by today. Shockingly, findings in Keeney's research indicate that the impact of bad decision making has increased with time. While in 1900 only 5% of deaths could be linked to poor decisions, in 1950, deaths linked to bad decision making increased to 20%–25%, and nearly 60 years later, the share had become 45%. An in-depth analysis shows that for groups within ages 15–64, the percentage rises to 54%–59%. As the author states these deaths were "avoidable by readily available personal choices." This sad truth is also established by McGinnis and Foege (1993), who study the leading causes of death in the United States in 1990 and established that they all can be linked back to poor decisions: tobacco, drinking, poor dieting, and exercising. A decade later, Mokdad and colleagues raised alarm that the share of deaths attributable to these causes is increasing, and they emphasized the need for policy and healthcare solutions that focus on prevention (Mokdad, Marks, Stroup, & Gerberding, 2004).

In essence, this also contradicts the idea that with enough opportunity and information, people always make the optimal decision. For example, with time, the advance of medicine, and scientific research, we know as a fact that smoking, drinking, poor diet, and lack of exercise lead to serious health conditions and death. Yet studies, including the ones cited above, show that with time, these behavioral decisions increase and lead to more deaths.

In addition to failing at optimal choice selection in long-term contexts, people seem inclined to easily accept life risks in the short term too. In his introduction to *The Behavioral Economics Guide 2015*, Ariely (2015a) uses texting while driving as one simple illustration of bad decisions that do not comply with traditional economic models for rational choice and utility maximization. Most individuals that engage in such behavior have enough information to know how dangerous it can be to text or use your phone in other ways while driving but still do it, influenced by overconfidence bias (e.g., I can text and drive, as I am a more skilled driver than the people who get into car crashes while texting) and present bias (e.g., it is more important to me to send this text to my friends right now than wait until I get to my final destination). This illustration explains the failures of decision making that lead to bad outcomes regardless of education, intelligence, and mental capabilities.

Legislation and the legal system

The past two decades have shown a rise in psychological research that contradicts our beliefs about perceptions and memory. The term "invisible gorilla" has become a symbol of the redefined limitations of human perceptions. In one of the most popular experiments on perception, Christopher Chabris and Dan Simons demonstrate that focusing one's attention on a specific task leads to "inattentional blindness," or missing of an obvious but unexpected object, despite it being right in front of one's eyes (Chabris & Simons, 2010, p. 6). In many contexts of everyday life, this phenomenon does not have dangerous consequences, but in others it has led to grave developments. As the opening story in Chabris and Simons' book *The Invisible Gorilla* (2010) reveals, within legal context, what one has noticed can be basis for key eyewitness testimonies shaping verdicts. Evidence subject to inattentional blindness poses serious risks on personal lives and the fairness of the judicial system, as it leads to unjust verdicts and unpunished wrongdoing. An academic discussion seeking explanation for the unexpected economic crash in 2008 has also proposed inattentional blindness as viable explanation (Coyle, 2011).

Research on memory has also produced findings that have serious implications for the effectiveness of legal systems. One of the most recognized scientists in the field of memory, Elizabeth Loftus, has focused much of her research on the malleability of human memory and phenomena such as memory contamination and fake memories (for an overview of her work, see Loftus, 2016). Many of the experiments and cases covered in her work establish that events occurring after a certain experience can modify how people remember it and can lead to the so-called misinformation effect (Loftus & Hoffman, 1989); or that fake recollections of events that never occurred can be planted in one's mind to feel as genuine as real events they have experienced (Bernstein & Loftus, 2009; Loftus, 2007). Misremembering and reporting fake memories as genuine have fewer implications when memories are incorporated in a fun story shared with friends but pose serious threats when the memories become key evidence in a legal trial. Legal trials are heavily influenced by the availability of eyewitnesses, and as Loftus herself has found, such availability has dramatic effect on the certainty with which jurors declare a verdict compared with the same criminal scenario without an eyewitness, even if the eyewitness is formally described as one with poor vision (Loftus, 2016).

In addition to these phenomena, which mostly relate to unconscious effects, science has revealed behavioral specifics, which create legal system failures related to wrong assumptions about conscious choices. Dervan & Edkins (2013) have studied the innocent defendant's dilemma and exposed what they describe as the plea bargaining's innocence problem, which refers to the many legal cases in which innocent defendants have pleaded guilty under plea bargaining procedures despite their innocence. In addition to analyzing real legal cases, the researchers set up an experiment that engages students in solving logic tests as part of a psychological study and subjects them to fake accusations of cheating. Students accused of cheating are presented with two options: (1) admitting guilt and losing the promised payment for participating in the psychological study but avoiding a trial before the Academic Review Board or (2) proceeding to the Review Board and risking losing the trial, which would mean loss of compensation, informing of the faculty advisor, and required enrollment in an ethics course. The surprising results revealed that more than half of the innocent students were willing to admit guilt and eliminate the risk of potentially losing the trial (Dervan and Edkins, 2013).

As the examples from these three fundamental domains in life—money, health, and justice—demonstrate, our contemporary socioeconomic realities hide a lot of imperfections that stem from incorrect behavioral assumptions. Ariely (2015) describes these imperfections as "design challenges" in our society systems, which are grounded on the assumption that people have limitless cognitive capacity and make logical decisions without emotional interferences. Sunstein (2014) points that in some service contexts, free markets actually reward exploitation of human errors and create settings in which they are encouraged (p. 11). With the advance of behavioral economics, there is an opportunity to recognize these challenges. Designs in markets and societies can be moved to align with the realities of human behavior and to redefine what is *common sense*.

History of behavioral economics

The story and key names in the field

Behavioral economics is a new field of study. Its true contemporary popularity began rising after 2002 when psychologist Daniel Kahneman was awarded the Nobel Prize in Economics for bringing psychology into the field of economics. Awareness on the field was further fueled by the 2008 financial crisis, which prompted Alan Greenspan to state in front of the US Congress that he was shocked that some of the key assumptions at the heart of economic policy did not hold true (Ariely, 2009; Greenspan, 2008). Another important milestone was realized in 2010 with the establishment of a formal behavioral economics unit informing policy design by the then prime minister of the UK David Cameron. The unit, called the Behavioral Insights Team (BIT), began producing and suggesting effective policy design tweaks that led to impressive success in domains where traditional approaches were both extremely expensive and ineffective (Halpern, 2015, p. 4). The findings and successes of BIT fueled interest in behavioral economics, which was further stimulated by a series of books published on the topic, such as *Nudge* by Richard Thaler and Cass Sunstein (2009), David Kahneman's *Thinking Fast and Slow* (2011), and Dan Ariely's trilogy *Predictably Irrational* (2009), *The Upside of Rationality* (2010), and *The (Honest) Truth About Dishonesty* (2012). Awareness of the opportunities revealed by this new field were further fueled by the popularity of the National Geographic TV show *Brain Games* and by Dan Ariely's (Dis) Honesty Project and documentary on dishonesty (Ariely & Melamede, 2015). Two recent Nobel Prizes in Economics, awarded to Shiller in 2013 and Thaler in 2017, further reinforced the importance of the knowledge generated by behavioral economists.

As in many other fields of knowledge, pinpointing the specific date when behavioral economics was born is difficult. There are hints about behavioral thinking that can be traced back to an essay written by Daniel Bernoulli and published in 1738 (Bernoulli, 1954) in which he discusses the psychological value (or happiness) that one amount of money can evoke, depending on the initial wealth of the recipient. The principle is referred to as diminishing sensitivity and is illustrated by the insight that gaining $100 would evoke much stronger sense of value in someone who has no wealth compared with another person who is wealthy and for whom this gain might go unnoticed. The novelty in Bernoulli's work, which is still frequently cited in economics, is in the focus on the *sense of value* or happiness that is determined not by the amount of monetary gain itself but by the *psychological response* to that amount. Bernoulli also makes observations about human dislike of risk, which motivates the work by Kahneman and Tversky (1979) on decision making under uncertainty. The two authors have found inspiration also in the work of psychologist and mystic Gustav Fechner, who lived and worked in the 19th century (1801–87) and whose work builds on Bernoulli's work by studying the relationship between psychological value and the strengths of the stimuli. His work later became the foundation of what is known today as the Weber-Fechner Law on the *just noticeable difference*, which is actively utilized in psychology and consumer behavior literature. It posits that the just noticeable difference in any change is proportional to the starting magnitude of the variable.

How does just noticeable difference apply in real market context?

People's response to change depends on the starting amount. This means that a change of a few cents in the price of a $4.50 cappuccino will likely go unnoticed by most customers, but a change of $1.00 will be above the just noticeable difference threshold and will be obvious to consumers.

The same mechanism explains why consumers treat one and the same amount of price savings differently depending on the original price of the product they are buying: when shopping for a $25 t-shirt, they are more likely to invest extra time and effort to walk to a further store where they can buy it for $10 less but are unlikely to initiate this extra effort to save $10 if they are buying a $625 suit.

In recent times, Herbert Simon has been identified as the true father of behavioral economics. Simons is a recipient of the 1978 Nobel Prize in Economics for his pioneering work on decision making within organizations. In his work, starting in the late 1940s, he questions the understanding for perfect rationality in the firm, which is at the core of economic thinking about the behavior of companies and organizations. In his work he proposes a new term, *bounded rationality*, suggesting that rationality needs to be viewed in the context of circumstances and certain conditions, and that decision making is characterized not by utility maximization but by *satisficing* (i.e., meeting the condition of being "good enough" given the respective context; Simon, 1948). The work of Simon is continued by his colleagues at Carnegie Mellon University, most notably George Loewenstein. Carnegie Mellon University is known as one of the knowledge centers in the behavioral economics field today and recently became the first university to launch undergraduate and doctoral programs specifically focused on behavioral economics.

A significant share of knowledge in the behavioral economics domain is attributed to Daniel Kahneman and Amor Tversky. These two psychologists had begun their collaboration at the Hebrew University in Israel and later continued working in the United States. Kahneman and Tversky started their active research on decision making in the 1970s. Their initial work had been focused in the field of psychology, but some of their pioneering work had been published in the leading economic journal of their time, *Econometrica* (Kahneman & Tversky, 1979).

As Kahneman later explains in his book, *Thinking, Fast and Slow*, the choice to publish their fundamental piece on *Prospect Theory* in *Econometrica* was not motivated by the topic of economics but by the fact that this journal happened to be a prime outlet for decision-making literature at the time (Kahneman, 2011). The choice of the journal later turned out to be critical for the article's impact and today it is one of the most cited articles in the social sciences. In their essay on *Prospect Theory*, Kahneman and Tversky challenge the alignment of the more commonly accepted utility theory with reality-based, decision-making behavior. They build on Bernoulli's work on diminishing utility of wealth and propose a change in the perspective toward wealth and utility that Thaler (2015a) describes as "radical" (p. 30). The proposition is that the value of wealth is experienced not based on the amount of wealth itself but by *changes* in this amount, and more precisely, by the direction of each change. Here is an example that Kahneman uses to illustrate the core idea:

> *Imagine that today Jack and Jill each have a wealth of $5 million. Yesterday, Jack had $1 million, so he gained $4 million to get to his current wealth level. Jill's fortune yesterday was $9 million, so she lost $4 million, which brought her to her current wealth level.*
>
> Kahneman (2011, p. 275)

Based on expected utility theory, both Jack and Jill should be equally happy, as their wealth levels are equal. However, the direction of the changes that led to these levels and the reference point (i.e., the original starting wealth) suggest that they are not. As part of the prospect theory, Kahneman and Tversky formulate another key term in behavioral economics—loss aversion. They find that people are likely to respond differently to the same amount of money depending on whether it is perceived as loss or a gain. Because people are inclined to be more active in preventing losses than in realizing gains, they might not be tempted to engage in a gamble if they have the opportunity to earn $500 but will likely enter in the gamble if it might prevent losing $500 they currently have.

Prospect theory

Prospect theory reveals that when faced with uncertainty and risk people choose on the basis of a reference point (e.g., their current wealth) and treat potential gains and losses differently. For example, if Peter is granted 100$ and then he is offered the chance to gamble to win another $100, there is higher certainty that he will opt out of the gamble and happily keep the earned $100. However, if he is handed $200 and told that he has the choice between voluntarily returning $100 (and keeping the other $100) or gamble to keep all $200, he is likelier to enter in the gamble.

In both cases Peter can end up with the same earning of $100 but in the first case, he perceives the second $100 as a gain while in the latter scenario he perceives it as a loss. When faced with the potential for loss, people are much likelier to engage in behavior to avoid the loss than they are in a situation with potential for a gain. Research shows that our loss avoidance is twice stronger than our interest in gain.

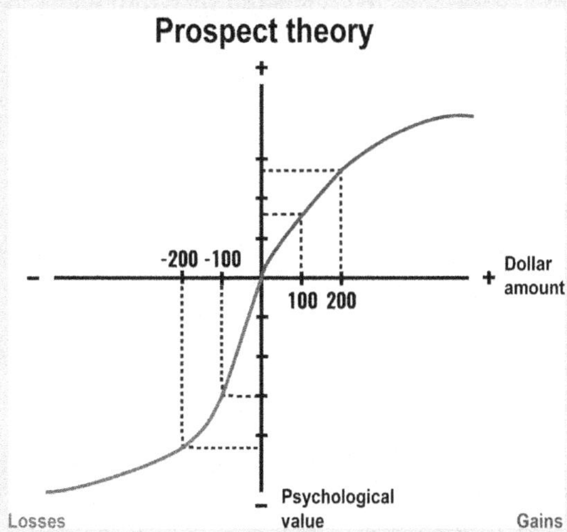

Kahneman (2011, p. 283).

In addition to prospect theory and loss aversion, Kahneman and Tversky are widely associated with insights involving the role of heuristics and biases in decision making (Tversky & Kahneman, 1974). They demonstrate that in the context of high complexity or lack of sufficient information, decision making is simplified by heuristic principles or rules of thumb, which make choosing easier. While they also highlight the benefit of such simplifications, Kahneman and Tversky demonstrate that the use of heuristics is associated with biases leading to systematic errors or deviations from rationality as defined by standard economics. Moreover, they reveal that the power of biases and heuristic is demonstrable among experienced scientists as well as among uneducated and less-knowledgeable individuals. The heuristic and biases literature makes an essential contribution to the behavioral economics field in advancing the idea that under the influence of biases and shortcut tactics, people make choices that are not optimal among the choices they had. Examples of biases and heuristic principles are discussed later in this chapter.

The influence of Kahneman and Tversky's theories in the field of economics is eventually facilitated further. They cross paths with economist Richard Thaler. His name is most often associated with the so-called *Nudge theory*, which advances the idea that by using choice architecture, individuals can be nudged toward making choices that are better for them instead of ones that deviate from rationality. His work involves applying the use of different nudges that help people pick better options, most notably in the area of retirement saving. Thaler's research inspired experiments with nudges that have yielded great successes in areas relating to healthy eating, energy saving, traffic control, and more.

Richard Thaler, along with his coauthor Cass Sunstein, advances the famous illustration explaining the deviation of traditional economic thought from the realities of human behavior with the concepts of *Humans* and *Econs*. *Econs* or *homo economicus* are imaginary species that reside in the theoretical world of economics and that "can think like Albert Einstein, store as much memory as IBM's Big Blue, and exercise the willpower of Mahathma Gandhi" (Thaler & Sunstein, 2009, p. 7). The real world, however, is populated with real people, or *homo sapiens* (humans), who in most cases "have trouble with long division if they do not have a calculator, sometimes forget their spouse's birthday, and have a hangover on New Year's day" (Thaler & Sunstein, 2009, p. 7). This analogy has become one of the most widely used in academic and popular literature explaining the difference between the assumptions made in traditional economics and in behavioral economics.

In the past years, behavioral economics is gaining more recognition across different fields. Specialized literature systematizing and advancing behavioral economics knowledge (e.g., Altman, 2015, 2017; Loewenstein, 2007; Zamir & Teichman, 2014) have fueled spread of behavioral thinking across different academic fields. Academic journals across social science fields prominently feature behavioral research.

In recent years, behavioral thinking has been stimulated also by the proactive efforts of numerous organizations studying and applying behavioral economics approaches to produce innovative solutions to a wide array of social and environmental challenges. Examples include the following: The BIT, a mission-driven organization that grew out of the UK government's behavioral unit and that designs policy and social solutions on the basis of behavioral economics knowledge; ideas42, a mission-driven organization initiated on Harvard University's campus by a group of researchers and students, and currently executing projects of different scale from New York City to the Philippines; Center for Advanced Hindsight, a behavioral economics lab at Duke University initiated by Dan Ariely that focuses on promoting new insights and knowledge-based solutions in the area of healthy eating and financial behavior; Behavioral Economics Group, the largest behavioral science group that publishes the prominent annual BE Guide and reports on advances in behavioral economics; iNudgeyou, a Danish organization generating and applying behavioral solutions across different social contexts; Mind, Behavior, and Development Unit, a World Bank unit testing and applying behavioral solutions for poverty alleviation and economic growth. Blog articles or publications by the World Economic Forum, the World Bank, the European Union, and OECD regularly cover behavioral economics knowledge developments and successful solutions inspired by the field.

New field or economics 3.0?

As a young field, behavioral economics is in a dynamic growth period with much new research flowing in and more attempts to systematize new insights in theoretical pillars. This process reflects the scope and scale of the ambitions within behavioral economics thought. The initial research and theories focused on individual decisions. They mostly sought to establish and explain errors people make by deviating from existing models of rationality (Camerer, Issacharoff, Loewenstein, O'Donoghue, & Rabin, 2003). Bias-prone thinking and irrationality explain the systematic nature of what are described as *mistakes* in decision making.

With the evolution of behavioral research and accumulation of theoretical content, the field advances with the newer thinking that it is incorrect to view human decision-making processes as error prone and individuals as irrational. Rather, the systematic discrepancies behavioral economists study should lead to updating the definition of rationality (Camerer et al., 2003). If the original definition for what is *common sense* is too limited or behaviorally unrealistic, then benchmarking against it leads to reinforcing the wrong golden standard (Altman, 2017a). Many leading researchers in the field are promoting the thinking that the true knowledge revolution behavioral economics claims over traditional economics cannot be achieved by studying individual, small-scale elements of choice dynamics. In fact, decision making can be understood only if the entire system (the decision-making individual and the surrounding context) is considered, and the proposed solutions are system-wide (Neth & Gigerenzer, 2015).

In this context, while at the beginning of its rise, behavioral economics was described as source of thinking that opposes the traditional economic field, more recently, the commonly shared belief is that behavioral knowledge has simply enhanced our understanding of economics in general and should be treated simply as *contemporary economics* (Avent, 2017). According to OECD, behavioral insights can no longer be dismissed as "a fashionable short-term foray by public bodies" and have proven to strengthen the effectiveness of the way many policy bodies and institutions across different countries work (Organisation for Economic Co-operation and Development, 2017). As one of the active contributors to the field Gerd Gigerenzer explains, behavioral economics is simply economics that is grounded "in more realistic assumptions" offering a perspective to socioeconomic phenomena without the idealized assumptions about unbounded rationality, unbounded self-interest, unbounded willpower, and unbounded computational accuracy (Gigerenzer, 2015, p. 226). These assumptions were adopted in traditional economic thinking to enable the development of grand and simple models that can be applied universally but that have broken ties with reality. With the added behavioral dimension, scientists and practitioners are in a much better position to build models that reflect actual human behavior and that include more variables facilitating improved understanding and ability to predict decision outcomes in social and economic situations (Altman, 2015a).

If the basic definition of economics describes it as a study of how society manages its scarce resources allocated by the "combined choices of millions of households and firms," and if 8 of the 10 fundamental principles of economics relate to how people make decisions and how people interact (Mankiw, 2017, p. 4–7), then the view that behavioral knowledge is simply part of contemporary economics seems to make sense. Moreover, the type of changes that behavioral thinking is injecting into the field of economics is not new; the field has promoted models that assume perfect competition, perfect information, and perfect rationality, but with time, these assumptions have been relaxed to give rise to newer and more realistic models of operation in the marketplace and society. In this context, the advance of behavioral sciences is leading to nothing more than another extension of economics, which relaxes the assumption of perfect rationality (Camerer et al., 2003).

Prominent themes and concepts in behavioral economics

This section provides a brief overview of prominent themes and concepts that constitute the theory in behavioral economics and key points at which it departs from the thinking in traditional economics. Main assumptions that are representative of conventional economic models and rejected by behavioral economists are summarized as follows (based on Altman, 2017c):

Conventional economics assumptions	Behavioral economics assumptions
The choices of individuals remain consistent across all bundles of goods and services, and through time *Example: if one likes going on inclusive holidays at the Caribbean, they are likely to continue taking this type of vacations for the rest of their lives*	Individuals make different choices across different product/service situations, and their preferences evolve over time *Example: one may have expressed preference for all inclusive Caribbean holidays for years but prefer to book only hotel and leave food options flexible when travelling to explore Italy*
Individuals are assumed to have thorough knowledge of all available options and are able to process it all without any limitation of their computational ability	In most situations, individuals lack thorough knowledge or do not have information about all possible options; even if they have complete information, they lack computational power to estimate and compare the outcomes associated with all options
Example: when deciding on the next skiing holiday destination one holds extensive information on all possible places in their choice set and the potential experience that each of them will offer, making a final decision on the basis of perfect and unbiased comparison across all choice factors	*Example: one cannot really know whether three months from now when they plan to go skiing, they will end up having the best possible weather conditions and skiing experiences in St. Anton (Austria), Zermatt (Switzerland) or Megève (France)*
Individuals are capable of forecasting the future implications and consequences of their decisions	Individuals have a hard time imagining their future selves as well as the consequences of decisions with future outcomes, especially when the context is over a long period of time
Example: one knows exactly how much they will enjoy holidaying in the Caribbean every year if they invest in that timeshare opportunity	*Example: one invests in a timeshare opportunity miscalculating the fact that after a few years of going to the same place, they experience the desire to holiday in different places but feel guilty to spend on travel to other destinations instead of spend time where they have already invested*
Individuals never regret past choices, as they are always optimal in terms of maximized utility and well-being	Regret is part of decision-making realities, and on many occasions, regret over past choices significantly influences current and future decisions

(*Continued*)

(Continued)

Conventional economics assumptions	Behavioral economics assumptions
Example: one never regrets previous destination choices and holiday formats even if they discover new places that offer more diversity or better experiences	*Example: after starting to use holiday periods to explore different countries and experience new cultures around the world, one regrets having "wasted" so many summers to passive beach all-inclusive holidays*
Controlling for risk, utility maximization is consistent with wealth or income maximization *Example: when making decisions about next holiday, one's choice is driven by affordability given their income (wealth status)*	Wealth and income maximization are not the only nor the most important sources of utility *Example: when making decisions about next holiday, one's choices are driven by the experience they are likely to get and it is possible that they make an effort to save for a long period of time to be able to afford a holiday that is outside of their normal budget but that will offer memorable experiences*
Individuals' ability to calculate and make efficient choices is irrespective of age, experience, education, or social context *Example: a young traveller at 21 is capable of the same analysis and comparison of holiday alternatives as an experienced traveler at 45 with a travel career of more than 20 years*	Individuals learn over time and adapt their decision toolbox depending on new knowledge, experience, and ecological considerations *Example: travelers with longer travel careers have more experience and knowledge to compare and choose, and avoid choices that may involve potential for service failure*
Individuals' behavior is independent of context and characterized with the same calculating manner toward maximizing utility *Example: a young traveler is likely to make the same choice for summer holiday regardless of the choices of their friends and regardless of whether at the time of the choice they are alone at home or out in the company of friends*	Behavior and decisions can only be properly explained through the prism of the immediate environment and the decision-making capability of the decision maker *Example: a young traveler is likely to be highly influenced in their choice of summer holiday by the choices of their friends and is likely to make very different decisions depending on whether the decision is being made while they are on their own at home or while they are out with their friends*

Over the past decades, behavioral economists have been recording and analyzing instances when people's preferences do not comply with the assumptions of conventional economics and lead to questions about the descriptive validity of standard economic models. Based on advancing knowledge in psychology and neuroscience, behavioral economists are promoting the thinking that the rational choice paradigm needs to evolve to include normal bounds of rationality in the context of economic choice (Camerer et al., 2003).

Rationality 2.0: bounded and ecological

There are situations in which risk is calculable and then statistics-based decision making makes sense, but in many everyday situations, alternatives are linked to uncertainty that is impossible to measure. For example, consider the uncertainty brought on by these questions: Who to marry? Where to invest? Which destination will offer a better experience for the upcoming holiday? When all alternatives are not clearly spelled out, there is limited knowledge about the possible consequences of the different options. It is also impossible to account for seemingly unrelated factors that may influence the outcomes, even in scenarios that seem to be clear: one suitor for husband may lose his health and end up being a more miserable alternative than another who may seem less caring at first; or an unexpected political crisis at the selected holiday destination may lead to nightmare experiences compared with seemingly less attractive other locations that do not encounter crisis.

The concept of "bounded rationality" was first introduced by Herbert Simon to explain the type of rationality that is observable in everyday realities but that does not align with the assumed, in conventional economics, "perfect rationality." In his Nobel Memorial Lecture, Simon states that with the concept of perfect rationality, which is at the core of many fundamental models, economic science "has focused on just one aspect of Man's character, his reason, and particularly on the application of that reason to problems of allocation in the face of scarcity." In reality, decision makers are indeed rational but constrained by their cognitive limitations in terms of knowledge and computational capacity (Simon, 1990).

Bounded rationality is advanced as alternative to perfect rationality, which assumes that decision makers seek to identify the optimal option on the basis of knowledge about all existing alternatives and that they have the ability to calculate consequences of each. In realistic settings, knowledge about all possible alternatives is rarely available, and human computational capabilities are limited. Under such circumstances, decision makers cannot be driven by optimization and instead aim for an alternative that is good enough under the given circumstances (*satisficing*, i.e., finding a satisfying and sufficient option) and based on a reasonable amount of calculation under conditions of incomplete information (Simon, 1948).

The more contemporary rationality concept advanced in behavioral economics is that of "ecological rationality," formulated by Gigerenzer, Todd, and ABC Research Group (2012). At the core of the concept is the idea that human beings apply multiple cognitive tools when making decisions, most of which are made in an environment of uncertainty. In this, they demonstrate ecological rationality (i.e., ability to select and apply the most appropriate decision-making tactics depending on the particular decision-making context; Gigerenzer, Fiedler, & Olsson, 2012, p. 3, 15).

The decision-making context is made up of the physical environment and relevant biological, social, and cultural factors. It can be deliberately designed to influence decision making, for example, through institutions and policies, or can be formed over time by the interactions of multiple decision makers (Gigerenzer, Fiedler, et al., 2012, p. 19).

Heuristics

One of the key terms in behavioral economics is *heuristics*, that is, simple rules of thumb used by people to make quick judgments under conditions of limited time and brainpower resources (Thaler, 2015a, p. 22). This theory serves as an alternative to the other two main theories: logic and estimating probability (e.g., Gigerenzer, Hertwig, & Pachur, 2011, p. xvii). When using heuristics to arrive at a judgment, decision makers ignore part of the available information to make a quick and frugal decision (Gigerenzer, 2015, p. 111).

The use of heuristics is associated with a tradeoff between accuracy and effort with two possible interpretations. First, it is a rationally made tradeoff motivated by the fact that not all decisions justify spending time and resources to arrive at an optimal choice. Second, cognitive limitations as barriers to rational choice lead to heuristics and thus to errors in judgment (Gigerenzer, 2015, p. 114). Heuristics allow decision makers to process information with less effort compared with an optimal decision rule. According to Shah and Oppenheimer (2008), all heuristics are based on one or more of the following effort-reduction methods: examining fewer cues, reducing difficulties with retrieval and storage of cue values, simplifying principles for cues, integrating less information, or examining fewer alternatives.

More recent thinking leads to understanding heuristics as smart tools that enable rational decision making in an environment of uncertainty (Neth & Gigerenzer, 2015). The most advanced theoretical analysis of heuristics comes from Gerd Gigerenzer's theory on ecological rationality, where heuristics are described as tools people use in response to an environment's specifics and their current mental capacities (Gigerenzer, 2015, p. 114). When weighing decision choices, failure to think statistically should not be treated as a cognitive limitation but as output of the situational dynamic between mental state and context. The use of heuristics is an element of smart decision making and serves as a means for arriving at fast and frugal decisions in an environment of uncertainty, rather than a suboptimal alternative to more precise decision-making tactics.

In some of Gerd Gigerenzer's recent publications and public talks, he criticizes the fact that heuristics have been positioned in literature with negative connotation. There is sufficient knowledge that heuristics are a natural mechanism for smart decision making, which in certain contexts produces more precise results than complex analytical models (Gigerenzer, 2016). Among the examples he uses to illustrate this point are the fast and frugal decisions that a sports player makes when estimating where the ball is likely to fall while it flies in the air and he runs after it (Gigerenzer, Fiedler, et al., 2012 p. 6) or the immediate decision made by a doctor in an emergency room who receives a patient with strong chest pains and needs to determine quickly whether intensive care is needed (Gigerenzer, 2015, p. 130). Heuristics can be fast and frugal as the smartest decision tactic for specific contexts, such as recognition memory, frequency monitoring, object tracking, ability to imitate, all of which evolve with time, learning, and experience (Gigerenzer, 2015, p. 113).

Eisenhardt and Sull (2001) confirm the utility of heuristics and introduce the idea of strategy as simple rules. Even as contemporary advancement of technology and data availability grow in sophistication, it is more effective to use "shortcut strategies that save time and effort by focusing our attention and simplifying the way we process information," which are effective only if tailored to the situation or person applying them (Sull & Eisenhardt, 2015, p. 5). There is growing evidence of the so-called less-is-more effect, which proves that under certain circumstances and contexts, using heuristics is optimal and produces sounder decisions (Gigerenzer & Brighton, 2011).

Biases

Another key concept in behavioral economics is *bias*. In many analyses, biases are studied in combination with heuristics as connected mechanisms explaining deviation from conventionally defined rationality. In fact, the work of Tversky and Kahneman, launched with their seminal article on the topic in 1974, is frequently referred to as the "heuristic and biases program." Heuristics and biases are often understood to belong together, because biases are thought to fuel heuristics (i.e., "I prefer to avoid losing money, so out of all options I will go with the one that makes it least likely that I will lose").

Biases are most often defined as intuition-driven systematic deviations from optimal choices (as traditionally defined by neoclassical economics) or violations of basic probability laws (Gilovich, Griffin, & Kahneman, 2003, p. 3) that lead to suboptimal decisions. As with heuristics, there are different views as to whether biases should be treated as failures of judgment (Tversky & Kahneman, 1974) or as smart tools that make sense considering the environmental context in which they are applied (Gigerenzer, Fiedler, et al., 2012).

Biases can be based on impressions or attitudes that cannot be traced back to their origin but that influence the opinion and behavior of the person (Kahneman, p. 11). For example, behavioral experts believe that the biased attitudes formed by false news and selectively consumed information driven by confirmation bias (accepting only messages that confirm one's current opinion and ignoring opposing views) explain the surprising outcomes of the last United States elections and the Brexit referendum in the United Kingdom (Harrell, 2016).

Optimism bias

Overestimating the probability of positive events and underestimating the probability of negative events.

Overconfidence bias

Overestimating ability or judgment, or somehow having an unjustifiable belief that all will be fine.

Confirmation bias

Seeking out or evaluating information in a way that fits with one's existing thoughts and preconceptions.

Delusion of competence

(Dunning-Kruger effect) Lacking reflexive acknowledgement that one is not equipped to make a decision or to act appropriately in relation to the demands of a situation.

Endowment effect

Overvaluing a good that one owns, regardless of its objective market value.

Status quo bias

Showing preference for things to stay the same by doing nothing or by sticking with a decision made previously.

Hindsight bias

Revising one's own history of beliefs in light of what actually happened and arriving at a distorted judgment in estimating of the probability of occurrence of an event ('knew it all along' effect).

What are some common biases?

- Optimism bias: overestimating the probability of positive events and underestimating the probability of negative events.
- Overconfidence bias: overestimating ability or judgment, or somehow having an unjustifiable belief that all will be fine.
- Confirmation bias: seeking out or evaluating information in a way that fits with one's existing thoughts and preconceptions.
- Delusion of competence (Dunning–Kruger effect): lacking reflexive acknowledgement that one is not equipped to make a decision or to act appropriately in relation to the demands of a situation.
- Endowment effect: overvaluing a good that one owns, regardless of its objective market value.
- Status quo bias: showing preference for things to stay the same by doing nothing or by sticking with a decision made previously.
- Hindsight bias: revising one's own history of beliefs in light of what actually happened and arriving at a distorted judgment in estimating of the probability of occurrence of an event ("knew it all along" effect).

Based on BE Guide (2017).

In the past few years, it has become fashionable to identify biases and generate lists of biases that lead to inefficient choices, especially in regard to consumer choice (e.g., Desjardins, 2017).

In response to the advancing knowledge about biases and how they influence decision making, behavioral literature has explored mechanisms for debiasing (i.e., using choice architecture techniques to reduce biases and counteract their effects). Debiasing is seen as an option addressing bounded rationality in social context (Eberl et al., 2013) or in legal context when steps are taken to stimulate rational thought processes (Jolls & Sunstein, 2004) by analyzing different information, providing additional information, or changing the format in which the information is presented.

Systems 1 and 2

The core idea advanced by Daniel Kahneman, based on his long collaboration with Amos Tversky, regards the duality of the human mind. He proposes that decision making depends on two systems that roughly correspond to intuition and reasoning. The nature of the decision-making process triggered by each of the two systems is significantly different: System 1 (intuitive) decisions are fast and driven by heuristics (shortcut), associative, and often influenced by emotions. For example, deciding to walk into one of two restaurants on the street because it has three occupied tables compared with one occupied table in the alternative across the street is a System 1 decision biased by social conformity (going with the obvious choice of the majority). System 2 decisions take longer and require effort and analysis of different options. For example, responding to the need to calculate 45 × 164 will require engagement of System 2 decision making (Kahneman, 2011).

Which system will dominate the decision-making process depends on the context and specific state of mind of the decision maker. System 1 is likely to take lead when System 2 is distracted or engaged in other activities, such as in situations of time pressure or in emotional states. System 2 dominates when a decision has high importance and relevance, and when the setting allows for concentration and slower decision processing.

One of the functions of System 2 is to control and "review" the suggestions arrived at with by System 1 solutions. However, experiments reveal that this control function is not always triggered and that, at times, System 1 errors are not revised by System 2 reasoning (Kahneman, 2011).

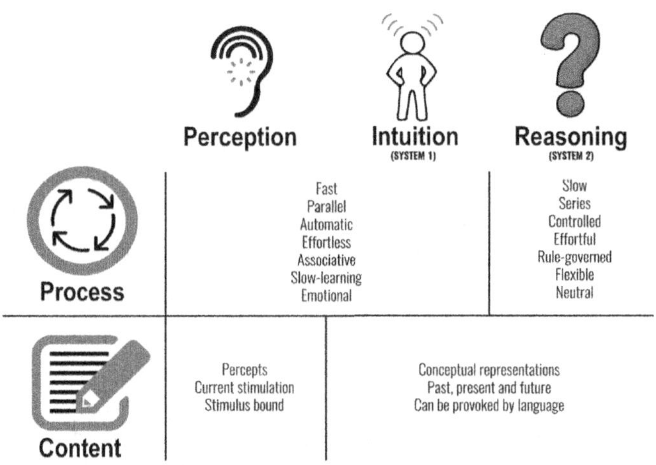

Based on Kahneman (2011)

Libertarian paternalism and nudges

Libertarian paternalism is a concept advanced by Sunstein and Thaler to define a form of paternalism that steers people's choices toward the most beneficial option without eliminating freedom of choice (Sunstein & Thaler, 2003). It is defined as "a weak, nonintrusive type of paternalism" that does not eliminate options but keeps choices available and simply makes the optimal alternative easier to select (Sunstein & Thaler, 2003). The justification for promoting paternalistic thinking is that nonpaternalism is grounded in the assumption that all people, at all times, make choices that are in their best interest and that are better than the choices that would be made by a third party. But what if this assumption is wrong? Is this ground for promoting some forms of paternalism?

An earlier notion of behaviorally justified, mild paternalism is presented by Camerer et al. (2003) and is referred to as *asymmetric paternalism*, meaning use of choice architecture principles that create benefits for the decision maker by nudging them toward the option that is more favorable. The asymmetry in the paternalism promoted by the authors comes from the fact that by definition it generates significant benefits for the ones who are likely to make an error (the boundedly rational) without imposing limitations or harm on the ones who are fully rational. The author's justification for asymmetric paternalism is that forcing or preventing choices for the individual's own good is similar to the type of care parents impose on their children when it comes to limiting their freedom to skip school or eat unhealthy food. Another justification for the acceptability of paternalistic thinking is that society is already accustomed to restrictive measures in domains such as drug control that limit the possibility for drug abuse, safety, and health regulations that force employers to guarantee acceptable work conditions, and compulsory education programs that are justified by the fact that education is proven to make people better off, etc. (Sunstein, 2014). Such policy-facilitated imposing or elimination of options is grounded on the philosophy that such methods help individuals avoid choices and costs, which are considered as unacceptable by modern society. In this sense, advances in behavioral knowledge justify merely extending the set of situations across which society acknowledges risks of harmful choices and costs, and accepts some form of paternalism as the vehicle for avoiding them (Camerer et al., 2003). Even educated and sophisticated individuals experience self-control failures, inability to process information, and update preferences, or estimation errors, and as result, make the mistake of choosing against their best interests. In light of this, behavioral economists suggest that if and when it is possible to predict situations of "apparent violations of rationality" (Camerer et al., 2003), there is reasonable justification for applying paternalistic approaches to prevent such mistakes. Recently acquired knowledge about how people make decisions and how they can make errors in determining what is best for them is highlighted as sufficient grounds for updating the firm belief against paternalism going back to the ideas of John Stuart Mill in *On Liberty* (Mill, 1966).

What is the belief advanced by John Stuart Mill?

Mill's philosophy is that the good of the individual is "not a sufficient warrant" for rightfully exercised power over any member of civilized community against his will. The only situation in which imposing control is perceived as acceptable is when this is a way to prevent the harm of others. Across all other situations, the individual holds full sovereignty over himself, his mind, and his body, including when he is likely to make a choice that is far from beneficial and far from the best available.

Mill (1960, p. 60).

The tools for executing libertarian paternalism are *nudges*: conscious attempt that use choice architecture design to modify the decision maker's behavior in a predictable way without eliminating any of the available options (Thaler & Sunstein, 2009, p. 6).

While Thaler and Sunstein (2009)'s definition of "nudge" and "acceptable libertarian paternalism" does not include forbidding options, in a discussion about asymmetric paternalism, Camerer et al. (2003) include limiting consumer choice as an acceptable mechanism.

Here are a few types of nudges that illustrate the application of libertarian paternalism as promoted by behavioral economists.

Defaults: the widely cited study of Johnson and Goldstein (2003) on the dramatic differences that defaults produce in organ donation program enrollment is a powerful demonstration of the significant welfare gains that no-action defaults can produce for society, including in domains such as saving lives through transplantation. Many experimental studies exploring the power of default-based policy solutions suggest that there is value in having no-action defaults (e.g., Araña & Carmelo, 2013). While in most cases gains for the society are unquestionable, researchers suggest the need to carefully account for the tradeoff between gains, potential errors, and costs (physical, cognitive, and emotional), and the need to seek *majoritarian defaults* (Camerer et al., 2003).

Why enrollment in organ donation programs varies dramatically across countries?

Johnson and Goldstein (2003) compare the enrollment in organ donor programs across a set of European countries and establish that in some countries enrollment is in the upper 90% while in the rest enrollment is really low (below 15%). The two researchers observed that these extreme differences were present when countries are culturally similar (e.g., enrolment in Germany was 12% while enrollment in Austria was 99.98%) ruling out cultural differences. Targeted

(Continued)

(Continued)

research revealed that in both countries with low enrollment and countries with high enrollment, the popular opinion was that donor donation programs were of great value to society and that enrolling in them aligns with good social values. This ruled out any value or attitude-related explanation.

The factor that was established to explain the extreme differences was the enrollment design and specifically the default option. In countries where the default option was enrollment (i.e., one has to proactive sign off the program or they are automatically enrolled), the participation rate was extremely high. In countries were the default option was non participation (i.e., one has to proactively make the choice to be part of the program), enrollment was exceptionally low.

Based on Johnson and Goldstein (2003).

Framing: framing relates to the rationally unjustified effect that difference in formulations of information with identical meaning produces on beliefs, preferences, and reaction (Kahneman, 2011, p. 364). Framing effects are produced by the different ways in which the presented problem is formulated. Framing is powerful and impacts decisions even among sophisticated professionals like doctors as demonstrated in an experiment conducted by Amos Tversky and colleagues at the Harvard Medical School (McNeil, Pauker, Sox, & Tversky, 1982). The experiment involved asking physicians to choose between two possible treatments of patients with lung cancer: surgery (with statistically proven higher short-term risk but a positively favorable 5-year survival rate) or radiation (statistically proven a safer option in the short term but with lower survival rate from a 5-year perspective). Two groups of physicians were given the same information, but for the first, the statistic for the treatment was framed as survival rate (i.e., "the 1-month survival rate of surgery is 90%") while for the second—as mortality rates (i.e., "there is 10% mortality in the first month following the surgery"). As result of the different formulation, 85% of the physicians in the first group chose surgery and 50% in the second group expressed preference for radiation.

Framing can be based on loss aversion and trigger preference for the option that is framed around avoiding a loss rather than the option framed as benefitting from a gain (Tversky & Kahneman, 1981). It can also be structured to highlight a more favorable characteristic of a situation or product. For example, a recent study demonstrates that framing a purchase as more experiential versus more material modifies readiness to borrow to pay for it (Tully & Sharma, 2017).

How does framing work when used to nudge certain behavior?

A good example of how framing effect can fuel a nudge is the different outcome that can be expected if a public campaign seeking to promote energy-saving behavior communicates one of the following messages:

1. *through energy conservation methods you can save $350 per year* (focus on gain) or
2. *without energy conservation methods you lose $350 per year* (focus on loss)

Given that loss aversion is more powerful and more likely to motivate proactive behavior, the information campaign encouraging energy conservation is likely to be more successful if it uses option (b) as a nudge

Thaler and Sunstein (2009, p. 37).

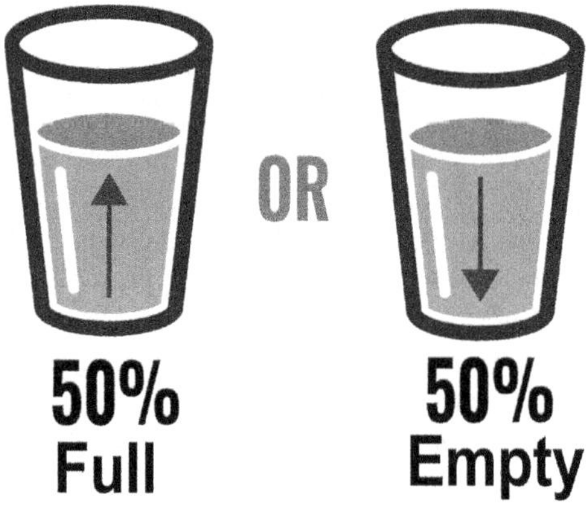

Disclosing and salience of information: making information salient is another nudge-like mechanism. Disclosure policies, such as consumer protection policies, policies regulating lottery activities, licensing requirements, and others are part of contemporary institutional systems. At their core is the principle of making specific information salient to guide decision making without de facto introducing specific prescriptions about behavior. An easy example is the Hazard Communication Standard issued by the US Occupational Safety and Health Administration in the 1980s, which requires that all employers adopt a hazard communication program and inform workers of the relevant risks. This policy has used mandatory disclosure as a mechanism of making workplaces significantly safer without de facto requiring change of the behavior of employers or employees (Thaler & Sunstein, 2009, p. 191).

Influencing disclosure or salience is relevant also in cases when the decision makers are educated enough and have the relevant knowledge. For example, at the moment of purchasing a car, well-educated consumers might be overwhelmed with other features of models they are considering and might simply not be sufficiently salient to the benefits of energy-efficient vehicles. Such lack of salience might lead them to neglect energy efficiency as attribute, even though it would be in their economic interest and in the interest of society (Sunstein, 2014). In this sense, making energy efficiency salient can nudge a car buyer to consider this factor in their choice process and may influence their final decision.

Disclosure and salience are especially relevant when it comes to complex choices or choices with future consequences, as these situations produce many deviations from optimal choice (Tversky, & Kahneman, 1983). One way of making information salient in such contexts is by mapping or translating likely outcomes of complex or abstract choices into easy-to-imagine options. For example, instead of leaving workers to self-navigate complex retirement scenarios, they can be told that their current plan will provide for a tiny hut as dwelling during retirement while the alternative could secure a comfortable two-bedroom condo (Thaler & Sunstein, 2009, p. 133).

Cooling off periods: cooling off periods represent an opportunity to overcome a hot emotional state and potentially adapt or change choices made during this hot state. This has been considered relevant because in many contexts people seem to make decisions with long-term implications in the heat of the moment without full consideration of associated future impacts. This phenomenon has been referred to as the *hot-to-cold empathy gap* or *projection bias* and is related to self-control problems, such as when people overindulge and show preference for short-term benefits driven by their current state of mind.

In commercial context, cooling off periods provide a chance for introspective reexamination of the made decision and create an incentive for sellers to ensure that decisions are made rationally. If a seller seeks to benefit from hasty consumer decision making, the cost of reversed consumer decisions during the cooling off period will be transferred away from the consumer and to the seller. Cooling off periods are most commonly implemented as guaranteed refund periods allowing buyers to return or exchange their purchases.

The main challenges with cooling off nudges is to determine the limit and design of the time period, so that they enable correction for hasty decision but do not create a barrier for those making good decisions (Camerer et al., 2003). Another complexity is associated with applying cooling off to social context to enable the adapting of life-changing decisions made in the heat of the moment, such as hasty decisions to marry or divorce. For example, some American states impose a mandatory waiting period before a couple who has filed for divorce can actually separate (Thaler & Sunstein, 2009, p. 253).

Limiting choice: there are varying opinions on whether elimination or limitation of choice is an unacceptable nudge. According to Thaler and Sunstein's (2009) definition of libertarian paternalism, choices need to remain available so elimination of options does not qualify as a nudge. Camerer et al. (2003) define asymmetric paternalism as one that leaves a rational decision maker uninfluenced, which also presumes access to all options. At the same time, they discuss limitation as an acceptable choice architecture mechanism, especially when it comes to introducing cut-off dates and deadlines. It has been demonstrated that deadlines nudge taxpayers to be more disciplined with their tax declarations and to benefit from tax incentives, and that scientists are more proactive in submitting proposals to benefit from calls for research grants (Camerer et al., 2003). Ariely and Wertenbroch (2002) also demonstrate that imposing cut-off dates for paper submission helps students avoid suboptimal planning of their course assignments, which is much more prevalent when there are no deadlines.

Limitation-based nudges receive a different level of support among researchers and policy makers, but they are a common form of regulation in many countries. Examples include limiting the movement of motorized vehicles as measure for air quality control in urban areas or limiting the number of visitors that can walk through a sensitive cultural attraction to manage footprint. A contemporary example for a limitation-based nudge is cafeterias without trays, which eliminate trays as a measure to reduce food waste and water usage (Thaler & Sunstein, 2009).

Sunstein (2014, p. 21) highlights the importance of recognizing that behavioral market failures justify policy solutions, including those that are based on some form of paternalism. He also reminds that in their core, autonomy-based objections to paternalism are motivated by people's welfare (based on the belief that governments make people's lives worse, not better). However, new behavioral knowledge demonstrates that due to choice overload and other factors, decision makers often compromise their autonomy and act against their own welfare (Sunstein, 2014). This, and the fact that choice architecture is already an inevitable part of socioeconomic life, contributes to the belief that some form of paternalism is acceptable and in the best interest of the individual and society.

Culture and BE

Some of the initial behavioral studies exploring heuristics and biases in decision making suggest that many of the observed mechanisms are stable across different cultural contexts. Ariely reports that, to his own surprise and that of his research collaborators, the experiments on dishonest behavior across a number of countries (Canada, Italy, China, Israel, and among others) consistently yielded results that were comparable to those found in the United States (Ariely, 2012). His explanation is that the tasks that were at the heart of the experiments were culturally neutral, so culture was not a significant factor in this specific context. That said, he suggests that there is need for further research exploring how culture leads to and impacts different levels of dishonesty in different societies. In the context of moral relativity, varying culture-dependent acceptability of certain behaviors, such as smoking, infidelity, or academic cheating means that culture influences moral thresholds and norms (Ariely, 2012, p. 191).

Recent studies are shedding light on linkages between culture and different levels of corruption across countries, and conclude that specific dimensions, such as uncertainty avoidance, individual collectivism practices, and human-oriented practices, encourage corruption (Seleim & Bontis, 2009). Culture has also been used to explain differences in ethical behavior and adoption of sustainability principles (Leonidou, Skarmeas, & Saridakis, 2018), varying levels of tax morale, and associated differences in shadow economy presence across countries (Alm & Torgler, 2006). Levinson and colleagues explore cultural specifics in economic and financial decision making in China and the United States. They established dramatic differences in financial value estimation, property ownership judgments, and readiness to consider social or contextual information (Levinson, Richardson, & Peng, 2007).

The relationship between culture, decision making, and behavioral dynamics is certainly a domain with great potential for new and interesting insights. Many of the most typical indicators used to measure cultural differences directly relate to key mechanisms studied in behavioral economics. Examples include the following: attitudes about power; uncertainty avoidance; feminine-style consensus-seeking versus masculine-style competitiveness; individualism versus collectivism; long- versus short-term orientation; indulgence versus restraint (Hofstede, Hofstede, & Minkov, 2010) and future orientation; institutional collectivism; human orientation; performance orientation; gender egalitarianism; assertiveness (House, Dorfman, Javidan, Hanges, & Sully de Luque, 2013); and preferences regarding risk, timing of rewards, reciprocity, altruism, and trust (Falk et al., 2015).

Ethics

The discussion on ethics and behavioral economics has two aspects that deserve attention: the ethical challenges associated with how behavioral knowledge is applied, and the understanding behavioral scientists have on what is moral behavior.

Ethical application of behavioral knowledge

Redefining the limits of ethics when it comes to using behavioral insights for different purposes is a considerable challenge. In recent popular articles and interviews, the Nobel Prize winning author of the nudge theory, Richard Thaler, emphasizes the importance of ensuring that nudges are applied ethically by following three fundamental rules:

- being transparent and avoid misleading,
- opting out should be easy to choose and pursue, and
- providing a clear explanation for how the nudged option benefits the decision maker.

Unfortunately, many commercial applications of nudges seek to profit from misleading customers by exploiting psychological mechanisms, such as fear of missing out, default effects, anchoring effects, or by manipulating perceptions, expectations, and emotions (Gigerenzer, 2016). A recent book by Nobel laureates George Akerlof and Robert Shiller is devoted to economic mechanisms that fuel opportunities for market success through deception and manipulation, leading people to make decisions they name "NO-ONE-COULD-POSSIBLY-WANTs" (Akerlof & Shiller, 2015, p. xii). Dan Ariely's most recent book explains the wide variety of mistakes commonly made with decisions about money is built entirely on real-life examples illustrating the market practices of banks, financial, and insurance companies (Ariely, 2017).

As behavioral scientists produce more insights that are incorporated in formal education, academic and popular literature, and popular media, awareness of the good and bad ways of applying behavioral thinking will grow. The hope is for corrections of policy and market mechanisms that enable manipulative use of behavioral tools. More aware consumers are also more likely to put pressure on companies for more responsible behavior and to punish misuse of psychology by brands.

Behavioral perspective on moral behavior

Morality is viewed through the prism of the bounded rationality theory and the fact that behavior is function of personal and environmental factors, and is thus largely dependent on the context (Gigerenzer, 2011). This suggests that environmental designs can influence the strictness with which one will adhere to their own internal moral standards (Ariely, 2012). This is different from the view on crime and dishonest behavior advanced by Nobel Prize winning economist Gary Becker suggesting that illegals acts can be explained by basic cost versus benefit analysis that involves calculating the gain that the act of dishonesty will yield, the likelihood of being caught, and the expected punishment if one is caught. Recent experiments demonstrate that neither an increase in the benefits produced by a potential act of dishonesty nor the likelihood of being caught produces change in likelihood and magnitude of the act (Ariely, 2012, p. 9).

The mentioned earlier study on enrollment in organ donation programs (Johnson & Goldstein, 2003) suggests that morality cannot be explained only by internal factors, such as empathy, for example, because when asked, people declare strong agreement with the value of participating in organ donation programs and with the statement that "this is the right thing to do." Yet when presented with the choice to enroll, their actual behavior is highly influenced by the design of the decision operationalization and enrollment is highly dependent on the default option. A similar experiment focused on switching to a greener energy mix for household needs confirms this. While people express firm support for the importance of moving toward the use of greener energy, their decision to actually switch is highly dependent on the default option. When the default option is a greener mix, the majority of customers switched to it, but when the default option remained grey energy, the majority did not switch to more environmentally friendly sources (Pichert & Katsikopoulos, 2008).

Considering the importance of the environmental context on encouraging and supporting moral behavior, Gigerenzer (2011, p. 219) suggests that "the causes of moral behavior are not simply inside the mind and that understanding the interplay between minds and environments is a useful starting point for moral policy." Currently, institutions often apply policies that rely on people's internal motivators, such as an organ donation programs designed around the belief that enrollment is driven by moral beliefs and is independent of situational factors. The alternative, Gigerenzer (2011, p. 219) suggests, is to adopt *moral sufficing* thinking and understand that acts of dishonesty or crime are driven by heuristic decision making, which is influenced by the decision-making setting. In that sense, dealing with unethical acts would mean identifying the heuristic, which most likely fuels undesired behavior and creating an environment that suppresses the likelihood for its triggering. This is the logic applied in the proposed "broken window theory" (Kelling & Coles, 1997), which suggests that making the environment in a city or neighborhood tidier by eliminating broken infrastructure and street waste combined with zero tolerance measures leads to substantive change in behavior and significant decrease of petty crime.

In his research program on dishonesty, Dan Ariely supports the thinking that (dis)honest behavior should be treated as function of internal and environmental factors, and that redesign in the environment can significantly influence the likelihood of unethical acts (Ariely, 2012). His work focuses mainly on small acts of dishonesty conducted by people who otherwise identify as moral and ethical. In fact, the leading internal mechanism that influences ethical behavior is an individual's self-concept and the need to maintain a positive one that is aligned with one's internal moral standards (Mazar, Amir, & Ariely, 2008b). As observed by other researchers, however, many individuals with positive self-concept are *moral relativists* and easily engage in partial dishonesty or in acts that constitute small deviations from the rules (e.g., underreporting the number of copies made on the office copy machine) (Goldstone & Chin, 1993). The extent to which this moral relativity will lead to unethical behavior depends on external mechanisms. Examples include: the existence of basic control mechanisms (e.g., monitoring of submitted reports or checking the quality of completed tasks); salience of moral rules (operationalized through reminders of the institution's honor code to which one has committed or the ten commandments); the use of a medium, such as tokens or monetary rewards instead of cash (e.g., tokens earned for completed tasks; Mazar et al., 2008b); observable prevalence of others being dishonest in the same situation; and whether other violators belong to the same social group that the decision maker identifies with (Gino, Ayal, & Ariely, 2009). These and many contextual details seem to influence the likelihood for ethical misbehavior, but these deviations from honest behavior do not translate into updating a positive self-concept, and the majority of people still identify themselves as individuals of high moral standard. In everyday situations presenting an opportunity for dishonesty, the majority of individuals are likely to cheat but not to the fullest extent possible. This allows them to rationalize their act as one that is below the cut-off line for dishonest behavior and enables the preservation of their own moral identity (Mazar, Amir, & Ariely, 2008a).

An important contribution to the new behavioral perspectives on morality and ethics is focused on small acts of dishonesty by otherwise ethical people. While they continue to be treated quite differently from deliberate criminal behavior, the magnitude of the impact and cost to society aggregated by many such small acts justifies the pursuit of mechanisms to limit them. For example, estimates reveal that the tax gap generated by small-scale underreporting or misrepresenting of information on tax forms in the United States is much larger than the one attributed to deliberate tax fraud. This leads to the need for new ways of thinking about policy and market designs that rely on the combination of mental and environment factors (Ariely, 2012; Gigerenzer, 2011). Effective designs could make engaging in unethical behavior more difficult and could foster an atmosphere of openness and transparency (Rick & Loewenstein, 2008). Specific tactics could include increasing the salience of ethical standards and limiting the possibility for justifying dishonesty, minimizing anonymity and strengthening the sense of identification, and closing the awareness gap between abstract perception of moral self and specific acts that constitute acts of dishonesty (Ayal, Gino, Barkan, & Ariely, 2015).

New perspectives or misunderstanding of ground assumptions

Behavioral economics is evolving quickly. While Nobel Prize Laureate Daniel Kahneman (2011), the author of *Thinking, Fast and Slow*, writes about systematic errors and the susceptibility of our minds to them, behavioral scientists today believe that deviations from *conventional wisdom* or maximizing behavior should not be automatically categorized as mistakes or lack of rationality (Altman, 2015; Gigerenzer, Fiedler, et al., 2012). Instead, they call for insights beyond simplistic thinking that human decisions are irrational, uninformed, biased, or vulnerable to illusions (or even delusions) (Smith & Argyros, 2017), and suggest that perhaps the neoclassical norms for rational behavior, which science has been relying on, were simply not ideal to start with (Altman, 2015a).

What has led to general acceptance of the concept of perfect rationality as core to conventional wisdom and other such norms? Some of the rationality-grounded models used in science and practice were imperfect and errors in the way that these models have been adopted and used over time may have brought on new assumptions. One recent explanation comes from the work of Gerd Gigerenzer and his colleagues who suggest that while rational actor models are simple and well-structured, they rely on the wrong methodology extracted from the origins of Bayesian decision theory (Gigerenzer, Todd, et al., 2012). In the work of Leonard Jimmie Savage, who is considered as the father of modern Bayesian decision theory, he outlines the specific context in which his theory works—a constrained settings within which all alternative outcomes and probability distributions are known with certainty. In these "small worlds," as he calls them, choice is driven by optimization on the basis of perfect knowledge and perfect rationality (Savage, 1981). Unfortunately, most of the decision-making realities do not comply with the characteristics of these small worlds and represent "large world" settings with imperfect information and limited ability to calculate outcomes (Brighton & Gigerenzer, 2012). Given that in a large world the fundamental conditions of perfect knowledge and perfect information are altered, the principles of small world rational decision-making models cannot be expected to suffice. This mismatch of using a small world decision model in the context of a large world setting is seen as one of the reasons that today's understanding of conventional wisdom does not comply with reality (Gigerenzer & Todd, 2012).

Today's thinking is that the behavior of individuals, organizations, and markets does not align with traditional models of conventional wisdom and are highly dependent on psychological, institutional, cultural, and biological considerations that are relevant to the choice that is being made in the respective moment and specific setting (Altman, 2019; Gigerenzer, Todd, et al., 2012). Because of the systematic nature of these deviations and the deeper understanding of what leads to them, there are calls for the field to redesign and propose "alternatives or revisions to the conventional wisdom" (Altman, 2015, p. xvii) and to recognize that what is observed are not deviations but *ecological rationality* (i.e., smart considerations of the specific moment and context with application of smart heuristics from the adaptive decision-making toolbox; Gigerenzer, Todd, et al., 2012).

Criticism of behavioral economics

As discussed earlier, behavioral economics or behavioral thinking in economics is a young and fast-developing domain. While behavioral scientists have successfully provided explanations across many areas where traditional thinking has failed (see cases later in this chapter), limited experience with behavioral dimensions makes scientists and practitioners unclear about implications they will have in both theory and practice. On one side, active research and applied experimentation will continue uncovering new insights that strengthen the ability to explain and predict behavior. On the other side, there is lack of full clarity as to what other impacts might be unlocked by this new knowledge. Some leading authors point out that while behavioral knowledge is advancing quickly, there are still a large number of academic publications that focus on limited and narrow perspectives rather than contribute more evenly with different points of view (Altman, 2015). Gigerenzer (2016) states that there is need to develop models allowing for better *prediction* of human behavior than models that fit current or past behavioral patterns. He calls for stronger emphasis on methodologies that allow for exploring and comparisons of different explanations rather than using safe null hypothesis testing.

One of the first directions in which unlocking behavioral insights has produced undesirable effects relates to unethical applications of behavioral tactics, as discussed earlier. Companies seeking fast and dirty sales strive to apply behavioral insights and nudges (Thaler, 2015b, 2016) in product descriptions, pricing tactics, and promotions that seek to trick consumers (Samson, 2016).

In the introduction of the 2016 BE Guide, Gigerenzer (2016) criticizes the continuously reinforced in behavioral literature negative connotations around heuristics as associated with error and irrationality. An important part of Gigerenzer's research focuses on the idea that heuristics are part of a smart decision-making system that enables individuals to make *fast and frugal* decisions when the situation they are in requires such. He describes *smart heuristics* and demonstrates that fast and frugal decisions sometimes yield more reliable and smarter results than complex decision-making processes that meet conventional standards for rationality (Gigerenzer, 2015; Gigerenzer & Todd, 1999). Gigerenzer's theoretical insights in the past few years lead him to persistently call for reframing negative thinking around heuristics (as associated with errors) and for advancing knowledge about when heuristics work better than complex decision models.

The editor of two recent book collections on behavioral economics, Altman (2017), has highlighted that the initiated by Kahneman and Tversky heuristics and biases literature promotes conclusions about irrationality or systematic errors in human decision-making that need revision. Essentially, people's choices are benchmarked against the unrealistic neoclassical models of rationality. In his analyses, Altman rejects the assumption that errors and biases are hardwired in the human brain (2017b, p. 22) and calls for the formulation of a new gold standard for optimality in choice making rather than continuing benchmarking toward the same principles of neoclassical economics that behavioral scientists are rejecting.

Naturally, behavioral economics is subjected to rigorous criticism for ideas about different levels of paternalism involved in nudging and choice architecture. In a recent interview, Richard Thaler, the author of the term *libertarian paternalism*, recognizes that the idea for even mild forms of paternalism triggers different levels of resistance among many scientists and policy makers (Thaler, 2016). In the article that first introduced the term in literature, he and his coauthor talk about libertarian paternalism as being "a relatively weak and nonintrusive type of paternalism," which nudges toward certain choices but does not eliminate or fence off the rest (Sunstein & Thaler, 2003). While the choices remain available, the assumption made here is that the actual decision about which options make the individual better off is determined by a choice expert who is assumed to be more knowledgeable than the decision maker (Altman, 2017) and who is in position of making a fully rational, impartial judgment about the best path for the wellbeing of someone else. Even though policy solutions following libertarian paternalism as principle have worked successfully, there are examples of failures triggered by the "don't tell me what I can't do" syndrome. One of the most notable examples is the failed attempt of New York mayor Michael Bloomberg to introduce a partial ban on the sale of sodas in containers of more than sixteen ounces (Sunstein, 2014, p. 52).

The alternative to libertarian paternalism proposed by some behavioral economics researchers is to focus on redesigning the decision-making environment and enabling the smart decision maker to independently arrive at the best possible decision. This entirely *libertarian* approach still leaves the possibility for experts and institutions to play a role, mainly in improving the overall decision-making environment and decision-making capabilities of the decision maker rather than nudging them toward one or another option (Altman, 2017). While theoretically a reasonable direction for the future, the main challenge is that, as revealed in the introduction of this chapter, we live in societies where existing institutions and systems have been shaped to a large extent around the assumption of traditional economic thinking. In that sense, the libertarian smart agent approach is an ideal that scientists should continue studying and societies can execute. Until then, much of the libertarian paternalism principles can add value and help navigate the behavior-unfriendly societal systems, as well as prevent some dramatic social trends linked to poor decisions (Keeney, 2008).

The applied side of behavioral economics

The practical value added of behavioral economics

The most important contribution of behavioral economics is the realism it brings to understanding and explaining how people choose and behave. With the new light it has shed on the factors that influence people's choices, it has become nearly impossible to develop theoretical models or design policies without questioning realism. In this sense, the success of behavioral economics lies in its ability to offer analyses that help explain problems in better ways than conventional approaches and to propose solutions that have more realistic explanatory and predictive power than conventional ones.

The power of this realism stems from the success behavioral economists have had in providing explanations, sometimes shockingly simple ones, for failures in past attempts to solve socioeconomic problems of large scale. Among these are unsuccessful policies in the areas of financial saving and retirement planning, incentives for healthier living, effectiveness of traffic rules, and so on.

Another important change that behavioral economics has brought to the field of economics is recognizing the need for multidimensional perspectives and borrowing of insights from across different knowledge domains. In this sense, behavioral economics stimulates multidisciplinary thinking, which relies on assumptions and insights not only from psychology but also sociology, law, political science, biology, etc. (Altman, 2015a). Based on these new insights, behavioral economics leads to an opportunity for building new theoretical models that (1) are more realistic and precise in reflecting actual behavior and (2) recognize that behavior contradicting neoclassical economic theory can still be rational and intelligent in the context of the specific situation in which the decision is being made (Altman, 2015a).

The following set of cases present some of the successful applications of behavioral thinking to real-world problems, which have not been effectively solved with traditional approaches. They come from different socioeconomic domains and reveal impacts of different scale.

Behavioral economics in action

- *Case 1: save more tomorrow program (public),*
- *Case 2: smarter lunchroom program (public/social),*
- *Case 3: traffic rules (public),*
- *Case 4: saving and loan repayment (private solution),*
- *Case 5: happiness policy (public),*
- *Case 6: fighting obesity with air miles (Canada),*
- *Case 7: student journey to graduation,*
- *Case 8: redesigning summons in NYC,*

- *Case 9: saving water*, and
- *Case 10: fire preparedness.*

Case 1 Save more tomorrow program for retirement planning in the United States

The challenge

One of the significant problems with the retirement savings system in the United States since the 1990s through current times is under saving. This leads to poor quality of life and severe social problems for older segments of the population and additional costs for society. According to official data cited by Benartzi (2012), around 50% of the US population does not save enough or does not have access to savings programs at all, because employers find them too complex to administer. Among the citizens who do have access, about one-third find it complicated to navigate required forms, so they procrastinate and eventually never join, foregoing tax benefits and employer contributions. This leaves only about 30% of the US population that saves for retirement. Because of the complexities involved in joining a retirement plan (such as even understanding finance terminology), many people are unable to choose properly and end up with savings rates of around 6%, while the rate recommended by retirement planning professionals is at least 10%. All of this leads to a risky state of retirement savings in the United States—less than 1% of the population is saving enough or more than enough for their post-working years (Benartzi, 2011).

The problem with voluntary saving in the United States is exacerbated by the changes in retirement policies over the years. When originally introduced, voluntary savings programs, known as 401(k) plans, were designed to serve as a supplement to other primary sources of retirement income. Due to legislative changes in the past few decades, 401(k) plans have become the main source of support for retirees, creating a serious problem across the population with low enrollment rates.

Assumptions that fuel the problem

The main issue with voluntary retirement savings policies in the United States is that they are grounded in the assumption that households aim to smooth out consumption over their life span and are capable of solving the relevant optimization problem in each time period before deciding how much to consume and how much to save for the future (Thaler & Benartzi, 2004).

In reality, household saving behavior deviates from this ideal due to two prominent behavioral phenomena: procrastination and status quo bias (Samuelson & Zeckhauser, 1988). Procrastination is driven mainly by the complexity of the financial decisions involved in retirement saving plan enrollment. Many of the choices that one must make are complex and technical, even for people with financial or economic education. This makes people procrastinate with enrollment or with updating of their retirement plans, despite the clearly recognized importance of such activities (Thaler & Benartzi, 2004).

According to traditional economic theory, retirement decisions are driven by rational choice making that should not be influenced by insignificant factors, such as default options. Madrian and Shea (2000), however, demonstrate that changes in default options can actually produce dramatic changes in retirement plan enrollment rates.

Because retirement policies in the United States have been informed by traditional economic theory, they are grounded on assumptions of perfect rationality as defined in ways that contradict observable human behavior.

The behavioral explanation for why the problem exists

There are three main behavioral obstacles that explain why traditional retirement saving policies in the United States failed and left too many people without sufficient savings for their retirement years.

The first behavioral explanation is the so-called *present bias,* which makes people focus more on immediate gratification rather than long-term benefits. This mechanism is usually at the heart of self-control failure, including when it comes to limiting current spending to save more for the future. It is strengthened by the so-called *ideal future self-bias,* which makes decision makers convinced that despite their failure to do "the right thing" today, they will certainly be able to do it tomorrow. In other words, present bias is further fueled by the belief that it is okay to fail now, because tomorrow we will be more disciplined and will behave in the right way.

The second obstacle is associated with the established power of default options. In a widely cited study, Johnson and Goldstein (2003) show that the default on a simple driver license form leads to dramatic differences in organ donor program participation rates. In countries where participation is the default option, enrollment is around 98%–99%, while in countries where the default is nonparticipation, rates are barely around a few percent. Because US volunteer retirement programs are traditionally based on personal choice, the de facto default option has been to not enroll in a pension plan. Since the default option of not doing anything is powerful, in the context of retirement planning context it leaves a large share of the population out of the system. This is further fueled by the fact that enrollment involves making more than 15 complicated financial choices. Complexity leads people to procrastinate with these choices and eventually to not enroll at all.

The third behavioral obstacle leading to the ineffectiveness of the traditional retirement system in the United States is *loss aversion*. This relates to the human inclination to be much more proactive in avoiding losses than to pursue gains. This mechanism kicks in when it comes to savings too, because emotionally and mentally, people frame savings as a loss (i.e., as money they are not able to spend now).

The behavioral solution

A proposed solution to the retirement savings problem in the United States is the *Save More Tomorrow* program, developed by two leading behavioral researchers: Richard Thaler and Shlomo Benartzi. They offer a retirement savings model that flips the behavioral challenges, explaining how low retirement plan enrollment rates can be turned into solutions that stimulate participation.

The first trigger incorporated in the program's design is based on the default mechanism. Workers are automatically enrolled in a retirement plan to benefit from the power of defaults. Default enrollment in retirement planning has been shown to produce dramatic shifts in enrollment rates (Madrian & Shea, 2000). The option to opt out of retirement saving still remains available, but to select it, workers have to proactively make the effort to choose to leave the program.

The second behavioral mechanism incorporated in the *Save More Tomorrow* program uses the power of ideal future self-bias, which makes people convinced that they will be much better at making the right choices tomorrow than they are today. Using this idea, the retirement plan program asks people to commit to save more in the future instead of today. This is achieved by a commitment to a plan involving increase of the rate at which they save for retirement each time they receive a salary raise. Because it relates to the future, people commit to this with ease and do not perceive the additional saving in the future as loss.

The third behavioral mechanism incorporated in the *Save More Tomorrow* program is to suppress loss aversion by extracting the increased savings amount (due to salary increases) before it gets to the worker's paycheck. By not seeing the money go to their savings account, people do not experience the emotional pain associated with loss and therefore do not experience the force of loss aversion.

These three mechanisms combined together are at the core of the Save More Tomorrow program, which has been incorporated in the most current Pension Protection Act in the United States.

Results and benefits of using the behavioral solution—comparative effectiveness, comparative costs, and more

The first trial of the *Save More Tomorrow* was executed at a US company where the dominant share of the workers were blue collar with low income and little background in finance and economics. This segment is considered to be the most vulnerable to under saving. In fact, most of the participating workers openly state that they cannot imagine saving at all, as they live from paycheck to paycheck.

The *Save More Tomorrow* program automatically enrolled all workers in retirement saving plans, resulting in an enrollment rate of 78%. The program asked participants to commit that every time they receive a pay raise, they will increase the rate at which they save by 3%. The program also made the savings amount go directly to the workers' savings account without appearing on the paycheck to suppress possible loss aversion.

As result of the *Save More Tomorrow* program, workers at the company saw a dramatic increase in their retirement saving rates. While in the first year (1998), the average savings rate was 3.5%, and just 5 years later, the savings rate quadrupled, reaching an average of 13.6%. This increase translated into savings that support a dramatically different quality of life.

As result of this natural experiment, many programs following the principle of *Save More Tomorrow* have been rolled out at more than 60% of large companies in the United States. The approach of the *Save More Tomorrow* program has also been incorporated in the most recent amendments of the Pension Protection Act in the United States.

References

Benartzi, S. (2011). Saving for tomorrow, tomorrow. TEDSalon NY2011: TED. Available from <https://www.ted.com/talks/shlomo_benartzi_saving_more_tomorrow> Accessed 09.01.18.

Benartzi, S. (2012). *Save more tomorrow: Practical behavioral finance solutions to improve 401 (k) plans*. New York: Penguin Group. Available from https://www.google.com/books?hl = en&lr = &id = WYD_Bm97ZRIC&oi = fnd&pg = PT10&dq = Save + More + Tomorrow: + Practical + Behavioral + Finance + Solutions + to + Improve + 401&ots = 57f_DtlHOA&sig = YFnfM38vE8wrxmx1J3M1r7kngro.

Johnson, E. J., & Goldstein, D. (2003). Do defaults save lives? *Science*, *302*, 1338–1339. Available from https://doi.org/10.1126/science.1091721.

Madrian, B. C., & Shea, D. F. (2000). *The power of suggestion: Inertia in 401(k) participation and savings behavior the power of suggestion: Inertia in 401(k) participation and savings behavior* (Working Paper No. 7682). Cambridge. Available from http://www.nber.org/papers/w7682.

Samuelson, W., & Zeckhauser, R. (1988). Status quo bias in decision making. *Journal of Risk and Uncertainty*, *1*, 7–59. Available from http://web.mit.edu/curhan/www/docs/Articles/biases/1_J_Risk_Uncertainty_7_(Samuelson).pdf.

Thaler, R. H., & Benartzi, S. (2004). Save more tomorrow: Using behavioral economics to increase employee saving. *Journal of Political Economy*, *112*(2). Available from http://www.journals.uchicago.edu/doi/pdfplus/10.1086/380085.

Case 2 Smarter lunchrooms movement

The challenge

Childhood obesity has become a dominant public concern in many developing countries, especially in the United States, where over 17% of children and adolescents are overweight (Skinner & Skelton, 2014). Children's obesity rates are even more disturbing among disadvantaged segments of society.

Childhood obesity is associated with high social and economic costs. Excessive weight is linked to increases in serious health conditions among children and reduced educational and employment opportunities (NIH Obesity Research Task Force, 2011).

The sharp increase of scientific research in the area of obesity and nutrition has produced numerous theories for a combination of factors that explain the fast growth of childhood obesity rates. While it is hard to point to one or two dominant factors, reasons seem to work in combinations with different impacts for different social groups (Cawley, 2015), and it is clear that the type of food consumed by children deserves consideration. The dominant consumption of energy-dense foods with limited nutritional value combined with a limited consumption of fresh fruits, vegetables, and other healthy foods is one of the main causes of obesity among children. This problem has been reinforced by school lunch services, as many US school cafeterias systematically provide limited and mostly unhealthy food options.

The assumption(s) that fueled the problem

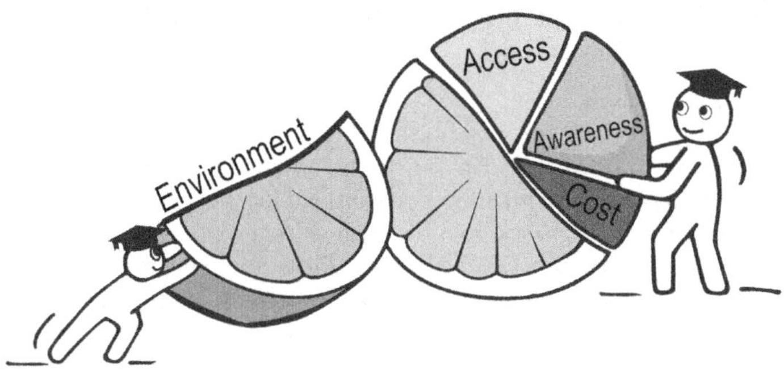

As discussed earlier, there are numerous factors thought to have led to the severity of the US child obesity problem. The main issue is a limited awareness on the importance of a balanced diet among responsible institutions and parents. This has led to the limited availability of healthy foods in school cafeterias where food choices are determined mainly on a cost basis. Lack of education about healthy eating has further reinforced the problem.

Food choices have been subject to general assumptions about decision-making as being driven by rational analysis of all available choices followed by selection of the one that offers most benefits. This underlies the belief that if both healthy and unhealthy options are available in a cafeteria, decision makers will weigh the benefits and choose the food option that is best for them.

Over time with the advance of obesity concerns, policy makers and researchers have made different assumptions that are easily questioned by behavioral scientists. Among these are assumptions that young people know how much they want to eat and when they are full, or that mindful awareness on calorie intake and portion control are sufficient to manage weight (Wansink, Just, & Payne, 2009).

The behavioral explanation for why the problem exists

One of the main problems that fuel the obesity epidemic is that children have limited knowledge about the importance of a healthy diet. Lack of information leads to inability to recognize which foods are healthy and unhealthy, and what food choices are good or bad for the child.

The availability and easy access to unhealthy foods is another major factor. For example, school cafeterias are traditionally known for featuring fast-food items along with sugary drinks, which obviously stimulates the consumption of such foods. Additionally, lunch times are often limited to less time than that needed to consume foods at a pace that is healthy digestively, so students must rush through their selections to have a reasonable amount of time to eat their mid-day meal.

Recent advances in behavioral research have also established the importance of factors such as heuristics (shortcuts) in choosing among available food options (Schulte-Mecklenbeck, Sohn, De Bellis, Martin, & Hertwig, 2013). The role environmental factors, such as setting and size of portion (Ebbeling, Pawlak, & Ludwig, 2002), as well as packaging, plate shape, lighting, available variety, and the social company affect food choices and volumes consumed.

The lack of awareness on the influence of such additional factors on food choice has led to assumptions that cafeteria design, information availability, and general setting do not have impact on the choices that children make when selecting food items for lunch.

The behavioral solution

One large-scale effort to improve the quality of eating in US schools is the Smarter Lunchroom Movement. The program was launched at Cornell University by two leading researchers on food decision-making and behavior, David Just and Brian Wansink. In 2010 the two researchers established The Cornell Center for Behavioral Economics in Child Nutrition Programs, which has initiated the Smarter Lunchrooms Movement. The aim of the movement is to use advances in behavioral science to identify lunchroom solutions and tactics that lead to healthier eating among school children. The National Office of the Smarter Lunchrooms Movement provides tools, training, strategies, and support for the many participants in the program seeking to create environments that "nudge" students toward better nutrition and improved overall health.

Results and benefits of using the behavioral solution (comparative effectiveness, comparative costs, etc.)

The Smarter Lunchrooms Program works with more than 30,000 schools across the United States. The main tool it offers to partner institutions is a handbook with 60 low-cost or no-cost simple tactics for healthier eating and a scorecard to monitor performance over time. Some examples of scientifically proven tactics incorporated in Smarter Lunchroom designs include (Just & Wansink, 2017):

- Making vegetables available at two locations in the cafeteria, which can result in students taking up to 40% more.
- Holding recess before lunch, which can increase vegetable and fruit consumption by 54%.
- Serving fruit in colorful fruit bowls (instead of the traditional stainless steel bowls) can double fruit sales.
- Using fun, descriptive names for healthy food choices (e.g., "superpower peas" for green peas) can increase their consumption by 30%.
- Serving fruits in slices can increase consumption by 70%.
- Simply suggesting to students to take a fruit increases the number of students eating (and not simply taking) a fruit by up to 70%.

Research that the Smarter Lunchrooms Program continues to generate is supported and used by numerous institutions, and it has begun informing policies related to children's nutrition, food services at schools and academic institutions, food labeling, and more.

References

Cawley, J. (2015). An economy of scales: A selective review of obesity's economic causes, consequences, and solutions. *Journal of Health Economics*, *43*, 244–268. Available from https://ac-els-cdn-com.proxygw.wrlc.org/S0167629615000296/1-s2.0-S0167629615000296-main.pdf?_tid = 33a2b938-e2b7-11e7-ae06-00000aab0f27&acdnat = 1513466393_2e29da9e048eeeea9f2a6c7aec943c49.

Ebbeling, C. B., Pawlak, D. B., & Ludwig, D. S. (2002). International epidemic of childhood obesity. *The Lancet*, *360*(9331), 473–482. Available from http://corcom130-sp10-advertising.wikispaces.umb.edu/file/view/Childhood obesity.pdf/132419279/Childhood obesity.pdf.

Just, D., & Wansink, B. (2017). *How to build a smarter lunchroom: The healthy choice, the easy choice*. Handbook by the Smarter Lunchrooms Movement National Office, Cornell Center for Behavioral Economics in Child Nutrition Programs.

NIH Obesity Research Task Force. (2011). *Strategic plan for NIH obesity research* (No. 11–5493). Available from https://www.niddk.nih.gov/about-niddk/strategic-plans-reports/strategic-plan-for-nih-obesity-research.

Schulte-Mecklenbeck, M., Sohn, M., De Bellis, E., Martin, N., & Hertwig, R. (2013). A lack of appetite for information and computation. Simple heuristics in food choice. *Apetite*, *71*, 242–251. Available from https://doi.org/10.1016/j.appet.2013.08.008.

Skinner, A. C., & Skelton, J. A. (2014). Prevalence and trends in obesity and severe obesity among children in the United States, 1999–2012. *JAMA Pediatrics*, *168*(6), 561. Available from https://doi.org/10.1001/jamapediatrics.2014.21.

Wansink, B., Just, D. E., & Payne, C. E. (2009). Mindless eating and healthy heuristics for the irrational. *American Economic Review: Papers & Proceedings*, *99*(2), 165–169. Available from https://doi.org/10.1257/aer.99.2.165.

Case 3 Making roads safer

The challenge

Traffic accidents are a leading cause of premature deaths in many societies. While automobile technology and road infrastructure design have been helping improve safety performance, many features of modern life have been having the opposite effect. Distractions due to mobile phones or other gadgets (Wang, Bao, Du, Ye, & Sayer, 2017) and overall stress levels (Useche, Serge, & Alonso, 2015) depleting self-control and limiting attention are among the most frequent causes for errors leading to accidents on the road.

Even though the United Kingdom is one of the countries in Europe with a lower rate of traffic accidents, they still constitute a significant cost to society. In 2016 traffic accidents in the United Kingdom caused more than 250,000 casualties, including 1792 fatalities and 24,101 seriously injured. In 21% of the cases in 2016, accidents were entirely or partially due to aggressive or reckless driving (Department of Transportation, 2017).

During an interesting trial of behaviorally framed interventions to minimize speeding offenses and improve collection of fines, the BIT collaborated with East Sussex

County Council and West Midlands Police to study causes of fatal accidents. The area sees 64% more accidents than the rest of England (Behavioural Insights Team, 2017).

The analysis of the BIT research team revealed that 10% of accidents and 7% of those involving fatalities or serious injuries are caused by people with at least one previous speeding conviction (Ruda, Silva, & Wieshmann, 2017). Despite previous offenses, these drivers continue to drive recklessly, disregarding traffic rules and speed limits.

The main task of the team was twofold: to increase compliance with speeding sanctions and to reduce repeat speeding offenses.

Assumptions that fuel the problem

Just like in many countries, traffic laws and enforcement procedures in the United Kingdom are designed around thinking that violators engage in such behavior on the basis of estimated risk, estimated chances of being caught, and benefits from the act. In reality, risk perceptions in driving context vary depending on contextual and personality factors (Eboli, Mazzulla, & Pungillo, 2017). In addition, drivers, in many cases, do not have enough information to estimate the actual risk they are taking when violating a traffic regulation (Useche et al., 2015). Research has shown that speed limit awareness is not enough to ensure compliance, even after reminders of the limit and the potential for being fined (Lu, Zhang, & Perloff, 2016). Regarding benefits, except in rare cases, speeding does not really yield major benefits, except perhaps saving some time.

The behavioral explanation for why the problem exists

There are multiple behavioral factors that can explain the tendency to violate speeding limits and to reoffend. In most cases, speeding is caused by the driver's limited attention or distraction caused by situational factors, overconfidence bias (leading drivers to believe that they are more competent and skillful that others on the road) (Deery,

1999), and present bias (O'Donoghue & Rabin, 2015), which motivates drivers to focus on the momentous thrill of speeding rather than mid- to long-term consequences of violating traffic rules. Optimism bias is also at play as drivers underestimate the probability of causing an accident due to speeding (Shepperd, Carroll, Grace, & Terry, 2002). Additionally, rationale behind speed limits is not salient, which leads to drivers ignoring the link between speed limit violations and the risk of an accident and loss of life.

The behavioral solution

The starting point for addressing this challenge was an in-depth analysis of multiyear collision data with an emphasis on behavioral findings. Analysis revealed that accidents are more likely to happen because of speeding, that overconfidence is often at play, and that a significant share of speeding violations are committed by repeat offenders. Accidents involving occupational drivers were not found to be more common than those involving regular drivers (a commonly held belief by the public).

Based on these findings and using the BIT framework for behavioral solutions (easy, attractive, social, timely), the intervention team proposed focus on lowering the rate of repeat speed limit violations through changes in the existing violation notification process for drivers who have been caught speeding. The notice that violating drivers received was redesigned to include visual and simple information that focused on the rationale behind why speed limits should be followed rather than on the sanctions and risks of noncompliance. The Notice of Intended Prosecution, the document that violators of a speed limit would receive, was completely revamped to provide understandable and easy-to-process information explaining the reasons behind the speed limits and risks associated with violating them. The new notice contains an image of flowers at a roadside area of an apparent deadly accident spot with the title, "No driver means to kill. They were just going too fast." This is followed by some statistics on the loss of children's lives as result of road accidents and the fact that speed is one of the main causes of accidents. This format of the communication shifts the focus to explaining why speed limits are in place and potential consequences of violating them.

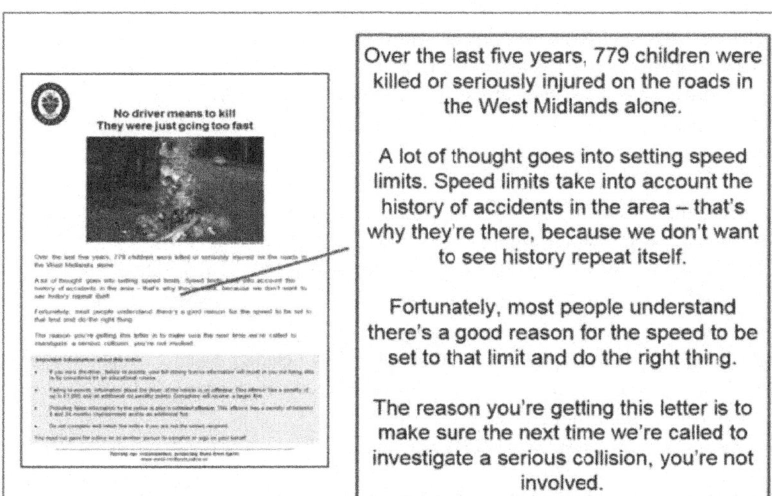

O-behave! (2017).

Results and benefits of using the behavioral solution

The solution was tested among 15,346 drivers who were caught speeding. The intervention (i.e., receiving the redesigned notice for the violation) reduced the likelihood for reoffending by 20% within 6 months of the offense. The timely payment of penalty notices was also increased by 13.7%, reducing the likelihood for prosecuting by more than 41% (Ruda et al., 2017). Based on data from the West Midlands Police and their home office, the BIT team estimated that if the solution were to be applied across West Midlands, annual savings would equal £1.5million for the criminal justice system and £25million if applied across England and Wales (O-behave!, 2017).

An important element of this behavioral intervention's success was the fact that it was very low-cost. One of the challenges presented to the BIT team was that the existing budget of involved institution did not allow for any significant modifications, so speed limit behavior had to be addressed with minimal cost.

Based on the success of this project, the intervention is now being replicated with the London Metropolitan Police.

References

Behavioural Insights Team. (2017). The behavioural insights team - Update report 2016-17 (pp. 1–58). Available from http://www.behaviouralinsights.co.uk/wp-content/uploads/2015/07/BIT_Update-Report-Final-2013-2015.pdf.

Deery, H. A. (1999). Hazard and risk perception among young novice drivers. *Journal of Safety Research*, *30*(4), 225–236. Available from https://ac-els-cdn-com.proxygw.wrlc.org/S0022437599000183/1-s2.0-S0022437599000183-main.pdf?_tid = 838c2f40-f8ad-11e7-9b45-00000aab0f6b&acdnat = 1515881166_46a835ffe732b9284dbf356f4cb61813.

Department of Transportation. (2017). *Reported road casualties in Great Britain: 2016 annual report*. Available from https://www.gov.uk/government/uploads/system/uploads/attachment_data/file/648081/rrcgb2016-01.pdf.

Eboli, L., Mazzulla, G., & Pungillo, G. (2017). Measuring the driver's perception error in the traffic accident risk evaluation. *IET Intelligent Transport Systems*, *11*(10), 659–666. Available from https://doi.org/10.1049/iet-its.2017.0084.

Lu, F., Zhang, J., & Perloff, J. M. (2016). General and specific information in deterring traffic violations: Evidence from a randomized experiment. *Journal of Economic Behavior & Organization*, *123*, 97–107. Available from https://ac-els-cdn-com.proxygw.wrlc.org/S0167268115003339/1-s2.0-S0167268115003339-main.pdf?_tid = c9c2e55e-f8b1-11e7-8a03-00000aacb35f&acdnat = 1515882994_d9fbe9e0c600da85cf810b746ace4604.

O-behave!. (2017). Making our roads safer - The 2017 Nudge Awards: Nudge for good. *O-Behave! Blog*. Available from http://o-behave.tumblr.com/post/162708993447/making-our-roads-safer-the-2017-nudge-awards.

O'Donoghue, T., & Rabin, M. (2015). Present bias: Lessons learned and to be learned. *American Economic Review: Papers & Proceedings*, *105*(5), 273–279. Available from https://doi.org/10.1257/aer.p20151085.

Ruda, S., Silva, M. W., & Wieshmann, H. (2017). Improving road safety: New results. *The Behavioral Insights Team Blog*.

Shepperd, J. A., Carroll, P., Grace, J., & Terry, M. (2002). Exploring the causes of comparative optimism. *Psychologica Belgica*, *42*, 65–98. Available from https://s3.amazonaws.com/academia.edu.documents/34145086/PsychBelgica2002.pdf?AWSAccessKeyId = AKIAIWOWYYGZ2Y53UL3A&Expires = 1515895939&Signature = yIw3Cn26QfQ%2BFmFbeKeqWPJDtHE%3D&response-content-disposition = inline%3B filename%3DExploring_the_Causes_of_Comparative_Opti.pdf.

Useche, S., Serge, A., & Alonso, F. (2015). Risky behaviors and stress indicators between novice and experienced drivers. *American Journal of Applied Psychology*, *3*(1), 11–14. Available from https://doi.org/10.12691/ajap-3-1-3.

Wang, Y., Bao, S., Du, W., Ye, Z., & Sayer, J. R. (2017). Examining drivers' eye glance patterns during distracted driving: Insights from scanning randomness and glance transition matrix. *Journal of Safety Research*, *63*, 149–155. Available from https://doi.org/10.1016/j.jsr.2017.10.006.

Case 4 Using behaviorally-friendly design to encourage loan payoff

The challenge

According to data from the Federal Reserve Bank of New York as of December 31, 2016, total household indebtedness of US households was $12.58 trillion, marking a 1.8% increase from the third quarter of 2016 and 12.8% from the second quarter of 2013. As of December 31, 2016, 4.8% of US household outstanding debt ($607 billion) was in some stage of delinquency, and 3.3% ($412 billion) was seriously delinquent (at least 90 days late or "severely derogatory") (Federal Reserve Bank of New York, 2017).

A large share of household debt is associated with mortgages. In 2014 the total number of households using more than 30% of their income for housing increased to 40 million, with almost 20% of households using more than 50% of their income to pay for housing costs (Common Cents Lab, 2016). Long payoff periods generate additional debt burden due to interest, higher risk of default, and lack of savings.

To respond to this need, fintech startup *APASave* developed a smart software-based service that intelligently syncs household income and expenses to enable faster mortgage payoff and thus an increased savings rate. Even though the opportunity offered by the young company is easy to use and translates to obvious benefits such as decrease in loan term by over 5 years and faster building of net worth through saving money, consumers are very hesitant to enroll and benefit from this opportunity.

Assumptions that fuel the problem

According to traditional thinking, debt repayment decisions are a tradeoff between the desire to minimize current and future total costs over the life of the loan. If this reflects typical consumer behavior, most debtors would base their repayments on a calculated amount that offers optimal balance between minimizing current costs and total costs depending on the household's income. However, behavioral scientists have established that due to a strong anchoring effect, minimum required payments strongly determine the decision for what amount the consumer will pay (Navarro-Martinez et al., 2011). Making information about future cost of the debt salient has also proved to influence debt repayment behavior, suggesting that under regular circumstances, consumers do not consider future cost and do not seek to optimize against their current ability to pay.

Another traditional assumption, which seems to be violated here, is that consumers optimize when choosing between different options available to them. If that was the case, making debtors aware of the APASave service should be sufficient to motivate them to choose the service, as it provides a favorable optimization between current costs and long-term wealth accumulation.

The behavioral explanation for why the problem exists

Previous research in the area of behavioral finance has revealed that average consumers seek to simplify financial decisions and often use heuristics. Biases, such as anchoring, have powerful influence on the decisions that consumers make, including when deciding on what payment amounts to make on their debts (Navarro-Martinez et al., 2011).

One common heuristic used by consumers to simplify debt payment decisions is rounding. According to Wang and Keys (2014), two-thirds of the consumers who stick to minimum rate payments when repaying their credit cards round up within $50 of the required amount. Analysis of mortgage repayment data conducted by the Common Cents Lab and *APASave* also revealed that many people are paying more than required due to rounding of payment amounts to the nearest $5 or $10. This suggests that the voluntary inclination of debtors to make higher payments is part of a decision simplification tactic rather than rational effort to optimize current and future costs.

Resistance to switching to the more favorable *APASave* service could be explained by two effects. One is inertia or status quo bias, which has been shown to have strong influence on consumers' financial decisions, preventing them from benefiting from apparently superior options (Madrian & Shea, 2000). The second effect is associated with the perception of savings as loss (seeing earned money as money that cannot be spent).

The behavioral solution

To respond to the challenge, *Common Cents Lab* and *APASave*took a behaviorally informed approach. First, to suppress the association between savings and loss, communication messages promoting the company's services were reframed around earning money back rather than saving. The value proposition of the service was changed from "save money on a mortgage" to "earn money back from a mortgage." As part of that intervention, the name of the company was also changed from *APASave* to *EarnUp* (Common Cents Lab, 2016).

The second intervention revolved around battling the anchoring effect of minimum payment rates. To overcome the inertia of choosing to make a monthly payment that equals the required minimum, *EarnUp* proactively prompted consumers to overpay by explaining the advantage of increasing monthly payments by even a small amount. Given that the average mortgage amount for a new loan in the United States is $312,700 at a 30-year-fixed interest rate of 3.76%, adding just an extra $25 a month to the repayment amount will translate to savings of over $7000 and early full repayment by a whole year (Common Cents Lab, 2016). Using knowledge about rounding up as heuristic, the team tested two prompt designs: (1) prompt to overpay by rounding up and (2) prompt to overpay without a suggestion for rounding up.

Results and benefits of using the behavioral solution

The emphasis on earning versus saving in the value proposition and in the name of the company translated to a sharp increase of the interest among consumers exposed to advertisement. The new framing of the marketing messages led to an increase of click-through rates on online advertisements by 59%.

Direct prompts for overpaying provided rationale and also led to change in repayment behavior. Both conditions (prompt to overpay and prompt to overpay by rounding up) increased individual monthly payments, but the rate observed for the roundup group was higher (13% compared with 10% for the general overpay prompted group). In both conditions, the average amount by which consumers decided to overpay was $60, which translated to about $8000 of savings over the life of a loan and a total of $1,300,000 in interest saved for *EarnUp* users who agreed to pay more than their minimum payment. A full 86% of the people who agreed to overpay declared that they had never before done that with any other loan (Common Cents Lab, 2016).

Based on insights on financial behavior, *EarnUp* continues to successfully grow its business of integrating loans and optimizing their repayment. Using heuristics-based design in messaging and service, the startup simplifies financial decision-making and optimizes repayment and saving in a way that is favorable for debtors and profitable for the company.

References

Common Cents Lab. (2016). *Common cents lab end of year 2016 report*. Available from https://advanced-hindsight.com/wp-content/uploads/2017/01/Using-Psychologically-Satisfying-Numbers-to-Pay-Off-Loans-Faster-EarnUp.pdf

Federal Reserve Bank of New York. (2017). *Quarterly report on household debt and credit*. New York. Available from https://www.newyorkfed.org/medialibrary/interactives/householdcredit/data/pdf/HHDC_2016Q4.pdf.

Madrian, B. C., & Shea, D. F. (2000). *The power of suggestion: Inertia in 401(k) participation and savings behavior the power of suggestion: Inertia in 401(k) participation and savings behavior* (Working Paper No. 7682). Cambridge. Available from http://www.nber.org/papers/w7682.

Navarro-Martinez, D., Salisbury, L. C., Lemon, K. N., Stewart, N., Matthews, W. J., & Harris, A. J. L. (2011). Minimum required payment and supplemental information disclosure effects on consumer debt repayment decisions. *Journal of Marketing Research, XLVIII*(Special Issue 2011), S60–S77. Available from https://www2.bc.edu/linda-salisbury/Navarro-Martinez_Salisbury_etal_2011.pdf.

Wang, J., & Keys, B. J. (2014). *Perverse nudges: Minimum payments and debt paydown in consumer credit cards* (Penn Wharton Public Policy Initiative No. Book 25). Available from http://repository.upenn.edu/pennwhartonppi.

Case 5 Designing policy with happiness in mind

The challenge

In recent years, leading economists have initiated a discussion as to whether GDP continues to be the most appropriate measure of progress, yet it remains to be the most commonly referred to indicator. Nearly all global country ranking sources and growth indices consider GDP to be its leading or one of its leading elements. GDP is used to judge whether a country is advancing or lagging behind in economic growth and providing for a better quality of life for its citizens.

The challenge with this is that the prioritization of economic growth as measure for how a country is doing has made it synonymous with measure for the wellbeing of its residents. The majority of contemporary societies are driven by the idea that higher income and purchasing power are associated with higher quality of life. Strategic decisions made by policy makers and government leaders are based on this assumption. At the same time, multiple scientific studies reveal that increasing income and GDP are not correlated to well-being measures, and that in many of the most successful economies' happiness levels remain the same over the past decades or are falling (Easterlin, 1995; Layard, 2010).

In the past decade, an increasing number of researchers have raised concern with the fact that while societies and politicians assume there is a strong correlation between income and wellbeing, statistical data reveals that higher monetary gains do not produce better quality of life or higher levels of happiness. In light of these findings and as result of scientific advances in the area of happiness, researchers have been calling for moving away from policy design practices that focus on raising average incomes and GDP and replacing them with such that place well-being at their core (Diener, 2000; Kahneman, Krueger, Schkade, Schwarz, & Stone, 2004; Layard, 1980). With the notable exception of the country of Bhutan, where governance is based on the adopted Gross National Happiness Index instead of on GDP, few countries have made progress toward policy making that prioritizes happiness of their populations.

Assumptions that fuel the problem

For many decades, government decision making and policy design have been driven by the idea that improving the average income of a population leads to an improved quality of life. This, in essence, has equated *wellbeing* with *having*. Based on this assumption, policies and public investments have been designed with the priority to facilitate increase in the national income per capita. Similarly in countries that lag behind in their development, donor agencies invest in measures to improve the quality of life by increasing income levels.

The behavioral explanation for why the problem exists

Numerous scientists have already demonstrated that income and happiness do not go hand in hand. Studies report that across the economies in Europe, the United States, and Japan that have experienced significant growth after the 1950s, the level of reported happiness does not seem to change in any relationship with the increasing GDP and income levels (Easterlin, 1995). Reported levels of happiness in the United States have remained flat since the

1950s, despite the strong growth of the American economy (Layard, 2010). A chapter in the 2017 Happiness Report reveals a similar observation for China, which has been experiencing unprecedented growth levels, but this does not seem to translate to higher happiness levels.

A targeted analysis of the relationship between happiness and income in the United States revealed that while poverty (i.e., low income) impacts sense of wellbeing and exacerbates the impact of other unhappy events such as divorce or health problems, correlation between income and sense of wellbeing was observed until household income reached the average for the US $75,000. After this, income level did not have impact on the reported level of happiness (Kahneman & Deaton, 2010).

Results from the famous Harvard Study of Adult Development also support these insights and finds that the only factors seeming to have significant impact on perceived happiness are social and personal relationships (Waldinger & Schulz, 2010).

The behavioral solution

In principle based on traditional economic thinking, policies across different countries are designed to maximize the sum of cardinal utilities associated with higher income, more and higher paying jobs, etc. instead of utility in the form of population happiness and perceived wellbeing (Layard, 2010). An example of the different policy perspectives that focus on economic measures versus on happiness is provided by Layard (2010), who explains that the promotion of mobility policies makes sense for policy makers that seek to increase income, as mobility is proven to increase it. However, mobility also means separating from family members and social networks, which translates to loneliness and low levels of reported happiness. So from a wellbeing perspective, stimulating mobility is not a great policy solution.

Advances in scientific research in the area of happiness have enabled the identification of the key factors that lead to increased happiness and the ones that kill it. This has made it possible to promote national and international measures of happiness levels (Krueger & Stone, 2014), which are beginning to inform policy design.

Results and benefits of using the behavioral solution

One pilot effort to adopt happiness-driven policies comes from the United Kingdom as result of the pioneering work on happiness and policy from Professor Richard Layard, based at the London School of Economics. As part of the Wellbeing Program at the Center for Economic Performance founded by him, he and his colleagues confirmed that income is not important contributor to happiness but that leading contributors to unhappiness are anxiety and depression, which are increasingly prevalent in contemporary societies. Based on this finding, Professor Layard proposes policy measures that make mental support services widely available, especially through schools. According to the estimates of his team, the investment in the expansion of these public services is below the cost that British society would pay to address the effects of mental health problems at a later stage (Layard, n.d.). To test the effect of potential public mental health services in the early 2000s, CET launched trials of the 18-hour Penn Resilience Programme, designed to increase the mental resilience of young people, at 22 English schools. Based on the success of the pilot, the program has been expanded and later included 60 schools across 10 localities. Based on the positive results of these trials in 2007, the UK Secretary of State for Health announced the launch of a program for Improving Access to Psychological Therapies (IAPT), which became an integrated part of the National Health Services. According to the latest report, results the IAPT program is offering support and treatment services to 400,000 people a year and demonstrates 45 per cent recovery rates.

Meanwhile, the increasing attention to the need to account for wellbeing as part of measuring how well a country is doing has led to the rising influence of the World Happiness Report as well as to the initiation of 50 changes in the way that Eurostat and national statistical institutes across EU member states collect, report, and use data. Changes include the adding of measures of leisure time, health, the quality of social relationships, and subjective wellbeing reports (Fleurbaey, n.d.).

References

Diener, E. (2000). Subjective well-being: The science of happiness and a proposal for a national index. *American Psychologist, 55*(1), 34–43. Available from https://doi.org/10.1037//0003-066X.55.1.34.

Easterlin, R. A. (1995). Will raising the incomes of all increase the happiness of all? *Journal of Economic Behavior and Organization, 27*, 35–47. Available from http://ipidumn.pbworks.com/f/EasterlinIncomesandHappiness.pdf.

Fleurbaey, M. (n.d.). *Making sure economists count what really matters (case study).* Available from http://www.lse.ac.uk/researchAndExpertise/researchImpact/PDFs/ensure-economists-count-what-matters.pdf.

Kahneman, D., & Deaton, A. (2010). High income improves evaluation of life but not emotional well-being. *Proceedings of the National Academy of Sciences of the United States of America, 107*(38), 16489–16493. Available from https://doi.org/10.1073/pnas.1011492107.

Kahneman, D., Krueger, A. B., Schkade, D., Schwarz, N., & Stone, A. (2004). Toward national well-being accounts. *The American Economic Review, 94*(2), 429–434.

Available from https://s3.amazonaws.com/academia.edu.documents/36043016/nationalwellbeing.pdf?AWSAccessKeyId = AKIAIWOWYYGZ2Y53UL3A&Expires = 1516473805&Signature = XwDx5twIS2CnnxdZObuVfdq8iKM%3D&response-content-disposition = inline%3B filename%3DToward_National_Well-Being_A.

Krueger, A. B., & Stone, A. A. (2014). Progress in measuring subjective well-being. *Science, 346*(6205). Available from https://doi.org/10.1126/science.1256392.

Layard, R. (n.d.). *Making personal happiness and wellbeing a goal of public policy (a case study)*. Available from http://www.lse.ac.uk/researchAndExpertise/researchImpact/PDFs/happiness-wellbeing-public-policy.pdf.

Layard, R. (1980). Human satisfactions and public policy. *The Economic Journal, 90*(360), 737–750. Available from http://www.jstor.org/stable/2231740.

Layard, R. (2010). Measuring subjective well-being. *Science, 327*(5965), 311–338. Available from https://doi.org/10.1126/science.1184703.

Waldinger, R. J., & Schulz, M. S. (2010). What's love got to do with it? Social functioning, perceived health, and daily happiness in married octogenarians. *Psychology of Ageing, 25*(2), 422–431. Available from https://doi.org/10.1037/a0019087.

Case 6 Fighting obesity with air miles[1]

The challenge

Just like many countries, Canada is facing a challenge with growing obesity rates among its population. Over 30% of its youth and 60% of the adult population are overweight or obese (Organisation for Economic Co-operation and Development, 2017). Obesity is associated with significant social and economic cost to society as it leads to deteriorated health, social stigma, and limited employment opportunities.

Recent studies show that Canadians with a body mass index that is higher than 30 kg/m^2 are several times likelier to have diabetes, high blood pressure, and to experience heart disease, and that people who are already obese or overweight are getting heavier faster compared with the baseline population (Kirk, Tytus, Tsuyuki, & Sharma, 2012). Analyses have demonstrated that the total direct costs attributable to overweight and obesity complications in Canada are $6.0 billion, which corresponds to 4.1% of total Canadian health care expenditures. This rising economic burden threatens the sustainability of the Canadian health care system (Anis et al., 2010).

One of the main contributors to growing obesity levels is the widespread lack of exercise culture and the relatively inactive lifestyle of Canadian people.

Assumptions that fuel the problem

There are several popular assumptions that the obesity paradigm shift initiated by Canadian health institutions leaves behind. The first is that the increasing problem with being overweight is a problem of the individual and not a problem of

1. This case is based on a study published in a case study collection of behaviorally informed policy practices issued by Organisation for Economic Co-operation and Development (2017) and has been supplemented with additional research and data.

the society. The fast rise of obesity levels and associated problems with them include a rise in chronic medical conditions, such as heart disease, diabetes, and others, which leads to swelling healthcare costs and social costs, such as limited employment opportunities and stigma. In this context, Canadian researchers, mission-driven organizations, and institutions make an important shift in their thinking by agreeing to treat obesity as a significant problem of the society and as one that requires investment and behaviorally informed tactics.

One of the explanations for rising obesity levels is the assumption that making information and weight-loss options available are sufficient to prompt people who need to lose weight to engage in what is clearly beneficial and healthy for them. Behavioral research has established that inability to address obesity is not linked to lack of information or recognition of the problem. Individuals who are aware of the need to lower their weight and know the effective steps to doing so are failing at executing or sustaining the habits that are needed.

The behavioral explanation for why the problem exists

A number of decision errors described in behavioral literature explain the irrational resistance to corrective actions among people who are obese or overweight. One reason is inertia, which makes it easier to stick to current habits rather than to introduce new ones. The second is present bias, which fuels the attractiveness of instant gratification of enjoying food compared with the benefit of restriction leading to a better future self. A third challenge is the difficulty associated with imagining the future self and envisioning the future effects of current choices, especially if they are in the further future as pertains to results from dieting and exercising. Procrastination is also at play, as most individuals find it easier to postpone the start of a diet for the next day, influenced by the overconfidence effect.

The behavioral solution

As part of an overall shift in obesity public policy, the Public Health Agency of Canada is adopting a different perspective to the problem. Driven by medical and behavioral research initiated through the Canadian Obesity Network, society and institutions are recognizing that the scale of the obesity epidemic and the wrong reliance on the assumptions that individuals can resolve weight problems on their own require innovative measures. These include developing capacity and funding behavioral and medical interventions that can address and alleviate obesity depending on the level of severity (CCDP, 2015).

Given that one of the main causes of obesity is a sedentary lifestyle with a lack of a regular exercise routine, the Centre for Chronic Disease Prevention, under the Public Health Agency of Canada, launched a pilot program for motivating Canadians to engage in more regular exercise. Grounded on knowledge from behavioral sciences, the program design utilizes the nudge theory and places focus on attractive incentives rather than on explaining benefits of exercising.

Loyalty programs are very popular in Canada, and Canadian households are among the highest users of loyalty programs, collecting points from an average of eight loyalty programs at a time. To transform this popular love for loyalty programs into a nudge to exercise, the CCDP partners, with the leading provider of reward programs LoyaltyOne Inc. and YMCA Canada fitness clubs, to offer air mileage rewards in exchange for physical activity (Organisation for Economic Co-operation and Development, 2017).

Results and benefits of using the behavioral solution

The program initially includes two offers: a base offer (one air mile for every two visits to a fitness club) and a bonus offer (10 air miles for every week in which the participant completed two fitness visits or 20 air miles if the visits to the gym are three times per week or more). A few months after the launch, the design of the program is modified deliberately: the base offer is eliminated to test whether the base of participants driven by loss aversion will seek to avoid losing their accumulated rewards by switching to the bonus option.

The program ends up enticing 98,000 participants, which is four times the target set before the start of the pilot. Results show that 62% of the active YMCA members visited the fitness center at least one more time each week, and that enrolled members visited their gym, on average, 17% more frequently than those who were not enrolled.

While initial results are optimistic, more detailed analysis of observed behavioral effects are still underway. The project is also evaluated by using a Social Return On Impact analysis, which reveals that every Canadian dollar invested in the program translates into the value of 3.5 Canadian dollars saved in total costs attributable to overweight and obesity conditions (Organisation for Economic Co-operation and Development, 2017).

References

Anis, A. H., Zhang, W., Bansback, N., Guh, D. P., Amarsi, Z., & Birmingham, C. L. (2010). Obesity and overweight in Canada: An updated cost-of-illness study. *Obesity Reviews, 11*(1), 31–40.

CCDP. (2015). *Improving health outcomes: A paradigm shift (strategic plan 2016–2019).* Available from http://www.phac-aspc.gc.ca/cd-mc/assets/pdf/ccdp-strategic-plan-2016-2019-plan-strategique-cpmc-eng.pdf.

Kirk, S. F., Tytus, R., Tsuyuki, R. T., & Sharma, A. M. (2012). Weight management experiences of overweight and obese Canadian adults: Findings from a national survey. *Chronic Diseases and Injuries in Canada, 32*(631233). Available from https://www.canada.ca/content/dam/phac-aspc/migration/phac-aspc/publicat/hpcdp-pspmc/32-2/assets/pdf/ar-01-eng.pdf.

Organisation for Economic Co-operation and Development. (2017). *Behavioral Insights and Public Policy: Lessons from Around the World.* Paris: OECD. Available from http://dx.doi.org/10.1787/9789264270480-en.

Case 7 Improving the likelihood for enrollment and graduation of unprivileged college students[2]

The challenge

According to the latest data from the National Center for Education Statistics, the 6-year graduation rate for first-time, full-time undergraduate students at 4-year, degree-granting institutions is 59%. The graduation rates are naturally highest at institutions with selective admissions criteria and lowest at institutions with open admissions policies (National Center for Education Statistics Fast Facts, n.d.).

Despite the high rate of high school graduates who apply for a college degree (70%), many do not end up enrolling to start and others fail to complete their education. The challenge with young people who intend to start college but never do, or who fail to complete it, is significant over their lifetime in two ways. The first is associated with the missed opportunity to improve their

2. This case is based on the report *Nudging for Good* (ideas42, 2016), presenting the work of the nonprofit organization ideas42 on numerous projects with tertiary education institutions supported by multiple donors.

capabilities and to open new potential venues for career development and personal success. An analysis by the Georgetown Center on Education and the Workforce (Carnevale, Rose, & Cheah, 2012) finds that a bachelor's degree in the United States is worth, on average, $2.8 million over a lifetime, and that holders of undergraduate degrees earn 84% more than those with only a high school diploma. At the same time, just above 40% of the US. adult population actually has a completed college degree.

The second aspect with failed college graduates is associated with the fact that some end up repaying student loans for the education they started but never completed, putting themselves at a double disadvantage of burdening their budget without receiving the opportunity to benefit from the return on their investment (ideas42, 2016).

A dominant reason for starting but not completing education is inability to fund studies. Despite the availability of federal and other sources of financial aid, many students fail to access them and end up interrupting their studies and never graduating.

Assumptions that fuel the problem

Among the most widely cited assumptions that prevent university administrations from seeing and solving such challenges is the belief that as long as information about financial aid is made available, students will make the right choice. The format of the content and the channels through which it is made available are underestimated as factors that may lead to ineffective consumption or understanding of the information.

Traditional thinking also disregards the importance of context, leading to lack of consideration that when overwhelmed by academic work and many other responsibilities, students operate with thinner cognitive resources and limited attention. This leads to a limited ability to process or remember information about deadlines or steps they need to take to benefit from financial aid. As part of this undermining context, administrations often do not consider the fact that applying for financial aid might also be associated with social stigma or self-confidence problems.

A third wrongful assumption is that if students are not applying, they must have found better alternatives and must have benefitted from them.

The behavioral explanation for why the problem exists

Based on their experience with numerous projects across different tertiary education institutions in the United States, *ideas42* analyzed the many different behavioral barriers that make the college student's journey a challenging one. They find that, for example, making the step to enroll in college after being accepted is associated with the anxiety of starting something new and unknown and also with the need to fit into a new context. Difficulties with building new relationships and adapting to new social realities are faced by many freshmen, and experiences include fear of being rejected or being lonely. These challenges are especially serious for those coming from low-income families, underprivileged minority backgrounds, or from families in which they are the first to enroll in college (ideas42, 2016).

The experience of the *ideas42* team reveals that a common reason for dropping out of college is that many students face challenges with maintaining their eligibility for federal aid, which is essential for their ability to fund their studies. In most cases, students lose federal aid due to conventional reasons, such as misunderstanding the need to reapply every year, missing reminders and subsequently missing deadlines, or procrastinating and forgetting to reapply altogether (ideas42, 2016).

Dealing with the experience of completing college is challenging, and extended over time, it adds to the cognitive burden of young students. The mental resources required to manage studies and many other daily obligations translates to a limited cognitive bandwidth and attention scarcity for dealing with problems and challenges (*ideas42*, 2016). The difficulty of imagining desired success (e.g., completing a difficult course or graduating) somewhere in the distant future exacerbates the challenge of dealing with difficult periods of time. This subsequently increases the likelihood that a student with problems will seek an easier way by dropping out of their studies.

The behavioral solution

In a series of projects, *ideas42* experimented with solutions that address some of the outlined behavioral challenges making the college student journey less bumpy. In one of them, they partnered with Arizona State University to ensure that more students can benefit from available financial aid to complete their studies. Data confirms that despite the availability of federal scholarships and need-based grants, more than $2.7 billion remains unused simply because not enough students apply for aid. At the same time, many students experience financial needs, and when they do, they are more likely to drop out of college.

Behavioral science reveals that especially in busy periods when people are experiencing limited cognitive bandwidth, they are likely to forget about upcoming events and miss deadlines. The specific analysis of the *ideas42* team demonstrates that among the main reasons why federal financial aid remains unused is that students forget about deadlines, misjudge their eligibility for scholarships, or get confused with the multiple steps of the application process and the different information needed in their applications. Often, they do not realize what information about their parents is needed, and they fail to collect it or try to do so at the last moment. In addition, the misconception that students applying for financial aid are a minority leads to additional problems associated with self-confidence and identity.

All these factors result in a large number of students in need who miss the opportunity to benefit from financial aid packages, while significant amounts of aid remain unused.

To address the outlined behavioral barriers, the *ideas42* team collaborated with the University administration to introduce a behavior-friendly communication process accompanying the application steps for financial aid. The redesigned communication includes a series of emails that encourages students not only to apply for financial aid but also to apply early to benefit from the maximum potential amounts for which they may be eligible. Content and visual design aims to trigger the following effects:

- Persistently emphasize priority deadlines to make forgetting or missing them harder.
- Encourage students to speak to their parents about their application and obtain all information that the application requires in advance (including household financial information).
- Make it easier for students to judge eligibility correctly and see information about what they are required to provide through the use of visual charts and graphs.
- Boost social conformity effects and suppress self-confidence barriers by presenting information about the fact that a majority of students rely on some financial aid and that students applying for aid are not a minority.
- Present the entire application process as an easy-to-understand series of small steps that are easy to follow and keep track of.

In addition to optimizing communication with students, the intervention includes experimental communication with parents.

Results and benefits of using the behavioral solution

The experimental intervention at State University of Arizona produced impressive results. Combining student and parent communications led to a 72% increase of early applications. Early applications enabled an increase in the average financial aid students received by between $269 and $643, which translated to significant amounts over the period of their entire study. Overall, continuing communication increases the total submissions for federal aid. As a result, 1124 more students filed for federal aid, receiving a total of $27 million more in scholarships and grants replacing loans.

The estimates of the *ideas42* team reveal that the cost of the additional communication introduced in the process is less than $0.15 for each additional student who files before the priority deadline. Given that more effective use of financial aid translates to higher likelihood for graduation and lower post-graduation financial burden associated with student loans, the cost and effort invested in this simple intervention seem insignificant.

References

Carnevale, A. P., Rose, S. J., & Cheah, B. (2012). *The college payoff: Education, occupations, lifetime earnings*. Available from https://cew-7632.kxcdn.com/wp-content/uploads/2014/11/collegepayoff-complete.pdf.

ideas42. (2016). *Nudging for success: Using behavioral science to improve the postsecondary student journey. American Enterprise Institute (Anuj Shah)*. Available from http://www.ideas42.org/wp-content/uploads/2016/09/Nudging-For-Success-FINAL.pdf.

National Center for Education Statistics Fast Facts. (n.d.). <https://nces.ed.gov/fastfacts/display.asp?id = 40> Accessed 21.01.18.

Case 8 Reducing the use of disposable plastic bags in Chicago[3]

The challenge

Americans use 100 billion plastic bags a year with every US family taking home 1500 plastic shopping bags annually, only to use each of them for an average of 12 minutes in total. Despite the fact that many plastic bags are recyclable, only 1% of them are returned for recycling. Most of them end up at landfills (Center for Biological Diversity, n.d.). Given that plastic bags in landfills take more than 500 years to degrade, they represent an excessive environmental cost.

In search for a sustainable solution to the problem, many government authorities roll out bans on the use of single-use plastic bags. For example, in 2015–16, Chicago City Council banned all chain stores from providing disposable plastic bags at checkout. The ban covers single-use plastic bags but allows the use of plastic bags that are 2.25 mil or more thick and paper bags. This regulation's specificity makes it easy for stores to simply switch from using one kind of bag to another. Shoppers do not feel the difference and essentially continue using plastic bags at the same rate as before the ban. Ultimately, the ban does not lead to any change in the number of plastic bags used by shoppers (ideas42, 2017).

Assumption that fuel the problem

One of the main problems with the use of plastic bags is the fact that despite efforts to enable production of recyclable bags, the vast majority of shoppers continue treating them as single-use bags. The assumption that making the plastic bags recyclable can solve the pollution problem proves to be incorrect.

The fact that plastic bags differ and that their thickness is an indicator of single use or recyclable is expected to impact consumers and guide their usage behavior. In fact, shoppers do not differentiate between the different types of bags and simply apply the same behavioral patterns across the different categories. This is why the introduction of a ban on one kind of plastic bags merely leads to switch to another without any significant effect on the overall usage levels.

The behavioral explanation for why the problem exists

The partial ban on the use of bags at retailer outlets does not lead to any sensible behavioral change, because it provides an easy alternative that allows for sustaining the current usage model. This aligns with the inertia effect, which makes it easier to stay with the status quo model than create new habits.

3. This case is based on the project report made available on the *ideas42* blog (ideas42, 2017).

Behavioral knowledge suggests that encouraging behavioral change by providing information is also not effective. People experience resistance to negative information, such as information about environmental pollution, and are often unable to see the connection between their behavior and likely negative outcomes that are extended in the more distant future.

The behavioral solution

Chicago City Council's lack of success with their first ban provided motivation to explore alternative policies potentially more likely to trigger behavioral change among shoppers. Observations in some retailers show that introducing monetary incentives for shoppers to use reusable shopping bags is not effective either.

In November 2016, the City Council repealed the ban and replaced it with a seven-cent tax on all kinds of shopping bags provided by retailers. The use of taxes or fees on the use of plastic bags has been proven effective as a mechanism for changing shopper behavior in the United States and elsewhere (Poortinga, Whitmarsh, & Suffolk, 2012; Wagner, 2017).

The introduction of a fee on plastic bags triggers two behavioral effects. First, it triggers loss aversion, since it demands shoppers to pay for something that they are used to getting for no fee. This means that the change cannot go unnoticed, as had happened with the earlier ban resulting in a switch from one kind of plastic bags to another. The second is that the universal fee for all kinds of bags eliminates the easy switch to another kind of bag and motivates the effort to switch to reusable bags in the long run.

Results and benefits of using the behavioral solution

A study exploring the impact of the new policy included 14,168 customers of large grocery stores caught before and after the change. It reveals that prior to the launch of the tax, shoppers used, on average, 2.3 bags per shopping trip. The tax led to a 42% reduction of usage rates, pushing down the average to 1 bag per trip. Before the tax, 82% of shoppers used at least one disposable bag, and later on, the number fell to 49%. Associated with these results, the use of reusable bags increased from 13% to 33%, and the number of customers who did not use any bags at all increased from 8% to 21.5% (ideas42, 2017).

References

Center for Biological Diversity. (n.d.). Single-use plastic bag facts. <http://www.biologicaldiversity.org/programs/population_and_sustainability/expect_more_bag_less/facts.html> Accessed 22.01.18.

ideas42. (2017). *Preliminary study suggests Chicago's bag tax reduces disposable bag use by over 40 percent.* Available from http://www.ideas42.org/wp-content/uploads/2017/04/Bag-tax-results-memo-PUBLIC.FINAL_.pdf.

Poortinga, W., Whitmarsh, L., & Suffolk, C. (2012). *The introduction of a single-use carrier bag charge in wales: Attitude change and behavioural spillover effects* (WSA Working Paper Series ISSN 2050-8522 No. 01–2012). Cardiff. Available from http://orca.cf.ac.uk/73888/1/WSA-Working-Paper01-2012.pdf.

Wagner, T. P. (2017). Reducing single-use plastic shopping bags in the USA. *Waste Management, 70,* 3–12. Available from https://doi.org/10.1016/J.WASMAN.2017.09.003.

Case 9 Encouraging water conservation[4]

The challenge

Two thirds of the global population, or 4.0 billion people, experience severe water scarcity for at least 1 month per year. About half a billion people in the world experience severe water scarcity throughout the entire year (Mekonnen & Hoekstra, 2016). The fast-spreading threat of water shortage requires fundamental changes in attitudes toward water and in water consumption behavior.

In addition to the fact that only 3% of the world's water resources are fresh, pollution, drought, and a growing population have stressed many of the existing sources of fresh water. Climate change and human activities have led to the disappearance of more than half of the world's wetlands and many rivers and lakes. Experts expect that by 2025, two thirds of the population will face some form of water shortage (WWF, n.d.).

In addition to global efforts to address climate change and improve sustainable management of natural resources, the serious threat of water shortage requires fundamental changes in the attitudes toward this resource and in water

4. This case is based on the project report made available on the *ideas42* blog (ideas42, 2017) and Policy Research Working Paper #7283 by the World Bank (Datta et al., 2015).

consumption behavior, especially in communities that are already under stress. According to the World Bank, growing demographic and economic pressures have put water management as a policy priority even in relatively water-rich regions such as Latin America, which holds more than 30% of the world's freshwater resources (Datta et al., 2015).

A partnership project between the World Bank and behavioral consulting group *ideas42* executed a plan to reduce water usage in the water-constrained town of Belén in Costa Rica. Despite being located in a country with a humid tropical climate, fast population growth and expansion of the town have produced serious pressure on its resources and have led to water shortage. Analyses reveal that if current trends continue, the community will experience chronic water scarcity by 2030 (ideas42, 2017).

Assumptions that fuel the problem

One of the main sources of today's water scarcity problem is associated with the fact that until recently, water was treated as a freely given resource, so until it starts running low, communities and policy makers will not recognize that it is finite and requires management.

Traditional approaches policy makers usually resort to in case of water shortage include awareness campaigns, water price increases, or an introduction of taxes or fees. None of these measures produced significant results in Belén. Campaigns make people aware of the problem and the need to address water shortage, but having information does not lead to change in their behavior.

Water price increases also do not seem to lead to desirable results. The experience in Belén demonstrated that even a 70% increase of water prices does not translate to significant decrease in water consumption. It seems to take very little time for residents to adjust to new price levels, and over a very short period of time, they accept the new price and continue with their usual water consumption patterns.

The behavioral explanation for why the problem exists

Research conducted as part of the project in Belén reveals that resident awareness does not translate to a sense of personal responsibility to contribute to solutions to the water shortage problems. Findings suggest that people did not feel they were able cut their household water consumption. Part of the problem seemed to be the abstract idea that residents have about the quantity they consume and the meaning of the amount of cubic meters that they see on their bill. As result of this, people have a hard time deciding whether their own consumption is acceptable or requires adjustment. Findings revealed that even in cases when residents demonstrated willingness to do something about their water usage, they were unable to identify specific steps or actions that led to immediate lowering of their water consumption.

The behavioral solution

Based on the insights about the root of the problem, the *ideas42* team launched a behavioral solution that revolves around two main pillars: making sure that every resident receives easy-to-understand, personalized feedback on their monthly household water usage and is provided with specific water consumption reduction tips that help make the first step from intention to practice. The first

FIGURE 1.1 Water bill stickers indicating performance against neighbors. *Datta, S., Miranda, J. J., Zoratto, L., Calvo-González, O., Darling, M., & Lorenzana, K. (2015). A behavioral approach to water conservation: Evidence from Costa Rica (Policy Research Working Paper No. 7283). Washington, DC. Available from https://openknowledge.worldbank.org/bitstream/handle/10986/22156/A0behavioral0a0ence0from0Costa0Rica.pdf?sequence = 1&isAllowed = y.*

pillar was executed on the basis of the principle of descriptive social norms that provide a benchmark for individuals to compare their own performance or behavior against that of a social group they recognize as relevant. This mechanism was activated with a very simple solution—the use of happy face and sad face stickers that were placed on the residents' water bills. A happy face indicated that the water consumption of the respective household was below the average for their neighborhood, and a sad face indicated that the consumption level was above the average usage rate. This became an easy-to-understand indication of how people are performing against their neighbors (Fig. 1.1).

The second intervention, designed around the second pillar, involved mailing specially designed postcards addressed to each household in the town to enable specific goal setting and translation of intentions to specific steps. The card showed the average monthly consumption rate in the community and invited recipients to record their own water usage performance along with an improvement target for the following month. The card also contained a list of very specific and easy-to-execute measures that translate to lower water consumption, such as turning off the tap while brushing one's teeth, using less water in the garden, immediate repairing of water leaks (Fig. 1.2).

Results and benefits of using the behavioral solution

The results of both interventions were tested separately and produced significant results. The group of the population that received water bills with stickers benchmarking their performance against neighbors achieved a decrease of water consumption by 3.7%–5.6%. The households that received the goal-setting postcard lowered their water consumption by 3.4%–5.6%. Follow-up analyses revealed that these one-time interventions produced stable results for at least 4 months after their implementation (ideas42, 2017).

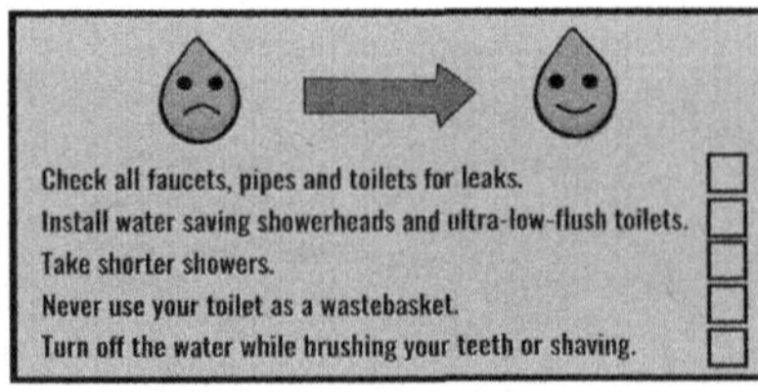

FIGURE 1.2 Postcard for goal setting and specific tips. *Datta, S., Miranda, J. J., Zoratto, L., Calvo-González, O., Darling, M., & Lorenzana, K. (2015). A behavioral approach to water conservation: Evidence from Costa Rica (Policy Research Working Paper No. 7283). Washington, DC. Available from https://openknowledge.worldbank.org/bitstream/handle/10986/22156/A0behavioral0a0ence0from0Costa0Rica.pdf?sequence = 1&isAllowed = y.*

References

Datta, S., Miranda, J. J., Zoratto, L., Calvo-González, O., Darling, M., & Lorenzana, K. (2015). *A behavioral approach to water conservation: Evidence from Costa Rica* (Policy Research Working Paper No. 7283). Washington, DC. Available from https://openknowledge.worldbank.org/bitstream/handle/10986/22156/A0behavioral0a0ence0from0Costa0Rica.pdf?sequence = 1&isAllowed = y.

ideas42. (2017, January). Encouraging water conservation: Inexpensive, replicable behavioral interventions. *ideas42 Blog*. Available from http://www.ideas42.org/wp-content/uploads/2017/02/Project-Brief_Belen.pdf.

Mekonnen, M. M., & Hoekstra, A. Y. (2016). Four billion people facing severe water scarcity. *Science Advances*, *2*(2). Available from https://doi.org/10.1126/sciadv.1500323, e1500323–e1500323.

WWF. (n.d.). Water Scarcity I Threats I WWF. <https://www.worldwildlife.org/threats/water-scarcity> Accessed 31.01.18.

Case 10 Nudging companies toward timely tax return registration[5]

The challenge

As in most countries, companies in Denmark are required to submit tax returns and VAT to the tax authorities each year. Even though the tax reporting system in the country is quite advanced and user friendly, 35% of Danish companies report taxes with delay, which triggers a significant administrative burden for the tax authorities and for the companies themselves (Hansen, 2017).

Assumptions that fuel the problem

The challenge described above is considered, to a large extent, to be tax evasion, and just like many other instances of rule-breaking behavior, it is result of a cost-benefit analysis. Negative consequences that weigh in include the potential to be caught and the power of authorities to determine one's inclination to pay

5. This case is based on the blog post describing this project by *iNudgeyou* (Hansen, 2017).

taxes on time or not (Kirchler, Hoelzl, & Wahl, 2008). Studies show that tax paying behavior is also influenced by the level of trust in the system and the perception of tax institutions' fairness, in addition to accepted social norms related to taxes (Walsh, 2012).

Denmark is a country with a high level of trust in their institutions and a social belief that paying taxes is the right thing, or respectively, the social norm. This suggests that the high rate of delays in tax return registration requires a different explanation.

The behavioral explanation for why the problem exists

The Copenhagen-based applied behavioral sciences group *iNudgeYou* undertook the mission to understand the problem with tax return delays and produce an effective solution. One key insight of the team working on the project was that at the core of the problem is the confusion that may exist between tax return registration rules for individuals and those for companies. In Denmark individuals are not required to submit tax return registrations annually, as by default their previous information is automatically resubmitted without any involvement on their part. Their responsibility is to proactively provide information if there is a change in circumstances, and therefore the information from the previous year is no longer applicable.

Companies, on the other hand, are required to proactively register their tax returns every year. The team working on the project found that a significant share of delays is linked to new company owners who are confused about rules and assume by default that just like with personal taxes, companies do not have to proactively summit returns every year.

While this feels like a plausible explanation of the problem at hand, it must be noted that in many cases, people forget to complete important administrative steps even if they generally acknowledge their importance.

The behavioral solution

Based on the insights from the preliminary research the *iNudgeYou* team undertook an experiment with potential interventions. The project focused on 119,000 companies that had not reported their tax returns a week before the final deadline of July 1, 2016. While the tax authorities had previously tried to send reminders, which have produced some effect, in this case, the reminding message was designed to increase the saliency of the approaching deadline and to incorporate some effective nudges. All target companies received a message with the clear heading, "Remember to report tax on time, to avoid a tax surcharge of up to 5000 kr." to reinforce a loss aversion effect.

The body of the email message itself was modified and tested in three versions, each designed around an additional nudge:

1. Strengthening salience by using the word "NOTICE" in front of the text.
2. Activating ego-consistent actions by drawing attention to whether the company had previously made commitments to report taxes on time.
3. Combination of salience and ego-consistency with specific instructions on how to report taxes.

Results and benefits of using the behavioral solution

Given that the subject line was consistent, the rate of opening of the email message among target recipients was largely the same for all three groups. The three different designs were effective and demonstrated similar strength in triggering the desired behavior. The overall impact of the behavioral design produced an increase of the share of companies that report taxes on time from 65.3% in 2015 to 74% in 2016, which translates to an average effect of 8.7% across the three versions of the email.

The experience of iNudgeYou demonstrated that sometimes minor adaptations in communications may address seemingly insignificant behavioral issues, which cause unnecessary administrative burden and costs. The insignificant investment that was necessary to produce significant increase in timely tax return submissions is proof for the value of investing in proper diagnosing of behavioral barriers in such contexts.

References

Hansen, P. G. (2017). We nudged danish companies to report their tax returns on time in 2016 - iNudgeyou. Available February 6, 2018, from http://inudgeyou.com/en/we-nudged-danish-companies-to-report-their-tax-returns-on-time-in-2016/.

Kirchler, E., Hoelzl, E., & Wahl, I. (2008). Enforced versus voluntary tax compliance: The "slippery slope" framework. *Journal of Economic Psychology*, *29*, 210–225. Available from https://doi.org/10.1016/j.joep.2007.05.004.

Walsh, K. (2012). Understanding taxpayer behaviour - new opportunities for tax administration. *Economic and Social Review*, *43*(3), 451–475.

References

Akerlof, G. A., & Shiller, R. J. (2015). *Phishing for phools: The economics of manipulation and deception*. Princeton University Press.

Alm, J., & Torgler, B. (2006). Culture differences and tax morale in the United States and in Europe. *Journal of Economic Psychology*, *27*(2), 224–246. Available from http://m.crema-research.ch/papers/2004-14.pdf.

Altman, M. (2015). *Handbook of contemporary behavioral economics: Foundations and developments*. Routledge.

Altman, M. (2015a). Introduction. In M. Altman (Ed.), *Handbook of contemporary behavioral economics: Foundations and developments. Routledge* (pp. xv–xxii). New York: Routledge.

Altman, M. (2015b). In M. Altman (Ed.), *Handbook of contemporary behavioral economics: Foundations and developments*. New York: Routledge.

Altman, M. (2017). *Introduction to smart decision-making. Handbook of Behavioural Economics and Smart Decision-Making*. Edward Elgar Publishing.

Altman, M. (2017a). Introduction to smart decision-making. In M. Altman (Ed.), *Handbook of behavioral economics and smart decision making* (pp. 1–8). Northampton: Edward Elgar Publishing.

Altman, M. (2017b). Rational inefficiency: Smart thinking, bounded rationality and the scientific basis for economic failure and success. In M. Altman (Ed.), *Handbook of behavioral economics and smart decision making* (pp. 11–42). Northampton: Edward Elgar Publishing.

Altman, M. (2017c). In M. Altman (Ed.), *Handbook of behavioral economics and smart decision making*. Northampton: Edward Elgar Publishing.

Altman, M. (2019). Implications of smart decision-making and heuristics for production theory and material welfare. Mind & Society, *18*(2), 167–179.

Araña, J. E., & Carmelo, L. J. (2013). Can defaults save the climate? Evidence from a field experiment on carbon offsetting programs. *Environmental and Resource Economics*, *54*(4), 613–626. Available from https://doi.org/10.1007/s10640-012-9615-x.

Ariely, D. (2009). *Predictably irrational, revised and expanded edition: The hidden forces that shape our decisions*. London: HarperCollins Publishers.

Ariely, D. (2010). *The upside of irrationality: The unexpected benefits of defying logic at work and at home*. London: HarperCollins Publishers.

Ariely, D. (2012). *The (honest) truth about dishonesty: How we lie to everyone - especially ourselves*. London: HarperCollins Publishers.

Ariely, D. (2015). Behavioral economics: An exercise in design and humility. In S. Samson (Ed.), *The behavioral economics guide 2015 (with an introduction by Dan Ariely)* (pp. v–x). Available from www.behavioraleconomics.com.

Ariely, D. (2009). The end of rational economics. *Harvard Business Review*. Available from www.hbr.org.

Ariely, D. (2009). The end of rational economics. *Harvard business review*, *87*(7–8), 78–84.

Ariely, D. (2017). *Dollars and sense: How we misthink money and how to spend smarter*. HarperCollins.

Ariely, D., & Melamede, Y. (2015). *(Dis)honesty: The truth about lies*. Documentary feature film, The (Dis)Honesty Project.

Ariely, D., & Wertenbroch, K. (2002). Procrastination, deadlines, and performance: Self-control by precommitment. *Psychological Science*, *13*(3), 219–224. Available from https://wolfweb.unr.edu/homepage/pingle/Teaching/BADM 791/Week 7 Procrastination, Impatience and Hyperbolic Discounting/arielydeadlines.pdf.

Avent, R. (2017). Moneytalk: A nudge in the right direction. *The Economist Radio*. Available from https://radio.economist.com/.

Ayal, S., Gino, F., Barkan, R., & Ariely, D. (2015). Three principles to REVISE people's unethical behavior. *Perspectives on Psychological Science*, *10*(6), 738–741. Available from https://doi.org/10.1177/1745691615598512.

Bernoulli, D. (1954). Exposition of a new theory on the measurement of risk. *Econometrica*, *22*(1), 23–36. Available from http://links.jstor.org/sici?sici = 0012-9682%28195401%2922%3A1%3C23%3AEOANTO%3E2.0.CO%3B2-X.

Bernstein, D. M., & Loftus, E. F. (2009). How to tell if a particular memory is true or false. *Perspectives on Psychological Science*, *4*(4), 370–374. Available from https://s3.amazonaws.com/academia.edu.documents/30657399/How_to_tell_if_a_particular_memory_is_true_or_false14323.pdf?AWSAccessKeyId = AKIAIWOWYYGZ2Y53UL3A&Expires = 1510839580&Signature = stPSDUZD5orW5FSw5bzStZncZyw%3D&response-content-disposition = inline%3B fi.

Brighton, H., & Gigerenzer, G. (2012). Are rational actor models "rational" outside small worlds? In K. Binmore, & S. Okasha (Eds.), *Evolution and rationality: Decisions, co-operation and strategic behavior* (pp. 84–109). Cambridge, UK: Cambridge University Press. Available from http://pubman.mpdl.mpg.de/pubman/item/escidoc:2098745/component/escidoc:2098744/GG_Are_2012.pdf.

Camerer, C., Issacharoff, S., Loewenstein, G., O'Donoghue, T., & Rabin, M. (2003). Regulation for conservatives: Behavioral economics and the case for "asymmetric paternalism.". *University of Pennsylvania Law Review*, *151*(3), 1211–1254. Available from https://doi.org/10.2307/3312889.

Chabris, C., & Simons, D. (2010). *The invisible gorilla: And other ways our intuitions deceive us*. Harmony.

Coyle, D. (2011). *The invisible hand meets the invisible gorilla: The economics and psychology of scarce attention*. Available from http://idei.fr/sites/default/files/medias/doc/conf/psy/2011/summary.pdf.

Dervan, L. E., & Edkins, V. A. (2013). The innocent defendant's dilemma: An innovative empirical study of plea bargaining's innocence problem. *Journal of Criminal Law & Criminology*, *103*, 1.

Desjardins, J. (2017). Cognitive bias codex. Available from http://www.visualcapitalist.com/every-single-cognitive-bias/.

Eberl, C., Wiers, R. W., Pawelczack, S., Rinck, M., Becker, E., & Lindenmeyer, J. (2013). Approach bias modifaction in alcohol dependence: Do clinical effects replicate and for whom does it work best? *Developmental Cognitive Neuroscience*, *4*, 38–51.

Eisenhardt, K. M., & Sull, D. N. (2001). Strategy as simple rules. *Harvard Business Review*, *79* (1), 106–119. Available from https://pdfs.semanticscholar.org/e96a/58af7c8efd8cd672b05ff0e6e71b97a3214e.pdf.

Falk, A., Becker, A., Dohmen, T., Enke, B., Huffman, D., & Sunde, U. (2015). The nature and predictive power of preferences: Global evidence. In *CESifo Area Conference on Behavioural Economics, Munich, October 23–24, 2015* (pp. 1–76). Available from: https://doi.org/10.1007/s10273-011-1262-2.

Gigerenzer, G. (2011). Moral satisficing: Rethinking moral behavior as bounded rationality. In G. Gigerenzer, R. Hertwig, & T. Pachur (Eds.), *Heuristics: The foundations of adaptive behavior* (pp. 203–221). New York: Oxford University Press.

Gigerenzer, G. (2015). *Simply rational: Decision making in the real World*. New York: Oxford University Press.

Gigerenzer, G. (2016). Introduction: Taking heuristics seriously. In A. Samson (Ed.), *The behavioral economics guide 2016 (with an introduction by Gerd Gigerenzer)* (p. 184). Behavioral Science Solutions Ltd. Available from: https://doi.org/10.13140/RG.2.1.3623.2803.

Gigerenzer, G., & Brighton, H. (2011). Homo heuristicus: Why Biased Minds Make Better Inferences. In G. Gigerenzer, R. Hertwig, & T. Pachur (Eds.), *Heuristics: The foundations of adaptive behavior* (pp. 2–27). New York: Oxford University Press.

Gigerenzer, G., Fiedler, K., & Olsson, H. (2012). Rethinking cognitive biases as environmental consequences. In P. M. Todd, G. Gigerenzer, & ABC Research Group (Eds.), *Ecological rationality: Intelligence in the world* (pp. 80–110). Oxford University Press.

Gigerenzer, G., Hertwig, R., & Pachur, T. (2011). Introduction. In G. Gigerenzer, R. Hertwig, & T. Pachur (Eds.), *Heuristics: The foundations of adaptive behavior* (pp. xvii–xxii). New York: Oxford University Press.

Gigerenzer, G., & Todd, P. M. (1999). *Fast and frugal heuristics: The adaptive toolbox. Simple heuristics that make us smart* (pp. 3–34). Oxford University Press. Available from http://pubman.mpdl.mpg.de/pubman/item/escidoc:2102905/component/escidoc:2102904/GG_Fast_1999.pdf.

Gigerenzer, G., & Todd, P. M. (2012). *Ecological rationality: The normative study of heuristics. Ecological rationality: Intelligence in the World (evolution and cognition)* (pp. 487–497). New York: Oxford University Press.

Gigerenzer, G., Todd, P. M., & ABC Research Group. (2012). *Ecological rationality: Intelligence in the World.* New York: Oxford University Press.

Gilovich, T., Griffin, D., & Kahneman, D. (2003). In T. Gilovich, D. Griffin, & D. Kahneman (Eds.), *Heuristics and biases: The psychology of intuitive judgment.* New York: Cambridge University Press.

Gino, F., Ayal, S., & Ariely, D. (2009). Contagion and differentiation in unethical behavior: The effect of one bad apple on the barrel contagion and differentiation in unethical behavior the effect of one bad apple on the barrel. *Psychological Science, 20*(3), 393–398. Available from https://doi.org/10.1111/j.1467-9280.2009.02306.x.

Goldstone, R. L., & Chin, C. (1993). Dishonesty in self-report of copies made: Moral relativity and the copy machine. *Basic and Applied Social Psychology, 14*(1), 19–32. Available from https://doi.org/10.1207/s15324834basp1401_2.

Greenspan, A. (2008). Statement of the Chairman of the US Federal Reserve Alan Greenspan in front of US Congress (28 October 2008). C-Span TV.

Halpern, D. (2015). *Inside the nudge unit: How small changes can make a big difference.* London: Ebury Publishing.

Harrell, E. (2016). Blindsided by trump's victory? *Behavioral science explains. Harvard Business Review.* Retrieved from https://www.hbr.org/2016/11/blindsided-by-trumps-victory-behavioral-science-explains.

Hershfield, H. E. (2011). Future self-continuity: How conceptions of the future self transform intertemporal choice. *Annals of the New York Academy of Sciences, 1235*(1), 30–43. Available from https://doi.org/10.1111/j.1749-6632.2011.06201.x.

Hershfield, H. E., Goldstein, D. G., Sharpe, W. F., Fox, J., Yeykelis, L., Carstensen, L. L., & Bailenson, J. N. (2011). Increasing saving behavior through age-progressed renderings of the future self. *Journal of Marketing Research, 48*(Special Interdisciplinary Issue 2011), S23–S37. Available from http://www.jstor.org/stable/23033463.

Hofstede, G., Hofstede, G. J., & Minkov, M. (2010). *Cultures and organizations: Software of the mind* (3rd ed.). McGraw Hill.

House, R. J., Dorfman, P. W., Javidan, M., Hanges, P. J., & Sully de Luque, M. F. (2013). *Strategic leadership across cultures: GLOBE study of CEO leadership behavior and effectiveness in 24 countries.* SAGE Publications.

Johnson, E. J., & Goldstein, D. (2003). Do defaults save lives? *Science, 302*, 1338–1339. Available from https://doi.org/10.1126/science.1091721.

Jolls, C., & Sunstein, C. R. (2004). *Debiasing through law* (No. 495 (09/2004)). Cambridge. Available from http://lsr.nellco.org/harvard_olin.

Kahneman, D. (2011). *Thinking, fast and slow.* London: Penguin Books.

Kahneman, D., & Tversky, A. (1979). Prospect theory: An analysis of decision under risk. *Econometrica, 47*(2), 263–292.

Keeney, R. L. (2008). Personal decisions are the leading cause of death. *Operations Research Special Issue on Operations Research in Health Care or Forum*, *56*(6), 1335–1347. Available from https://doi.org/10.1287/opre.1080.0588.

Kelling, G. L., & Coles, C. M. (1997). *Fixing broken windows: Restoring order and reducing crime in our communities*. Simon and Schuster, New York. Available from http://archive.wilsonquarterly.com/sites/default/files/articles/WQ_VOL20_A_1996_Research.pdf.

Leonidou, C. N., Skarmeas, D., & Saridakis, C. (2018). Ethics, sustainability, and culture: A review and directions for research. In L. Leonidou, C. Katsikeas, S. Samiee, & B. Aykol (Eds.), *Advances in global marketing* (pp. 471–517). Cham: Springer International Publishing. Available from https://doi.org/10.1007/978-3-319-61385-7_19.

Levinson, J. D., Richardson, W. S., & Peng, K. (2007). Valuing cultural differences in behavioral economics. *The ICFAI Journal of Behavioral Finance*, *IV*(1), 32–47. Available from http://ssrn.com/abstract = 899688.

Loewenstein, G. (2007). *Exotic preferences: Behavioral economics and human motivation*. New York: Oxford University Press.

Loftus, E. (2007). Memory distortions: Problems solved and unsolved. In M. Garry, & H. Hayne (Eds.), *Do justice and let the skies fall: Elizabeth Loftus and her Contributions to science, law and academic freedom* (pp. 1–14). Mahwah, New Jersey: Lawrence Erlbaum Associates.

Loftus, E. F. (2016). Eavesdropping on Memory. https://doi.org/10.1146/annurev-psych-010416-044138.

Loftus, E. F., & Hoffman, H. G. (1989). Misinformation and memory: The creation of new memories. *Journal of Experimental Psychology: General*, *118*(1), 100–104. Available from https://pdfs.semanticscholar.org/0aff/06d6269856761c663780c3926803e140bf41.pdf.

Mankiw, N. G. (2017). *Principles of economics (Mankiw's principles of economics)* (8th ed). Boston: Cengage Learning.

Mazar, N., Amir, O., & Ariely, D. (2008a). More ways to cheat – Expanding the scope of dishonesty. *Journal of Marketing Research*, *45*(6), 651–653. Available from https://www-2.rotman.utoronto.ca/facbios/file/Mazar_MoreWaysCheat.pdf.

Mazar, N., Amir, O., & Ariely, D. (2008b). The dishonesty of honest people: A theory of self-concept maintenance. *Journal of Marketing Research*, *45*(6), 633–644. Available from http://econweb.ucsd.edu/~jandreoni/Seminar/OnAmir.pdf.

McGinnis, J. M., & Foege, W. H. (1993). Actual causes of death in the United States. *Journal of the American Medical Association*, *270*(18 (November 10)), 2207–2212. Available from http://www.heartlandcenters.slu.edu/pdf/1_7_ActualCausesofDeathintheUniteStates.pdf.

McNeil, B. J., Pauker, S. G., Sox, H. C., & Tversky, A. (1982). On the elicitation of preferences for alternative therapies. *New England Journal of Medicine*, *306*(21), 1259–1262. Available from https://doi.org/10.1056/NEJM198205273062103.

Mill, J. S. (1966). On liberty. In J. M. Robson (Ed.), *A selection of his works* (pp. 1–147). London: Macmillan Education UK. Available from https://doi.org/10.1007/978-1-349-81780-1_1.

Mokdad, A. H., Marks, J. S., Stroup, D. F., & Gerberding, J. L. (2004). Actual causes of death in the United States, 2000. *Journal of the American Medical Association*, *291*(10), 1238–1245.

Neth, H., & Gigerenzer, G. (2015). Heuristics: Tools for an uncertain World. In R. Scott, & S. Kosslyn (Eds.), *Emerging trends in the social and behavioral sciences: An interdisciplinary, searchable, and linkable resource* (pp. 1–18). New York: John Wiley & Sons, Inc. Available from https://doi.org/10.1002/9781118900772.etrds0394.

O'Donoghue, T., & Rabin, M. (1999). Doing it now or later. *The American Economic Review, 89*(1), 103–124.

Pichert, D., & Katsikopoulos, K. V. (2008). Green defaults: Information presentation and pro - environmental behaviour. *Journal of Environmental Psychology, 28*, 63–73. Available from https://doi.org/10.1108/07363760210420540.

Rick, S., & Loewenstein, G. (2008). Commentaries and rejoinder to "the dishonesty of honest people.". *Journal of Marketing Research, XLV*(December), 645–653. Available from https://www.researchgate.net/profile/Nina_Mazar2/publication/228377683_More_Ways_to_Cheat-Expanding_the_Scope_of_Dishonesty/links/00b7d51bc74cf403cd000000.pdf.

Samson, A. (2016). Behavioral economics in perspective: Nudging for good and bad. In A. Samson (Ed.), *The behavioral economics guide 2016 (with an introduction by Gerd Gigerenzer), Behavioral Science Solutions Ltd.* Available from http://www.behavioraleconomics.com.

Savage, L. J. (1981). *The writings of Leonard Jimmie Savage; a memorial selection.* American Statistical Association.

Seleim, A., & Bontis, N. (2009). The relationship between culture and corruption: A cross-national study. *Journal of Intellectual Capital, 10*(1), 165–184. Available from https://doi.org/10.1108/14691930910922978.

Shah, A. K., & Oppenheimer, D. M. (2008). Heuristics made easy: An effort-reduction framework. *Psychological Bulletin, 134*(2), 207–222. Available from https://doi.org/10.1037/0033-2909.134.2.207.

Simon, H. A. (1948). *Administrative behaviour: A study of the decision making processes in administrative organisation.* New York: The Free Press.

Simon, H. A. (1990). Bounded rationality. In J. Eatwell, M. Milgate, & P. Newman (Eds.), Utility and probability ((pp. 161–176). London: The New Palgrave. Palgrave Macmillan.

Smith, V., & Argyros, G. (2017). Foreword. In M. Altman (Ed.), *Handbook of behavioural economics and smart decision-making: Rational decision-making within the bounds of reason* (p. xix). Northampton: Edward Elgar.

Sull, D., & Eisenhardt, K. M. (2015). *Simple rules: How to thrive in a complex World.* New York: Houghton Mifflin Harcourt.

Sunstein, C. R. (2014). *Why nudge? The politics of libertarian paternalism.* New Haven, CT: Yale University Press.

Sunstein, C. R., & Thaler, R. H. (2003). Libertarian paternalism is not an oxymoron. *The University of Chicago Law Review, 70*(4), 1159–1202. Available from http://chicagounbound.uchicago.edu/cgi/viewcontent.cgi?article = 5228&context = uclrev.

Tversky, A., & Kahneman, D. (1989). *Rational choice and the framing of decisions. Multiple criteria decision making and risk analysis using microcomputers* (pp. 81–126). Berlin, Heidelberg: Springer.

Thaler, R. H. (2015a). *Misbehaving: The making of behavioral economics.* WW Norton & Company.

Thaler, R. H. (2015b). The power of nudges, for good and bad, October 31 *The New York Times.*

Thaler, R. H. (2016). The economist asks: Richard Thaler. *The Economist Radio.* Available from https://radio.economist.com/.

Thaler, R. H., & Sunstein, C. R. (2009). *Nudge: Improving decsions about health, wealth and happiness.* London: Penguin Books.

Tully, S. M., & Sharma, E. (2017). Context-dependent drivers of discretionary debt decisions: Explaining willingness to borrow for experiential purchases. *Journal of Consumer Research,*

44(5), 960–973. Available from https://watermark.silverchair.com/api/watermark?token = AQECAHi208BE49Ooan9kkhW_Ercy7Dm3ZL_9Cf3qfKAc485ysgAAAd8wggHb-BgkqhkiG9w0BBwagggHMMIIByAIBADCCAcEGCSqGSIb3DQEHATAeBglghkgBZQM-EAS4wEQQMBfNG9KCYi9jJrsfUAgEQgIIBkvsVOtFzL6Jxzt-pOwzfUQtOIX7FSui8sHqhXUN5UjQyl.

Tversky, A., & Kahneman, D. (1974). Judgment under uncertainty: Heuristics and biases. *Science*, *185*(4157), 1124–1131.

Tversky, A., & Kahneman, D. (1981). The farming of decisions and the psychology of choice. *Science*, *211*(4481), 453–458. Available from http://shookrun.com/documents/framingtv-kahn.pdf.

Zamir, E., & Teichman, D. (2014). In E. Zamir, & D. Teichman (Eds.), *The oxford handbook of behavioral economics and the law*. New York: Oxford University Press.

Chapter 2

Tourism and traditional thinking

Chapter Outline

Economics tends to concentrate on how markets work and how to increase economic efficiency and economic growth. It often incorporates somewhat unrealistic assumptions to enable modelling to take place.

John Tribe, The Economics of Recreation, Leisure and Tourism

Tourism economics thinking

Finally, the limitations of economics in analyzing the leisure world should be noted. Economics tends to concentrate on how markets work and how to increase economic efficiency and economic growth. It often incorporates somewhat unrealistic assumptions to enable modelling to take place. The market is in fact just one possible mechanism that decides which leisure goods and services will be produced and who will enjoy them. It lacks a human dimension, for that human dimension (which includes the dimensions of caring, or emotion, or hope, or justice, or empathy, or love) is especially barred from the subject by its positivist rules. It does not raise or answer the questions about what leisure goods and services should be produced or who should enjoy them or indeed about what kind of a leisure society would be desirable. Such questions

Behavioral Economics for Tourism. DOI: https://doi.org/10.1016/B978-0-12-813808-3.00002-2

are generally tackled under ethics and philosophy and neatly sidestepped by mainstream economists.

Tribe (2015, p. 15)

This paragraph from the introduction of one of the leading textbooks in economics for travel and leisure summarizes the gaps, and limitations of conventional thinking that has guided, and continues to guide, decision-making, and policy design in the tourism sector. The partial approach in analyzing and influencing market phenomena, the disconnecting of tourism economics from psychology and sociology, the artificial separation of tourism growth and tourism sustainability as themes belonging to different domains, have all contributed to the many of the complex challenges that the industry is facing today.

This chapter will provide an overview of the fundamental beliefs that have traditionally guided planning, management, and policy development in the tourism domain. It highlights some of the unrealistic assumptions or gaps that conventional thinking about the tourism sector relies on and that are becoming obvious with the advance of insights in behavioral economics. The first part of this chapter focuses on assumptions and decision-making patterns that relate to decision-making about destination management, planning, and management of tourism while the second part zooms on assumptions that have guided thinking about traveler behavior.

The complexity of a single system

In her book *Thinking in Systems*, Donella Meadows defines a system as "a set of things (...) that are interconnected in such a way that they produce their own pattern of behavior over time" (Meadows, 2008, p. 2). She explains that if a challenge or an opportunity within one system is not analyzed and discussed considering the system as context, adopted solutions become partial or ineffective. Not recognizing that the system serves as a context leads to wrong assumptions about the source of the problems and to wrong conclusions about the potential solutions. Respectively solutions that are not system-harmonized lead to limited resolutions or to the distortion of other balances in the organism that respectively trigger different problems. Unfortunately today's tourism industry offers an abundance of examples of problems triggered by failure to adopt systems thinking.

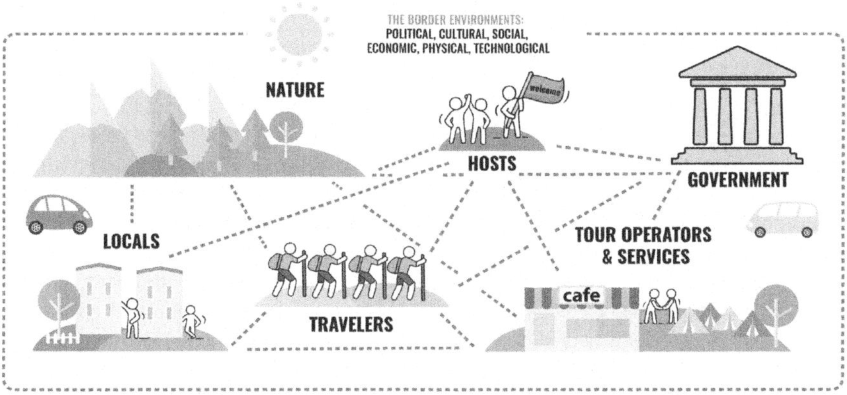

Even though scientific literature has recognized the power of applying systems thinking to tourism planning, management, and policy making, this philosophy has enjoyed limited attention in practical realities (Carlsen, 1999). The complexity of the tourism industry and the different layers of influences, which can impact it, leads researchers to propose systems thinking as appropriate lens toward understanding, planning, and managing this industry (Leiper, 1979). Hall states that a systems approach to understanding and planning tourism help to understand the potential social, economic, environmental, and political impacts that can be triggered by tourism development (Hall, 2008, p. 84). Identifying and managing these impacts is essential due to tourism's "systematic relationship" with the natural environment, which is both extractive (e.g., fresh water and local produce extracted from the place that tourists visit) and aesthetic (e.g., mountain vistas or marine landscapes which become the setting for enjoyment of leisure activities) (Carlsen, 1999). Systems thinking applied to tourism enables planning and management that considers all relevant ecological (natural assets) and social (local community) elements, as well as the interaction between these elements and the overall environment (Dimmock & Musa, 2015; Hall, 2008). It also offers a temporal dimension allowing for growth scenarios, cumulative effects of relationships, and development dynamics (Lutz, 1994).

Modeling system dynamics to enable realistic decision-making and policy development: the case of Mauritius

An interesting example of a systems thinking approach that weaves in tourism development comes from Mauritius. In the early 1990s a group of researchers from the International Institute for Applied Systems Analysis, the University of Mauritius, the Government of Mauritius and the United National Population Fund initiated the development and testing of a computer-based model that explores the interactions among population dynamics, socioeconomic development, and environmental factors. Socioeconomic aspects are linked to three leading for Mauritius sectors, including tourism, and are placed in the context of the complex interactions that occur between population, development, and the environment.

The systems thinking approach is operationalized through a model that allows for exploring the ways in which different elements interact with each other and develop over time. It looks at how growth in different economic activities, including tourism, impacts society, and the environment in ways that enable considerations in multiple aspects. First there is recognition that the prioritization of different economic sectors produces different employment and social benefits, and requires different investments in public education and skill development. Second it becomes very clear that economic sectors depend on different natural resources and produce very different impacts on the environment. As one of the members of the team states in the book presenting the Mauritius experience: "It matters to the environment whether the people are engaged in growing sugar, dyeing woolens, or international banking. Sugar production requires large amounts of land and water, and dumps organic waste into the rivers; dyeing woolens requires little land but a great deal of water, and dumps chemical waste into the rivers; international banking by itself, on the other hand, requires almost no interaction with the environment (although the consequences of international banking action on a country's economy may affect its environment)" (Lutz, 1994, p. 234). Third considering not only the socioeconomic benefits but also resource needs of economic activities, including tourism, allows for balanced planning and development decisions that consider trade-offs. As the case reveals Mauritius uses different tactics to stimulate growth in the sector but prevent overdevelopment: limiting investment to specific tourism zones, careful management of access by consciously prohibiting charter flights, capping the overall volume of the hotel capacity on the island and the size of individual accommodation facilities, and so on. "The raw material used for tourism development comprises basically natural and/or manufactured attractions, a mild climate, social tranquility, and political stability. … The success of tourism very often gives way to temptation for further exploitation of resources which can, in the long term,

(*Continued*)

(Continued)

prove detrimental to the fundamental interests of tourism itself. Tourism is therefore condemned to abide strictly by the rules of nature conservation for its own survival" (Lutz, 1994, p. 190).

The benefit of taking a systems view to tourism development allows for realistic consideration of both sides of the equation in Mauritius. It helps to gain a clear understanding of the types of socioeconomic gains that tourism growth can yield while also revealing the required investments (in education and training, infrastructure development, expansion of utility systems, etc.) and potential environmental trade-offs (sacrificing natural areas to development, increased consumption of water and other natural resources, pollution, etc.).

Despite the obvious benefits discussed in academic literature, in practice systems thinking does not seem to be frequently applied to planning and policy design. Tourism is complex and among the factors that have contributed to the generation of wrong assumptions guiding decision-making is the fact that it is multispectral, multidimensional, and in many ways difficult to define or even clearly outline in scope (Darbellay & Stock, 2012). This complexity naturally leads to the temptation to break tourism into smaller components or subindustries that are viewed, analyzed, and managed separately. For example, the hospitality sector in a country is usually regulated and overseen by a tourism institution (ministry of tourism, tourism agency, or department of tourism in a ministry of economy). At the same time another group of key players for the tourism sector—taxi companies and transportation service providers—are under the umbrella of a ministry of transportation and infrastructure. Ministries or agencies dealing with food and agriculture, usually supervise food service providers such as restaurants and catering companies. Cultural attractions such as museums fall under the umbrella of a ministry of culture, and national parks and natural areas are in the portfolio of ministries of environment. Within this line of thinking it is worth mentioning also public services such as safety and security, which include passport control of incoming arrivals and safety on the streets of the destination as they are essential for tourism too. They usually are responsibility of interior ministries. Health and emergency services are also quite relevant to the sector and are managed by ministries of healthcare or emergency agencies.

In addition to failure to account for the real interactions and potential implication of tourism development decisions for the destination (the supply aspect), this reality leads to inefficiencies from demand perspective as well. It means artificial division of the elements that constitute one offering—the traveler experience—into very different institutions with very different thinking and very different approaches to policy and decision-making. From a traveler perspective, the entire trip is essentially an amalgam of products, services, and experiences (Murphy, Pritchard, & Smith, 2000) delivered through a network of providers but from a supply side, it is a disconnected set of elements that are not thought about, let alone managed, as one system.

Why is this a behavioral problem?

The lack of a systems thinking approach to tourism development, management, or policy development is a behavioral problem because it boils down to the framing of issues and decisions with strategic implications. Big-picture framing of decisions versus focus on more specific immediate effects leads to different consideration of the common interest and tends to produce different decision outcomes (Stillman, Fujita, Sheldon, & Trope, 2018). If decision makers take a partial view and focus on the correlation between some elements in the system without recognizing the full context, they make partial decisions that may produce solutions to a particular issue while triggering negative ripple effect elsewhere in the system. For example, the story with the government official Mr. Smith at the start of this book illustrates how a partial focus on growing arrival numbers can produce decisions that are harmful for the system overall. Mr. Smith decides to use public funds for subsidies that are provided to big operators bringing foreign tourists to the country. Subsidies enable these operators to lower prices below the realistic market levels, which enables fast growth of arrival numbers but triggers several other effects. First it distorts competition as nonsubsidized operators are put at a significant disadvantage of competing with unrealistic market prices. Second lowered prices attract value-oriented travelers who are motivated in their destination choice and booking behavior mainly (or solely) by low price. This distorts the targeting strategy of a destination, especially if it is positioned on nonprice attributes (such as being home to an extraordinary natural or cultural attraction, or being known for high quality culinary offerings) and draws value-oriented travelers who may have less appreciation (and respectively desire to pay) for exceptional nature-based or culinary experiences. The presence of value-oriented travelers in the destination leads to a third effect—suppressed profitability for local tourism service providers who are "stuck" with a price-sensitive audience that is less- or not willing to pay for additional offerings (such as extraordinary culinary experiences). The fact that they occupy the accommodation capacities of the place creates a fourth, opportunity cost problem, as the lack of available accommodation limits the ability to attract other better-paying travelers at the same time. In this sense the decision to boost arrival numbers made without considering the full system leads to numerous negative effects that are destructive for the sector. Nonsystem framing of problems produce solutions that distort the system and that produce the many complex challenges that tourism faces today, including with leakages, low profitability, overtourism, unsustainable development, and so on.

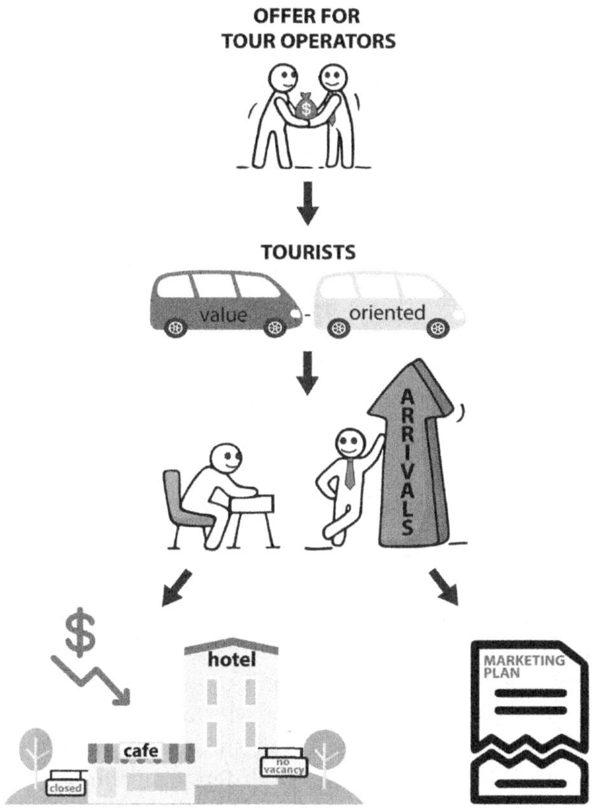

How to ensure the right framing?

One management framework that can provide solution to the conflict between the need to see tourism as a coordinated system and the practicality of how tourism is managed is the experience economy framework. It offers a perspective to decision-making through the lens of the customer buying the core offering—the traveler experience in its entirety. Taking the traveler experience perspective means realizing that the travel industry is a tourism experience network of stakeholders that surround the tourist and that need to be managed in coordinated manner. This includes all possible players that may influence the experience—private enterprises, public entities, voluntary organizations, and all experience-provoking elements from the surrounding environment (Sundbo & Sorensen, 2013).

Applying an experience-driven approach to decision-making would entail considering the connectivity between all elements and stakeholders that influence the offering consumed by the traveler. It facilitates a system thinking framing of issues and potential solutions. An experience-driven approach to planning and managing tourism would entail the application of experience tracking tools that allow for auditing of the traveler experience identifying gaps and failures requiring proper interventions (Nikolova, 2009; Nikolova, Bakker, Nevill, Metz, & Popovik, 2017). Such framing of the thinking offers a more systematic perspective to sectorial challenges and potential solutions.

Institutions and destination management

Tourism tends to be one of the industries for which institutional and organizational models across countries vary to a great extent. The choice of structures depends on the importance of tourism for the national economy, as well as the overall institutional and socioeconomic context in the respective country. In many countries where tourism is a leading sector, a special ministry leads its governance. In other cases the overarching institution is a ministry of economy supported by a tourism agency or a tourism board. The involvement of private sector in the different institutional models also varies greatly. Countries with more advanced economic development and traditions in tourism institutions have established formal mechanisms for collaboration with private sector. A summary of the most typical forms of destination governance across countries suggests that in most cases the models fall into one of the following categories: single public authority or a department within a single public authority, partnership of public authorities, public authorities outsourcing the delivery to private companies, some form of public–private partnership (could be in the form of a nonprofit making organization), or an association funded entirely through private sector (UNWTO, 2007, p. 136). The fundamental assumption behind the promotion of collaborative models is the idea that they combine the strengths of the two sectors and offset their weaknesses. For example, it is assumed that the public sector provides the more holistic and longer term strategic thinking while private sector complements with swift and tactical market thinking (UNWTO, 2007, p. 137).

National-level structures are usually supported by structures on regional and local levels. Local and regional tourism governance models vary from destination to destination to an even greater extent. An interesting analysis of destination models across 12 destinations in the Swiss Alps reveals that even if formal structures look similar on the surface deeper destination dynamics vary greatly leading to different decision-making patterns (Beritelli, Bieger, & Laesser, 2007).

This great diversity of institutional models and destination management practices across different countries and regions have made it very difficult to identify governance formats or even sets of factors that guarantee effectiveness. The majority of the studies on tourism institutions are based on individual cases rather than larger groups of models (Kim, Saha, Vertinsky, & Park, 2018) making it difficult to transfer knowledge from one place to another.

A look at the prescriptive thinking on tourism institutions and destination managements reveals that there is acknowledgment of the need to govern the sector on the basis of some form of partnership between public and private sector. Among the key recommendations on institutions and destination management frameworks are the importance of a strong and committed partnership that is united by a collective vision, and the essential role of a strong destination management organization that holds a leading position ensuring focus and long-term competitive orientation (UNWTO, 2007, p. 11–12). The earlier mentioned analysis of Beritelli and colleagues (2007), however, reveals that in reality even within one country formal destination management structures are complemented by deeper informal governance mechanisms, which in many cases become more influential that the formal ones. In some cases, these may be linked to individuals who are disproportionally influential while in others power asymmetries are associated with groups of individuals and/or enterprises. It is clear that in such cases the formal destination management structure is not able to play the expected leading role, and that management decisions are highly influenced by the particular interests of the informal leaders whose positions are based on their own-biased experiences, connections, knowledge, and attitudes toward the others (Beritelli et al., 2007). Because of these informal dynamics real understanding of the evolution of tourism policy, planning, and management processes within a destination is possible only if the lifecycle of influences and dynamics over time are tracked and understood in ways that step beyond single issues and appreciate the multilayer, cross-sectorial nature of the sector (Wray, 2009). This takes time and adds a lot of complexity, especially given that in many countries these dynamics and informal models shift with changes in political power. In any case the analysis of tourism governance and policy processes without a historic perspective, and consideration of the cultural political economic context might lead to their misinterpretation and inappropriate policy recommendations (Mellon & Bramwell, 2018).

In their theory overview Kim and colleagues (2018) establish that literature finds the effectiveness of tourism institutions to be dependent on a multitude of contextual factors such as crime and corruption, political and economic freedoms, trust and power dynamics, and that the quality of institutions has direct impact on the market performance of the destination translated to international arrivals and profitability (Kim et al., 2018). Generally poor governance triggers uncertainties with economic policies and affects not only incoming tourism flows but outbound tourism as well; thus impacting the performance of the tourism sectors in other countries, which are potential recipients of these outbound travelers (Demir & Gozgor, 2017).

Another great complication comes from the fact that traditionally destination management is driven by administrative factors and not demand factors. From a market perspective tourism destinations should be delimited on the basis of traveler consumption patterns rather than administrative boundaries. This, however, is super complicated, especially when it comes to destinations that cross different administrative regions and even countries (Blasco, Guia, & Prats, 2014).

The behavioral perspective to institutional complexities

The complexity of the dynamics and relationships underlying tourism governance reveals the misalignment between ideal assumptions and models, and the actual industry realities. Tourism requires coordination and integrated planning but actually there is no single CEO to lead the process, which is instead controlled and influenced by a network of government institutions, nonprofit organizations, and private commercial enterprises (Gunn & Var, 2002). The fact that tourism institutions and destination management structures need to behave as destination "factories" tasked with "achieving an excellent return on investment, market growth, quality products, a brand of distinction and benefits to all 'shareholders'" without having ownership or control over the employment processes (UNWTO, 2007, p. 12) often creates contradictions producing great deviations from ideal models. The dependence of tourism governance success on so many factors such as broader socioeconomic dynamics, cultural specific, political context, institutional failures, informal structures, power asymmetries, and so on has led to conclusions that success is sometimes dependent even on some level of serendipity (Blasco et al., 2014).

In addition, many countries where tourism is a significant contributor to the economy, suffer from political instability and frequent changes of government leaders. In such realities public institutions responsible for tourism governance and policy making often fall victim to permanent shifts in leadership and inconsistent policies. Short-term outlook limited to the current political term or upcoming elections eliminates one of the most important strengths of the public sector in tourism governance—the long-term strategic approach and concern for the wider public good (UNWTO, 2007, p. 137). This might be one reason that in some cases efforts initiated by the private sector tend to last longer or become permanent compared to such launched by public sector (Blasco et al., 2014).

An excellent and comprehensive overview of the realities of tourism governance is provided by Elizabeth Becker in her book *Overbooked* (Becker, 2013) in which she offers detailed stories from a wide variety of countries and destinations, including France, Costa Rica, Venice, Dubai, Cambodia, Zambia, and others. The stories in her book are about how tourism development was started and unfolded, how strategic decisions were made and by whom, and how often systems failed from assumed ideals because of wrong perceptions, human error, and self interest. Becker's brilliant overview of the realities of the industry reveals that rarely, if ever, tourism development has been guided by a balanced collaboration of public and private sector decision makers (perhaps with the notable exception of Costa Rica); that in many cases power asymmetries have caused terrible distortions in the trade-off between sacrifices made in the name of tourism development and benefits yielded from the sector; and that in most cases long-term strategic efforts to preserve globally significant natural and cultural assets have been made by private individuals, and philanthropists rather than governments.

The reality presented by *Overbooked* (Becker, 2013) reveals that assumptions and models guiding tourism governance often do not align with how things turn out. It signals that there is a need to take much more behaviorally realistic perspective to understanding how individual choices or group perceptions are likely to influence long terms strategic decisions for the sector, and adopt the system in a way that limits the risk of unwise development decisions. Both scientific knowledge and practical experience in the sector have accumulated sufficient insights about what aspects of the system design lead to obvious failures and damaging impacts.

Managing resources

Tourism is highly dependent on common pool resources or resources that are shared by all but owned by no one. These can include natural attractions (mountains, landscapes, and beaches), natural resources (clean air and water), traditions, cultural landscapes, community ambiance, or even beautiful sunsets. Common pool resources are often not only at the core of the tourism offering but also at the core of the quality of life of local residents. The need to share these resources in ways that are beneficial to both visitors and local residents constitutes one of the main challenges in tourism (Bosselman, Peterson, & McCarthy, 1999). Common pool resources in tourism, or *tourism commons* as they are referred to, include both tangible and intangible resources that are related to tourism product. In addition to the conventional resources such as air, water, oceans, ecosystems, fisheries, forests, wildlife, and other natural assets, nonconventional ones include streets, transportation systems, ports, urban areas, environmental and socioeconomic costs and benefits, the internet, intellectual resources, and others (Briassoulis, 2002). Shared resources in tourism are also linked to the concept of background tourism elements (BTEs) (Jafari, 1974), which serve as the context in which the traveler experience unfolds. According to Jafari who coined the concept (1974), BTEs can be *natural* such as oceans, seas, lakes, weather, and even sunshine; *sociocultural* such as history, religion, tradition, ceremonies, celebrations, and *man-made* such as buildings, monuments, architecture, and others.

In her recent book "Sustainable Tourism on a Finite Planet" Megan Epler Wood states that the problem with commons is twofold. First decisions about tourism growth that rely on core attractions do not account for their capacities and do not ask the questions: *How many people can this beach handle? How many people can be in this park at the same time and have an enjoyable experience without bumping into others? How many visitors can be handled by this archaeological site without the risk of damage?* Second there are no formal mechanisms for re-investing and maintaining of these resources by the market players that benefit from them, which leaves the responsibilities for the damage and associated losses in no one's hands (Epler Wood, 2017).

The behavioral challenge with tourism commons

Because common pool resources are at the core of the offering of many travel destinations and because they are shared but not owned, they become basis for many behavioral failures in the tourism system. The first failure is treating common pool resources as endless free resources that can be utilized without any consideration of carrying capacity or without accounting for the relative share of use that should be available to every community member. For example, this can relate to a beautiful and pristine natural area, which is used as recreational area and place for picnics. The capacity of the area is not endless and there is a point beyond which the presence of too many people looking to enjoy the scenery becomes overwhelming causing damaging footprint and making the expected experience of enjoying pristine nature practically impossible. Similarly growth of tourism in a community puts strain on its water resources and may lead to shortages simply because water was treated as a free endless resource, and no investments were made to prepare water supply systems for increased consumptions. Many popular tourism destinations, such as Mallorca in Spain, suffer from systematic water shortage that was triggered or exacerbated by failure to account for the limitations of this resource before tourism growth was stimulated (Koundouri, 2008). The case study on Belén in Costa Rica in the first chapter of this book is also relevant in this context.

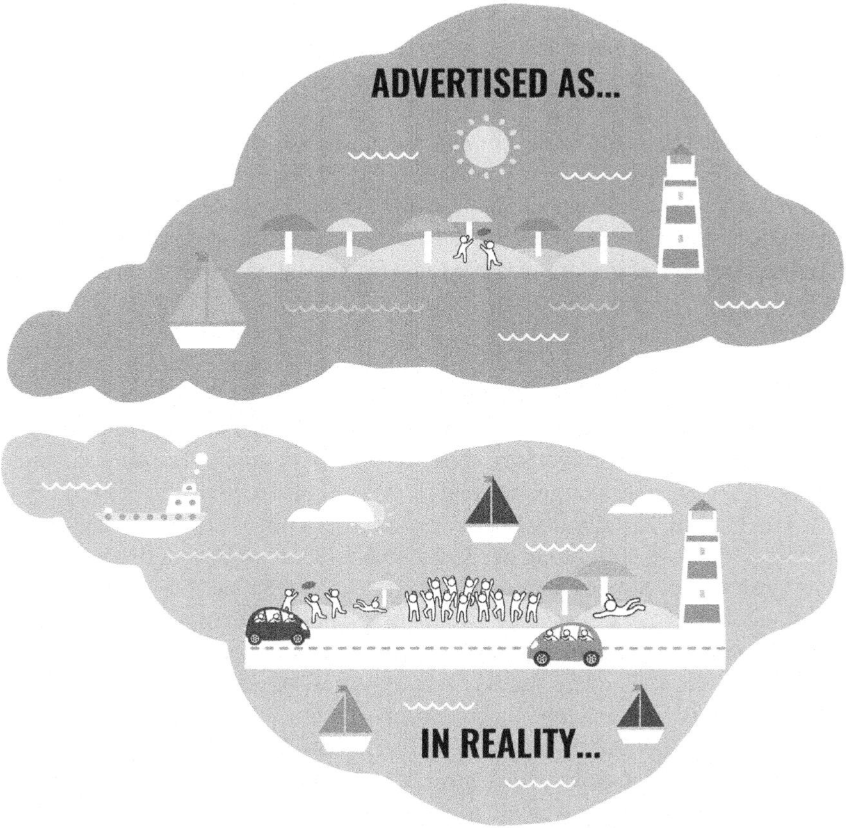

Another frequent failure related to common pool resources is the failure to imagine the impact that fast increase of consumption will have on them. This is associated with the fact that decision makers have a hard time imagining future outcomes, especially when they are extended over a longer period of time and that there are different ways to frame outcome (Kahneman & Tversky, 1983), that is, by putting emphasis on certain gains (e.g., potential profit from a certain development) while ignoring the sacrifice that they require (e.g., destroying the habitat of a local bird species). Ignoring impacts lead to focus on consumption rather than sustaining or maintaining the asset. For example, the significant increase of the number of daily visitors in a small traditional church leads to higher utilization and faster deterioration of its infrastructure, and significantly higher footprint (e.g., more generated waste in areas immediately surrounding the church). It also influences the overall ambiance, as the church is likely to be surrounded by groups of people for most part of the day making it impossible to experience it as a place for solitude and spiritual enjoyment.

Some of the failures in such cases are associated with the disconnection between responsibilities and incentives within the tourism system. For example, within one destination a tour operator or a transportation authority is incentivized by the potential for more profit to encourage more visitors to the area. So while they are motivated to invest in promoting the area as a place to enjoy nature or experience the unique setting of the local old town, they are not accountable for the impact that more visitors will have on the nature or the old town, and are certainly not responsible for investing in the maintenance or restoring of these shared resources. On this topic Megan Epler Wood states: "Around the world, as tourism escalates, there will be an increasing amount of pressure on beaches, monuments, and invaluable parks and protected areas. These places operate by and large without recompense from the industry or certainly without adequate resources to respond to the growing number of visitors that are now visiting and will visit in future. The value of public resources has generally been understood to be the burden of local citizens to pay for and protect. At best, the parks and protected area system may charge a special fee to foreigners to help cover the cost of their visit. But the majority of the global system does not value the tourism product offer or the cost of building necessary public water, sewer, and waste treatment systems to protect the underpinnings of sustainability at the most fundamental level. Tax systems for tourism are not designed to reinvest in the tourism product; they are designed largely to market tourism. As a result, tourism policy makers lack adequate funds to cover the cost of planning and public services. This causes an inevitable decline of destinations that lack basic funds for maintenance, protection, and upgrade" (Epler Wood, 2017, p. 31).

In many places commons that have been evaluated as holding significant potential for tourism are subjected to violation of ownership and access principles. Especially in countries with weaker legislation or institutions, powerful stakeholders take over the utilization of attractive resources. For example, if a pristine beach area is considered as having high value for tourism, powerful companies or individuals can benefit from power asymmetry and invest in building a large resort that changes the pristine nature of the beach, damages the experience for everyone else who may have been enjoying the beach in its undeveloped state and limits the potential for other users to benefit from this common pool resource. A rich collection of such stories is included in the earlier mentioned book by Elizabeth Becker *Overbooked* (Becker, 2013).

One framework that attempts to solve the tragedy of the tourism commons is the thinking of tourism as *ecosystem service*. The concept of *ecosystem services* is advanced by the Millennium Ecosystem Assessment (MA), a global initiative launched by the United Nations to assess how ecosystem change would affect human well-being (Millennium Ecosystem Assessment, 2005). *Ecosystem services* are defined as the benefits that people obtain from ecosystems contributing to human well-being (TEEB, 2010), which encompass goods, such as timber, fresh water, and medicinal herbs and services such as air purification, irrigation, and prevention of floods.

One of the most advanced initiatives that operationalize this thinking and links it to tourism is the European Union program *Natura 2000*, which is a European network of marine and terrestrial-protected areas aiming the preservation of landscapes, biodiversity, and habitats throughout the continent (European Commission, 2008). At the core of the *Natura 2000* philosophy is the idea that people and society derive benefits from protected areas and natural landscapes, and that these benefits should be framed as *ecosystem services*. They include not only supply of tangible resources such as water, clean air, crops, and timber but also cultural and recreational services such as maintaining cultural identity and restoring physical and psychological well-being through leisure activities (European Commission, 2013). The ecosystem services that relate to tourism include human perceptions and experiences such as enjoying an outdoors activity, benefitting from the pleasure of viewing a beautiful landscape, experiencing a sense of well-being, and stress reduction by contact with nature. This logic leads to the idea that the enjoyment of nature-based recreation and leisure opportunities is impossible without healthy and well-functioning ecosystems, and so societies must invest in their protections. Efforts to estimate the economic and social value of ecosystem services related to tourism and recreation aim to put a price tag on their potential destruction and demonstrate in an even more obvious way the economic sense of investing in the preservation and proper management of natural resources (see "Estimating economic, recreational and employment benefits generated by tourism in NATURA 2000 territories").

Estimating economic, recreational and employment benefits generated by tourism in NATURA 2000 territories

In 2011 the European Commission published a report "Estimating the economic value of the benefits provided by the tourism/recreation and Employment supported by NATURA 2000" that applies an advanced methodology calculating economic, recreational, and employment benefits derived from leisure activities in the NATURA 2000 territories. The study estimated that in 2006 the NATURA 2000 network attracted 1.7 billion visitor days, which translates to an average 184 visitors per day per NATURA site. The total generated visitor expenditure was between 50 and 90 billion Euro, which in turn generated employment opportunities producing additional income benefits of between 50 and 85 billion Euro. Employment estimates suggest that tourism and recreational activities in Nature 2000 support about 12 million of direct and indirect jobs.

Estimates allow for calculation of the benefits derived from NATURA 2000 areas down to the hectare revealing that in 2006 the value was between 150 and 330 Euro per hectare.

Based on BIO Intelligence Services. (2011). Estimating the economic value of the benefits provided by the tourism/recreation and employment supported by natura 2000 Final Report *prepared for the European Commission-DG Environment.*

The efforts to produce estimates of the value of natural resources are part of relatively recent efforts to advance *natural capital accounting* by measuring and valuing the environment in ways that are similar to the ways that countries track the economy. The ultimate goal of such efforts is to integrate systems for measuring and monitoring the health and changes in the environment with the national accounts that are kept by countries. This would allow national and international bodies to estimate benefits derived from natural resources, calculate the cost of their maintenance, monitor the state and quality of the environment, as well as to track the relationship between social, environmental, and economic dynamics. Efforts in this direction are led by the United Nations, the European Union, the Food and Agriculture Organization of the United Nations, the International Monetary Fund, the Organisation for Economic Co-operation and Development, and the World Bank, which have jointly produced the system of environmental–economic accounting (SEEA) to guide governments toward integrating economic, environmental, and social data into a single system enabling holistic decision-making (see "What is system of environmental–economic accounting").

What is system of environmental–economic accounting

System of environmental–economic accounting is a comprehensive statistical framework, which provides a compilation of consistent and comparable indicators for tracking and understanding the interactions between the environment and the economy. It enables countries to apply a system of internationally agreed concepts and definitions on environmental–economic accounting that can guide systematic and effective decision-making toward sustainable growth balancing economic benefits with the wise management of natural resources. Incorporating natural capital into national accounts can lead to relevant policy making and management decisions, as well as more informed decision-making by communities and private sector stakeholders that ensure the flow of benefits provided by natural resources but prevent their destruction and depletion.

Based on UN, EU, FAOUN, IMF, OECD, & WB. (2014). System of environmental–economic accounting 2012—Central framework. *New York: United Nations. Retrieved from <https://seea.un.org/sites/seea.un.org/files/seea_cf_final_en.pdf>.*

Given the novelty of these efforts and the fact that the societal systems that are currently in place have shaped well-rooted damaging behaviors toward the use of natural resources, there is a need to correct current human–nature interaction models. Existing markets, institutions, and policies fail to provide proper incentives for conservation and sustainable management of natural resources because of the asymmetry rewarding extractive production and failing to reward ecosystem service thinking (Guerry et al.,

2015). The application of tools that demonstrate in an obvious way the value of benefits derived from natural resources and that allow for calculation of the cost associated with their degradation is a step toward eliminating some of the behavioral failures. Once the value and cost are salient, the need to modify models becomes clearer. However, to produce a long-lasting systematic change of how natural resources are treated and managed by individuals, communities, businesses, and governments, there is need for further investigation of how contextual dynamics such as demography, poverty, education, sociopolitical, and cultural forces impact the way people use and treat the environment (Wolff, Schulp, & Verburg, 2015). Advancing knowledge in the area of behavioral economics, sociology, and psychology continue to enhance our understanding of these dynamics and of the principles that guide people's motivation, decision-making, and interaction with nature. Based on this new knowledge, behavior-smart thinking can help redesign societal and market systems to instill incentives for maintaining and enhancing natural capital. There is enough scientific and practical proof that behaviorally smart taxation, regulation, certification approaches, etc. can effectively change human–nature interaction models and encourage social norms for environmental stewardship (Guerry et al., 2015).

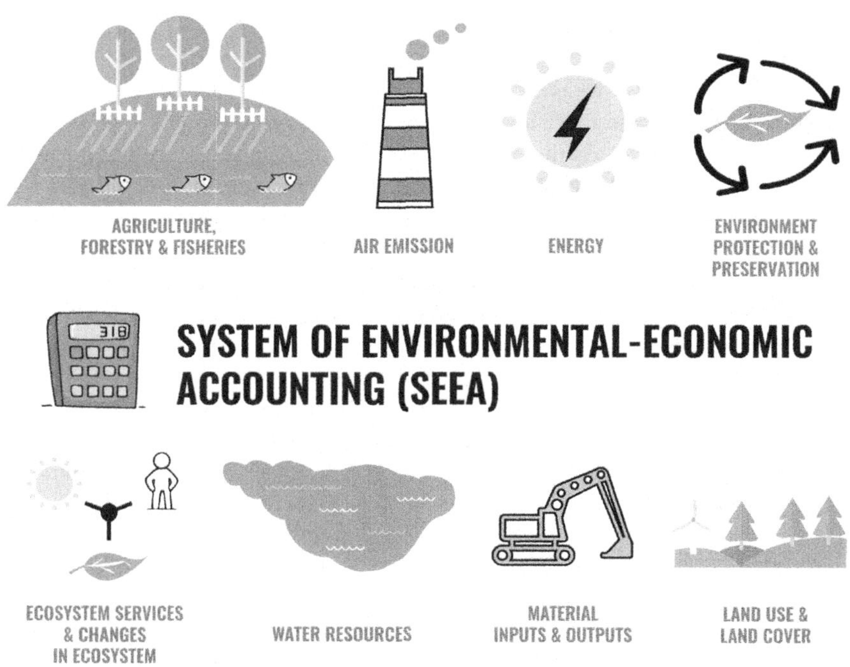

Based on UN, EU, FAOUN, IMF, OECD, & WB. (2014). System of environmental–economic accounting 2012—Central framework. *New York: United Nations. Retrieved from <https://seea.un.org/sites/seea.un.org/files/seea_cf_final_en.pdf>.*

Planning and managing growth

For many years texts on tourism development and planning have been promoting the idea that there are multiple approaches to planning tourism, and sustainable tourism is only one of them (Gunn & Var, 2002; Hall, 2008). The advancement in the past decades paradigms of ecotourism, responsible tourism, community-based tourism, pro-poor tourism, geotourism, and so on, have persistently been treated as specialized and niche approaches to planning and growing a tourism destination. Many public and private stakeholders perceive these as NGO-driven models that emphasize social care, environment protection, and equality—considerations that are typically not seen as responsibilities for mainstream market-driven tourism. In reality all these forms of tourism emphasize fundamental sustainability principles that provide equally valuable direction for any type of tourism anywhere around the world (Epler Wood, 2017). Ecotourism and geotourism emphasize the need to align market goals with the goals of protecting the natural resources and landscapes in destinations; pro-poor tourism and community-based tourism emphasize the need to ensure that tourism benefits local communities and that experiences offered to visitors are not disrespectful to local cultures; responsible tourism is grounded on the belief that travelers need to be conscious of the impacts that they can trigger with their behavior and to make choices that maximize positive and minimize negative impacts. All of these aspects are actually weaved into the views of the UN World Tourism Organization of what tourism should be: "UNWTO promotes tourism as a driver of economic growth, inclusive development and environmental sustainability... UNWTO encourages the implementation of the Global Code of Ethics for Tourism, to maximize tourism's socio-economic contribution while minimizing its possible negative impacts, and is committed to promoting tourism as an instrument in achieving the Sustainable Development Goals (SDGs), geared towards reducing poverty and fostering sustainable development worldwide" (UNWTO, n.d.).

Even though it has been wrongfully treated as a niche, in reality sustainable tourism is defined as tourism, which is "economically viable but does not destroy the resources on which the future of tourism will depend, notably the physical environment and the social fabric of the host community" (Swarbrooke, 2008, p. 13), which sound like principles for the development of any kind of tourism regardless of the intended scale (local, regional, and national) or targeted market segment (mass vs niche). Sustainability by definition means that planning and growth should not be based on choosing between market success, the environment and social responsibility but should be based on a balance between the three. Framing sustainability as a niche market segment has led to many decision-making mistakes that have produced tragic consequences across many popular tourism places. In essence many destination and business level decisions were made on the assumption that they have chosen an approach to planning and growing their destination that is different from sustainable, responsible or community-based tourism, and therefore they does not need to follow their principles. This has led to choices that have disregarded key tourism planning and growth management principles: the need to estimate the *carrying capacity* of places and communities, and plan investments and development in ways that do not lead to overtourism; the importance of identifying the *limits of acceptable change* for places and communities, and to develop destinations without overstepping them; the need to analyze and *manage visitor flows* in ways that minimizes pressures and avoids overcrowding and poor traveler experience.

Fundamental concepts in tourism planning

Carrying capacity relates to the capacity of a place or community to welcome people without suffering damaging impacts. Carrying capacity can be defined as a maximum number of people that can be present in one location at the same time or a maximum number of people that can visit within a certain time period (1 day, 1 month, and 1 year). Many sensitive natural and cultural attractions impose limitations on the number of people that can visit them based on the estimated impact of human presence and the maximum stress that the place can handle without suffering damage. Carrying capacity can be determined by purely physical factors (the church or square can hold this many people or a hiking trail can handle this many hikers at regular walking speed at the same time) or perceptual factors (having more than 100 people on the square gives local residents the sense of overcrowding or seeing other people on the trail while hiking damages the quality of the experience and ability to enjoy nature in solitude).

Limits of acceptable change relates to how much change linked to tourism development is acceptable to the local community and local stakeholders. If a destination is seeking to promote tourism around its beautiful coast, it needs to determine how much development it would accept as part of promoting tourism, that is, it is ready to sacrifice the wild beauty of its coast and accept that the coastline will look very different with infrastructure and resort buildings or it is not ready to lose the wilderness character of the area and prefers to explore forms of tourism that weave tourism facilities in nature rather than replace it. In some cases the identification of limits of acceptable change leads to decisions to limit tourism development or investment to certain zones or to a certain limit, that is, out of the 10 km wilderness coastline, development will be allowed only on 10% of the area.

Visitor flow management relates to the need to plan and manage the movement of visitors within a destination or attraction. Visitor flow management is much more visible on attraction level, for example, in museums or at archeological sites, where signage and walking paths guide visitors to move following a certain pattern. In protected areas visitor flows are managed through hiking/biking paths, markings, visitor infrastructure and maps that help keep people moving safely, and in ways that minimizes disturbances on biodiversity. Visitor flow management is possible and important at the destination level too as it can

(Continued)

(Continued)

prevent overcrowding and degraded visitor experience. Recent efforts to battle overtourism in hot spot cities such as Amsterdam and Barcelona have led to the experimental use of market tactics (prices that vary depending on day time, week of the day and season, promotion of less known attractions, etc.) that influence visitor flows and alleviate hot spots.

The painful lessons learned from destinations such as Venice, Barcelona, or Costa Brava serve as the living proof that tourism planning that does not consider economic viability along with impacts on the physical environment and social fabric ultimately runs into serious socioeconomic troubles. In this sense the traditions of presenting sustainability as a market niche rather than an essential guiding principle has led many destinations to ignore the basics of the triple bottom line in their planning efforts and has produced serious consequences such as overtourism and antitourism protests (Walker, 2018).

Discussion

In addition to the practices of assigning the management of different components of the tourism industry to different institutions, and the challenges of public–private collaboration, the planning of tourism is further complicated by the tendency to sacrifice long-term gains for short-term profits (Sessa, 1988). Taking a behavioral lens, there are several factors that explain this challenge. The first is that in general people have a difficult time imagining future outcomes, including the effects that specific behaviors or actions taken today will trigger in a few months or years, or the evolution of social or personal tastes with time and with changing sociocultural setting. In this sense even if a planning process is participatory and involves different representatives of the destination stakeholder network, many of them may be unable to imagine the impact of the different options they are considering.

In a situation of uncertainty or impossibility to imagine outcomes, individuals are much more likely to place more weight on short-term gains rather than long-term benefits. This is especially so if the gains are much easier to imagine and are especially likely to relate to them directly. For example, a local restaurant owner might be much more motivated to support a major new development if she/he associates this with potential increase of the visitor traffic near her/his restaurant than to support keeping of the current traditional state of things for the sake of preservation of community ambiance and avoiding overcrowding of the town. Similarly a politically appointed public servant may be more tempted to support a development that will enable her/him to report increased investments and growth in the number of visitors for the next election campaign rather than require analysis of the impacts of the development with the potential to reject it or postpone it for later in the future.

Another factor that may impede objective contribution to planning and growth management discussion is optimism bias. This, likely, has prevented many stakeholders across different destinations from learning from the failures and misfortunes of others before them and has led them to boldly repeat their very mistakes. Optimism bias is associated with overconfidence that one is better than the others and that the misfortunes of others in similar situations will not apply to them.

Measures of success

One of the biggest problems in contemporary tourism is the accepted measure of successful tourism growth. The number one indicator for tourism growth that is reported by destinations is number of tourist arrivals. In essence, this incentivizes tourism promotion and policy efforts to stimulate purely quantitative growth. The actual reality is that seeing the arrival of more heads reveals little about the socioeconomic impact that tourism has on the place. It also means that tourists are treated as numbers regardless of how they consume the destination (i.e., what is their footprint), how long they stay and most importantly, how much of what they spend stays in the local economy.

Related to the earlier discussion on tourism commons, there is little consideration of the fact that significant increase in physical presence produces physical impacts on the social and environmental context (crowding the streets and public areas in towns or overwhelming natural areas with human presence), increases pressure on and accelerates deterioration of infrastructure (more people walking the streets or trails means that they need to be repaired more frequently and maintained with a larger budget), accelerates usage intensity and potential exhaustion of resources (more visitors means more people consuming water for drinking and showering), increases the potential for damage on natural and cultural resources requiring different investment in their management (more visitors in a natural area or around an archeological site require investment in visitor infrastructure that supports higher intensity and guides visitor flows in ways that limits pressure on sensitive assets), etc. All these effects lead to the obvious realization that more arrivals in a place require more investment in assets management and infrastructure. However, the current norm in the industry is not to factor in the value of ecosystems and social capital or to account for the higher maintenance cost associated with increased intensity of tourism activities (Epler Wood, 2017).

What different tourism indicators reveal about economic impact?

An analysis of the impact of different traveler segments in Organisation of Eastern Caribbean States islands in the Caribbean reveals that arrival numbers alone do not say much about the economic impact of tourism. While the active cruise industry in the region generates an impressive number of arrivals, the average amount that each cruise passenger spends on the islands is $50. In contrast, overnight tourists who typically come on 5- to 7-day packages at all inclusive resorts leave on average $1000 per visit. Independent adventure travelers, visiting on flexible packages (8–9 days), and engaging in many experiences and services with local providers, can spend up to $2700 per trip.

As the following visual illustrates, this means that the same revenue that is generated by 200 cruise visitors ($10,000) can be earned by the destination from only 10 visitors on overnight packages or less than 4 independent adventure travelers. In this sense, while reporting only 4 arrivals may seem unimpressive in terms of numbers, the impact that this modest number triggers in the economy is equal to the hosting of 200 cruise visitors. If this estimate is taken further and combined with potential footprint (or the negative impact of hosting 4 vs 200 visitors on an island) the usefulness of using head count as success indicators makes even less sense.

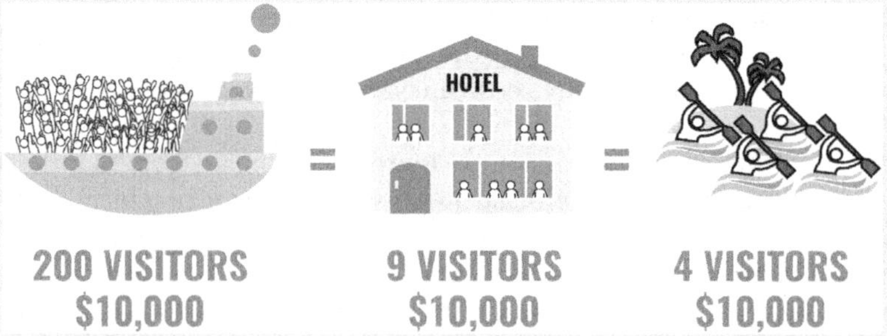

Based on Nikolova, M., Fernandes, E., & Shahidsaless, R. (2015). Strengthening tourism competitiveness in the OECS countries: Market analysis (OECS competitiveness project (P152117)). *Washington, DC.*

To really make sure that tourism growth generates relevant benefits for the destination and its community, it should be measured by the impact it makes on the place and its residents. In that sense increase of spending and in particular increase in the share of the spending that stays in the local economy is a much more meaningful indicators of positive performance of tourism than mere increase of the number of heads in beds (Dwyer & Forsyth, 1997). Another appropriate measure of success is length of stay as longer stay is always associated with higher spending (Barros & Machado, 2010). It is important to differentiate between the expenditures that travelers make and the share of these expenditures that stays in the local economy, as it is the latter that produces impact. Unfortunately in many destinations the design of tourism industry systems allows for revenues to be gained at the destination but to be transferred away from the local economy. This happens because large foreign outbound tour operators, resorts, and cruise companies, for example, sell holidays in a particular location but take the big share of the revenue they collect at their home economy rather than the destination where the consumption actually occurs (Gollub, Hosier, & Woo, 2003).

The focus on narrowly defined measures such as tourist flows and observable social and economic impacts ignores the fundamental factors underlying the effective functioning of the tourism system, that is, without an attractive environment that is preserved and maintained over time, and without a community setting that welcomes visitors, tourism cannot thrive effectively and sustainably (Carlsen, 1999). In this sense the failure to account for the quality of the experience of the traveler and the quality of life of the host communities as measures of success of tourism is problematic. If tourism is ruining local lifestyle and spirit, it is impacting the quality of life and as result inevitably influencing the quality of the traveler experience. An experience that leaves the visitor disappointed inevitably leads to poor market performance and eventual decline.

The behavioral implications of pursuing the wrong success indicators

Wrongful prioritization of arrival numbers as measure of success incentivizes decisions and interventions that do not help destinations. Just like the story in the introductory chapter about the government official Mr. Smith illustrates, purely stimulating arrival numbers leads to unwise choices such as extending subsidies to operators to drive arrival numbers up. Despite the fact that many researchers have proven that there are much better indicators for measuring the desired impacts of tourism (Dwyer & Forsyth, 1997; Dwyer, Forsyth, & Spurr, 2004; Juvan & Dolnicar, 2016) than arrival numbers, the standard practice continues to be to report tourism growth by quoting positive or negative trends in the number of tourists arriving at a destination.

Even though many tourism professionals understand the value of moving away from arrivals as leading indicator, the fact that it is prioritized determines the behavior of industry leaders and motivates the choices they make in terms of development, investment and policy. This is at the root of the most significant challenge that the industry is facing now—overtourism. A volume-oriented indicator for success produces volume-oriented growth.

References

Barros, C. P., & Machado, L. P. (2010). The length of stay in tourism. *Annals of Tourism Research, 37*(3), 692–706. Available from https://doi.org/10.1016/j.annals.2009.12.005.

Becker, E. (2013). *Overbooked: The exploding business of travel and tourism.* New York: Simon & Schuster.

Beritelli, P., Bieger, T., & Laesser, C. (2007). Destination governance: Using corporate governance theories as a foundation for effective destination management. *Journal of Travel Research, 46*, 96–107. Available from https://doi.org/10.1177/0047287507302385.

BIO Intelligence Services. (2011). *Estimating the economic value of the benefits provided by the tourism/recreation and employment supported by natura 2000 Final Report.* Brussels. Retrieved from <http://ec.europa.eu/environment/nature/natura2000/financing/docs/Estimating_economic_value.pdf>.

Blasco, D., Guia, J., & Prats, L. (2014). Emergence of governance in cross-border destinations. *Annals of Tourism Research, 49*, 159–173. Retrieved from <https://ac-els-cdn-com.proxygw.wrlc.org/S0160738314001108/1-s2.0-S0160738314001108-main.pdf?_tid = 5d855152-1692-11e8-b1e3-00000aab0f6c&acdnat = 1519168033_4d531434995d89903bd147c492f97773>.

Bosselman, F., Peterson, C., & McCarthy, C. (1999). *Managing tourism growth: Issues and applications.* Washington DC: Island Press.

Briassoulis, H. (2002). Sustainable tourism and the question of the commons. *Annals of Tourism Research, 29*(4), 1065–1085. Retrieved from <www.elsevier.com/locate/atoures>.

Carlsen, J. (1999). A systems approach to island tourism destination management. *Systems Research and Behavioral Science, 16*(4), 321–327.

Darbellay, F., & Stock, M. (2012). Tourism as complex interdisciplinary research object. *Annals of Tourism Research, 39*, 441–458. Available from https://doi.org/10.1016/j.annals.2011.07.002.

Demir, E., & Gozgor, G. (2017). Does economic policy uncertainty affect Tourism? *Annals of Tourism Research, 69*, 15–17. Available from https://doi.org/10.1016/j.annals.2017.12.005.

Dimmock, K., & Musa, G. (2015). Scuba diving tourism system: A framework for collaborative management and sustainability. *Marine Policy, 54*, 52–58. Available from https://doi.org/10.1016/j.marpol.2014.12.008.

Dwyer, L., & Forsyth, P. (1997). Measuring the benefits and yield from foreign tourism. *International Journal of Social Economics, 24*(1/2/3), 223–236. Available from https://doi.org/10.1108/03068299710161232.

Dwyer, L., Forsyth, P., & Spurr, R. (2004). Evaluating tourism's economic effects: New and old approaches. *Tourism Management, 25*, 307–317. Available from https://doi.org/10.1016/S0261-5177(03)00131-6.

Epler Wood, M. (2017). *Sustainable tourism on a finite planet: Environmental, business and policy solutions.* New York: Routledge.

European Commission. (2008). *NATURA 2000: Protecting Europe's biodiversity*. Oxford: Information Press.

European Commission. (2013). *The economic benefits of the natura 2000 network*. Luxembourg. https://doi.org/10.2779/41957.

Gollub, J., Hosier, A., & Woo, G. (2003). *Using cluster-based economic strategy to minimize tourism leakages* (Vol. 52246). UN World Tourism Organization. Available from https://doi.org/10.18111/9789284406166.

Guerry, A. D., Polasky, S., Lubchenco, J., Chaplin-Kramer, R., Daily, G. C., Griffin, R., & Vira, B. (2015). Natural capital and ecosystem services informing decisions: From promise to practice. *Proceedings of the National Academy of Sciences of the United States of America, 112*(24), 7348–7355. Available from https://doi.org/10.1073/pnas.1503751112.

Gunn, C. A., & Var, T. (2002). *Tourism planning: Basics, concepts, Cases* (4th ed.). London: Routledge.

Hall, M. C. (2008). *Tourism planning: Policies, processes and relationships* (2nd ed.). Edinburgh: Pearson Education.

Jafari, J. (1974). The components and nature of tourism: The tourism market basket of goods and services. *Annals of Tourism Research, 1*(3), 73–89. Retrieved from <https://ac-els-cdn-com.proxygw.wrlc.org/0160738374900346/1-s2.0-0160738374900346-main.pdf?_tid = 12bfcae8-1765-11e8-a87a-00000aacb361&acdnat = 1519258531_6b0fe3157a9a06ecd9549ffc872a8a08>.

Juvan, E., & Dolnicar, S. (2016). Measuring environmentally sustainable tourist behaviour. *Annals of Tourism Research, 59*, 30–44. Available from https://doi.org/10.1016/j.annals.2016.03.006.

Kahneman, D., & Tversky, A. (1983). Choices, values, and frames. *American Psychologist, 39* (4), 341–350. Available from https://doi.org/10.1037/0003-066X.39.4.341.

Kim, Y.-R., Saha, S., Vertinsky, I., & Park, C. (2018). The impact of national institutional quality on international tourism inflows: A cross-country evidence. *Tourism analysis, forthcoming*. Retrieved from <https://www.researchgate.net/profile/Young_Rae_Kim3/publication/321670227_The_Impact_of_National_Institutional_Quality_on_International_Tourism_Inflows_A_Cross-country_Evidence/links/5a2a462e0f7e9b63e535680c/The-Impact-of-National-Institutional-Quality-on>.

Koundouri, P. (Ed.), (2008). *Coping with water deficiency: from research to policy making (environment & policy series, book 48)*. Springer.

Leiper, N. (1979). The framework of tourism: Towards a definition of tourism, tourist, and the tourist industry. *Annals of Tourism Research, 6*(4), 390–407. Retrieved from <https://ac-els-cdn-com.proxygw.wrlc.org/0160738379900033/1-s2.0-0160738379900033-main.pdf?_tid = f6115af4-1a31-11e8-b154-00000aab0f6b&acdnat = 1519566432_f3169bf4ec9f348eaeed1cccb8272452>.

Lutz, W. (1994). In W. Lutz (Ed.), *Population development environment: Understanding their interactions in mauritius*. Berlin: Springer-Verlag/International Institute for Applied Systems Analysis.

Meadows, D. H. (2008). *Thinking in systems: A primer*. White River Junction, VT: Chelsea Green Publishing.

Mellon, V., & Bramwell, B. (2018). The temporal evolution of tourism institutions. *Annals of Tourism Research, 69*, 42–52. Available from https://doi.org/10.1016/j.annals.2017.12.008.

Millennium Ecosystem Assessment. (2005). *Ecosystems and human well-being: Synthesis*. Washington, DC: Island Press.

Murphy, P., Pritchard, M. P., & Smith, B. (2000). The destination product and its impact on traveller perceptions. *Tourism Management, 21*, 43–52. Retrieved from <https://ac-els-cdn-com.proxygw.wrlc.org/S0261517799000801/1-s2.0-S0261517799000801-main.pdf?_tid = 6262fbf2-168d-11e8-a52f-00000aacb361&acdnat = 1519165901_48e9adffd59aa7ffd06342d12efda855>.

Nikolova, M., Fernandes, E., & Shahidsaless, R. (2015). *Strengthening tourism competitiveness in the OECS countries: Market analysis* (OECS competitiveness project (P152117)). Washington, DC.

Nikolova, M. S. (2009). *Brand effects on retrospective evaluations of past consumption experiences*. The George Washington University.

Nikolova, M. S., Bakker, M., Nevill, H., Metz, M., & Popovik, G. (2017). Applying a visitor experience value chain for destination market performance assessment. In *ATLAS annual conference 2017: Destinations past, present and future* (p. 39). Viana do Castelo, Portugal. Retrieved from <http://www.atlas-euro.org/LinkClick.aspx?fileticket = nGjtRwuJTOA%3D&tabid = 263&language = en-US>.

Sessa, A. (1988). The science of systems for tourism development. *Annals of Tourism Research, 15*(2), 219–235. Retrieved from <https://ac-els-cdn-com.proxygw.wrlc.org/0160738388900849/1-s2.0-0160738388900849-main.pdf?_tid = 4f34d020-1a37-11e8-b71c-00000aab0f6c&acdnat = 1519568729_07bdb49400d1f149ca600043l1a8f37d>.

Stillman, P. E., Fujita, K., Sheldon, O., & Trope, Y. (2018). From "me" to "we": The role of construal level in promoting maximized joint outcomes. *Organizational Behavior and Human Decision Processes, 147*, 16–25. Retrieved from <https://ac-els-cdn-com.proxygw.wrlc.org/S0749597815303022/1-s2.0-S0749597815303022-main.pdf?_tid = f5e11438-4be1-453e-a001-c5aa71eb2ac8&acdnat = 1531803533_2a5671f9ce799708ac7f7f8c43ab04c7>.

Sundbo, J., & Sorensen, F. (2013). *Introduction to the experience economy. Handbook on the experience economy*. Cheltenham: Edward Elgar Publishing.

Swarbrooke, J. (2008). *Sustainable tourism management*. New York: CABI Publishing.

TEEB (2010), The Economics of Ecosystems and Biodiversity Ecological and Economic Foundations. Edited by Pushpam Kumar. Earthscan, London and Washington.

Tribe, J. (2015). *The economics of recreation, leisure and tourism* (5th ed.). New York: Routledge.

UN., EU., FAOUN., IMF., OECD., & WB. (2014). *System of environmental–economic accounting 2012—Central framework*. New York: United Nations. Retrieved from <https://seea.un.org/sites/seea.un.org/files/seea_cf_final_en.pdf>.

UNWTO. (n.d.). UNWTO: Who We Are.

UNWTO. (2007). *A practical guide to tourism destination management*. Madrid: UNWTO.

Walker, B. (2018). *Crowded out: The story of overtourism*. UK: Responsible Travel. Retrieved from <https://www.responsibletravel.com/copy/overtourism>.

Wolff, S., Schulp, C. J. E., & Verburg, P. H. (2015). Mapping ecosystem services demand: A review of current research and future perspectives. *Ecological Indicators, 55*, 159–171. Available from https://doi.org/10.1016/j.ecolind.2015.03.016.

Wray, M. (2009). Policy communities, networks and issue cycles in tourism destination systems. *Journal of Sustainable Tourism, 17*(6), 673–690. Available from https://doi.org/10.1080/09669580903071979.

Chapter 3

Tourism of the (near) future: growing, faster, on-the-go

Chapter Outline

Dynamics in the tourism sector

Once we see the relationship between structure and behavior, we can begin to understand how systems work, what makes them produce poor results, and how to shift them into better behavior patterns. As our world continues to change rapidly and become more complex, systems thinking will help us manage, adapt, and see the wide range of choices we have before us.

Donella H. Meadows Thinking in Systems: A Primer

Tourism is a large industry with linkages to multiple economic sectors and societal structures. Because of its vast scope and deep roots in socio-economic dynamics at large, it is actively influenced by trends and developments impacting today's societies. Many of these trends are shaping new realities and new behavioral patterns in the sector that require approaches than differ from what has been customary for public or business leaders.

This chapter zooms into several of the major trends and provides a behavioral perspective to the ways in which they are changing the global tourism system. Given the multitude of trends-tracking publications on the travel industry, the text does not emphasize on providing specific and most current data around each trend but will rather outline the general direction in which it is expected to shape the near future of the sector.

Behavioral Economics for Tourism. DOI: https://doi.org/10.1016/B978-0-12-813808-3.00003-4

Growth and overtourism

The rise of overtourism

Tourism is one of the largest global industries and in the past years it has been growing at rates that are increasingly faster (WTTC, 2018). As the figures of the UN World Tourism Organization, the United Nations agency that is consider the leading global body for the sector, reveal the increase in the number of people who travel internationally has been dramatic over the last decades. If just 30 years ago international arrivals were below 500 million, in 2012 they crossed the 1 billion mark and are expected to reach 1.4 million by 2020 (Fig. 3.1).

The main engine of international arrivals' growth in the most recent years has been the fast rise of new source markets where economic growth has fueled the expansion of a new middle class ready to spend disposable income on leisure travel. China has taken the lead to become the world's biggest market sending tourists abroad generating spending that is more than double

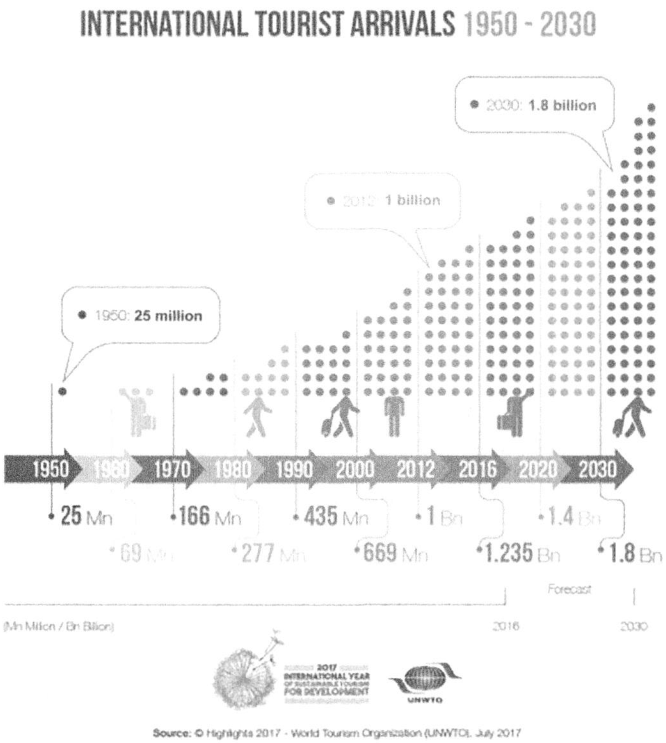

FIGURE 3.1 Trend in international tourist arrivals 1950–2030.

of what is spent internationally by United States travelers, the second biggest global source market (UNWTO, 2018b).

While the consistent increase in international tourism arrival has always been seen as a strong indicator for the health of the sector, it has produced one of the most worrying challenges for the sector today—overtourism. The term *overoturism* was coined by the influential media and trend-capturing platform Skift, and launched in their reporting on the mind-spinning growth of tourism in Iceland to describe the "potential hazards to popular destinations worldwide, as the dynamic forces that power tourism often inflict unavoidable negative consequences if not managed well" (Sheivachman, 2016). Since its introduction as a term overtourism has become focus of documentaries, news reports and industry analyses, and discussions around it have started leaving the boundaries of the industry drawing the attention of the public at large. Stories about tourism that has gone beyond the acceptable limits have started appearing in the most influential global media outlets such as The Economist, The Guardian, BBC, The New York Times, and others. In some of the most popular destinations in Europe public protests against tourism are raising a red flag to decision makers in the industry.

Overtourism has several dimensions that are important to outline. First, it relates to the presence of too many people or overcrowding that leads to deterioration of the traveler experience but even more importantly to the overwhelming of local places and local communities. Second, overtourism is not triggered by sheer volume, it is triggered by the lack of balance between volume and the capacity of the place. It means that even a few hundred visitors per day can cause an overtourism problem if the place or community have no infrastructure and support systems to meet the needs of these visitors, and to facilitate smooth visitor flow management preventing damaging footprint or pressure in hot spots. Third, overtourism effects can be associated with the clash between the behavior of visitors and the social norms of the destination. In that sense small groups of visitors may create high level of unease among local residents if they behave in ways that is considered disrespectful to the local culture or against social norms, including by damaging assets or attractions (Chien & Ritchie, 2018). Fourth, overtourism translates into a clash between the needs of visitors and the needs of residents. In some destinations this means that locals and guests are competing for the same scarce resource such as water, for example. In others, this means conflict between services and infrastructure for residents giving way to services and infrastructure for visitors. For example, shops that sell souvenirs or other products for tourists are taking over regular shops whose clientele are local residents. One of the most common recent expressions of the resident versus tourists problem is that in many places the market for long-term rentals geared toward residents focuses on short-term peer-to-peer accommodations changing the dynamics of local property markets and limiting living options.

In the words of local people:

"It has been a while since I have been thinking to give it up! I love the city, I love the way to live here, the way we had to live here. Now it is getting worse and worse."

"I think all the residents are facing this big question mark that no matter how much we love the city we consider our home, we are probably considering moving out to have a simpler and with more services and more comfort at the end."

"It would be nice if at least for once, the locals were a priority and not the tourists. Out of respect for the town and its history but also out of respect for the people who want to stay here who do not particularly want to take part in the tourism machine, and want to live like Venetians. This is slowly disappearing. Wear re a bit of an endangered species, if you like."

Quotes from the statements of residents of Venice and Barcelona featured in the documentary on overtourism by Responsible Travel (Walker, 2018).

Transport and accessibility

Cruises and low-cost airlines on the spot

What are the causes of overtourism? The recently produced by *Responsible Travel* documentary identifies several factors that are fueling the excessive growth of the industry (Walker, 2018) starting with the rise of low-cost carriers. Low-cost airlines brought to the market cheap flights making travel to many places highly accessible, mainly because of different forms of subsidies (Law, 2017). Low-cost airlines have played a positive role in opening up new places to tourism but have also contributed to the overcrowding of some traditional destinations, especially in Europe.

The second significant contributor to overtourism are cruises. With ever-bigger vessels and capacity to carry more and more people on board, cruise ships overwhelm the landscape in ports of call and contribute to massive overcrowding. A single large ship can disembark a couple of thousand people at a time and very often-popular ports of call, including compact towns and small island destinations, receive several vessels simultaneously. In addition to being a contributor to overcrowding, cruise tourism is characterized with strong misbalance between utilization of the resources of the visited destination and economic contribution. Spending just a few hours at the port of call with most shore activities planned and sold by the cruise line in advance, passengers spend very little money while away from the ship. An analysis of the spending behavior of different segments on some Caribbean islands revealed that cruise arrivals spend around $50 on average per arrival while every overnight arrival generates $1000 on average. At the same serving cruises is not only less economically beneficial for destinations but they actually produce a crowding-out effect that supresses growth of more profitable segments (Bresson & Logossah, 2011).

Increasing comfort of independent vehicles

A less talked about aspect of the changing transportation and accessibility landscape is the fast evolution in the personal transportation sector and namely the recreational vehicles, campervans, and other mobile camping solutions. The sense of independence, ability to escape to less visited places and freedom to initiate travel at any time fuels fast rise in the demand in this segment (RV Industry Association, 2018). Innovation has enabled fast improvements in the level of comfort offered by recreational vehicles alluring more and more buyers and renters much beyond the typical camping segment. The increasing number of recreational vehicles means that more and more people are engaging in independent outdoors holidays making their own decisions about where to go and where to stop. While in some urban areas there are regulations about recreational vehicle parking and access, in many natural areas access is at the discretion of the visitor. Because being in nature and using it is free, this new freedom enabled by mobile recreational solutions, fuels another form of misbalance between extracting benefits from the natural environment and paying for them. Some countries in Europe, especially in the Scandinavian region where access to nature is based on the principle of freedom to roam, are already experiencing an overtourism problem fueled by increasing flow of visitors on recreational vehicles who benefit from recreation in beautiful natural areas but who spend very little outside of gas contributing nothing to the local economy and to the management of the natural resources that are at the core of their choice to visit.

Similar dynamics are observed in the sailing segment, where recreational boating is gaining popularity as a new form of enjoying a holiday experience (ECSIP Consortium, 2015). The increasing accessibility of sailing experiences and the promise for more exciting interaction with water and coastal landscapes (Leposa, 2018) fuels rise in demand for sailing holidays that leads to overcrowding in popular sailing regions. Again, the independence of a sailing holiday means that a boat enables access to places that are inaccessible by land and increases human presence in more and more wilderness coastal areas. Again, while travelers enjoy the benefits of interacting with beautiful coastal landscapes there is no mechanism for them to pay for this service and secure the maintenance and management of these natural assets.

The changing accommodation landscape

Peer-to-peer accommodations

Another factor that is frequently identified as engine for overtourism is the fast rise of peer-to-peer rentals (Becker, 2013; Sheivachman, 2016; Walker, 2018) driven by the growing shared economy. Enabling the transformation of private living facilities into accommodation facilities has transformed the capacity of many destinations overnight. In the past destination growth cycles depended heavily on the rate with which new hotels are constructed, and add new rooms and beds to the available hotel inventory making it relatively easy to predict the maximum number of visitors that can arrive and stay overnight. They gave destinations and businesses time to develop additional infrastructure and support services, and adapt to the realities of the increasing number of visitors.

Today, peer-to-peer accommodations lead to fast swelling of accommodation inventories and make it hard to estimate how many rooms and beds are actually available, and how many of them are occupied at any given time. This fast but untraceable growth shocks places and eliminates the opportunity to plan and manage the impacts of increasing numbers of visitors.

That said, research around peer-to-peer accommodation platforms reveals that along with contributing to excessive growth of the number of visitors, they generate some desired effects such as increased spending that stays in the local economy, longer length of stay, higher level of engagement with the destination and its residents (Airbnb, 2018; Tussyadiah & Pesonen, 2016). Given that traditional industry players such as global hospitality groups, large tour operators and cruise companies, use accounting models that produce significant leakages of their revenues out of the destination (Ambrosie, 2015), and do not systematically produce all of the positive impacts associated with shared accommodation platforms, it may be that shared economy companies are source of more advantages and disadvantages.

Smart accommodations

Even thought it is in its infancy, there is another trend that is likely to change the accommodation sector and contribute to the multifaceted overtourism problem. Advances in architecture and energy technology have given rise to the creation of a growing number of off-the-grid accommodation solutions that can be moved around and installed anywhere. Some examples for such solutions include *Arkup* a floating home that is entirely self-sufficient and hurricane proof (Arkup, n.d.); Coodo, a mobile home designed from sustainable materials and installable in any natural environment (Coodo, n.d.); or *Dom.ai*—a self-sufficient off-the-grid three dimensional (3D)-printed home solution that can be installed anywhere.

Even though these innovations are relatively new and beginning to come to the market just now, they have the potential to revolutionize living and recreational realities. All of them place heavy emphasis on sustainability by using nature-friendly materials, incorporating cutting edge renewable energy technology and efficient waste management solutions. However, they also provide a new level of comfort combined with almost unlimited reach to natural places, which are currently accessible only to the more adventurous and hard-core fans of camping experiences. This new combination of comfort and contact with nature will likely lead to increased human presence in more wilderness areas further pushing the misbalance between extracting recreational benefits from nature and covering the costs for their maintenance and protection.

Social media

One of the factors that also seems to contribute to the problem with overtourism is the facilitated by social media sense of easy accessibility of popular tourist places and the sense of competition it triggers within one's social circle. A smiling selfie on top of a beautiful rock formation or at a picturesque old-town square triggers the curiosity and desire to have the same among social media friends (Leung, Law, Van Hoof, & Buhalis, 2013). Social media has activated the sense of competition among certain groups of travelers modifying the core motivation for travel and boiling it down to collecting selfies that are similar to those of friends rather than to experiencing new places.

The equalizing of a travel experience to an instant selfie produces another negative effect. It creates a fake sense of ease and accessibility of popular spots and makes travelers ignorant of the experience leading to the captured moment and the time and effort it may require. For example, Norway has been dealing with a dramatic increase of rescue operations for tourists who come determined to capture a selfie at the famous Preikestolen (Pulpit Rock) or the unique Trolltunga (Troll Tongue) but who are completely unaware of the fact that both spots are reachable only after one hikes for a few hours through a mountainous terrain and in dynamic weather conditions requiring proper preparation and outdoors gear (for more details see case at the end of this book). The fact that permanent connectivity gives travelers the options to figure things out on-the-go (Wang, Xiang, & Fesenmaier, 2014) and that social media moments form expectations that influence planning suggests that they lead to superficial motivation and poor planning decisions. The easy access to mobile services and peer-to-peer sharing produce overconfidence that one can always reach out and find information so they can ignore preliminary consultation with formal information and guiding services (Gretzel, 2010), which have been designed to prevent unrealistic planning.

Linkages and numbers

Another factor that has fueled the overtourism crisis is the broken tourism system, in which incentives for volume-based growth are disconnected from the costs required to support that growth. The players that package and sell a destination, and its assets are incentivized to sell more and more as this translates to direct profit. At the same time, they carry practically no responsibility for the cost of supporting more visitors in the destination, including increased consumption of water, electricity and other utility services, or the need for more infrastructure and higher cost of maintaining the existing one. Existing taxation systems in the industry are also designed in ways that do not account for the need for more investment in managing tourism assets as arrivals increase. Complicated ownership systems and accounting practices allow multinational players such as large tour operators, cruise companies and hospitality groups to avoid paying much taxes at the very destinations where they generate their profits (Ambrosie, 2015). In the cases when tourism taxes are collected by the destination, a significant share of them is invested in promotion activities aiming the attracting of even more visitors rather than in maintenance of tourism assets, and expansion and maintenance of tourism infrastructure (Ambrosie, 2015; Epler Wood, 2017). Part of that is explained with the discussed in Chapter 2 fact that the institutions and organizations that are responsible for tourism promotion are different and often disconnected from the ones that oversee the infrastructure and services that support tourist needs.

The changing profile of the traveler

New markets on the block

The rise of new economic powers has had major influences on market presence and global dynamics, including in tourism. China continues to strengthen its leadership as the number one source market in the world growing at much faster rates than the global average of the entire travel industry. The global average rate with which the industry continued to grow in 2017 is higher than in the previous few years and that is explained mainly by the rising significance of powerful new markets such as China, Brazil, the Russian Federation, and India (UNWTO, 2018a).

The rise of the new economic powers has modified dynamics within destinations seeking to attract international arrivals. While the European continent continues to be a leading source market for many destinations around the world, there is almost no country with a viable tourism industry that does not declare China and/or India as priority markets. In addition to the fact that this is explained by the continuing obsession of the sector with volume rather than quality, the massive pursuit of arrivals from the big new source markets is associated with several gaps in decision-making.

The first is that for many destinations the more rational and market-efficient option is to invest in some existing markets and seek to increase arrivals from them or to stimulate longer length of stay and higher average spending that translate to higher profitability. This typically requires tweaking of existing strategy or promotional efforts with some targeted investments that align with preferences that the host destination is already familiar with and capable of serving. On the other hand, the proper development of a new market, especially one that is culturally very different from the markets the destination is accustomed to, requires significantly more investment in research, promotion and likely adjustment of the destination's portfolio of offerings. All of this investment is made in a very competitive setting with multiple other destinations trying to establish presence in that same market alongside. In that sense, the massive pursuit of penetrating the Chinese and Indian markets for many decision makers on destination level might be explained with a more intuitive decision process rather than rational analysis of what might be most reasonable from a realistic market perspective. In many cases such decisions seem to be associated with the short-term political benefits of demonstrating alignment with buzz-worthy trends and avoiding a more effort-intensive route of explaining to constituents why market rationale suggests that there are better market opportunities that the destination should be pursuing.

Another problem is that interest in the Chinese and Indian markets is driven mainly by their sheer volume, which represent opportunity but also poses dramatic risks for many destinations. In the age of overtourism, accessing a market of such volume needs to come with careful planning and visitor flow management considerations.

New generations and new traveler behavior patterns

The entry of the new younger generations in the tourism market inevitably triggers changes in the demand landscape. While some of the consumption specifics of Millennial travelers identified by the many analyses published in recent years are associated with their lifecycle stage (e.g., price sensitiveness), others are distinctive for their demographic (e.g., fondness for technology-enabled services) (Barton, Fromm, & Egan, 2012). As a leading generational segment in the global travel industry Millennials are naturally introducing new traveler behavior patterns to the market that are picked up by older generations too. Peer-to-peer accommodation services, originally created by Millennials for Millennials, disrupted the accommodation market and are now mainstream. The inclination of Millennials to mix everyday with travel realities and the invention of the digital nomad model have also started spilling over to the other generations fueling the popping up of special coworking and coliving facilities that gear toward travelers who look to remain professionally active while being on the move (Levels, 2015).

We are frequently reminded that this is the generation that has grown up with technology and has developed a natural relationship with it in ways that blend online and offline experiences, including during travel. Having grown up with the topics of sustainability and climate change, they are also much more sensitive to them and much more inclined to make responsible traveler decisions (Barton et al., 2012; Phocuswright, 2015).

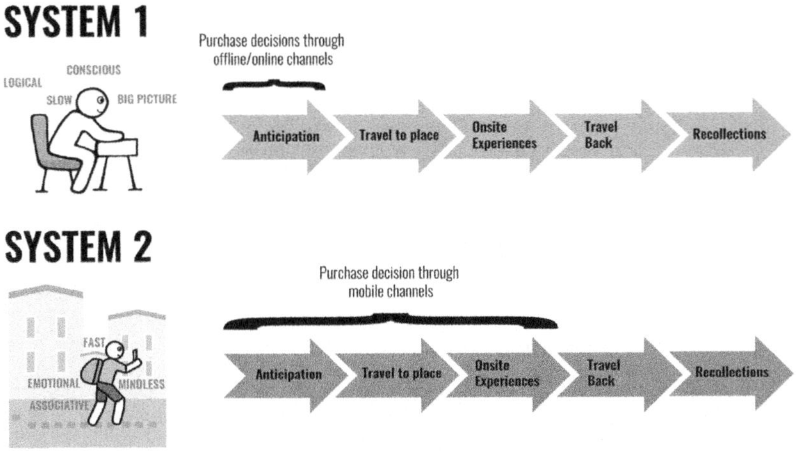

While less discussed in the industry, the advancing Generation Z that follows the Millennials cohort will also likely bring new models of experiencing travel. Many members of the Generation Z will naturally be much more experienced travelers from the start as for their generation traveling with the family and visiting different places during childhood is much more common that for previous ones (TMS Family Travel, 2017). The early start of a travel career will certainly shape different preferences for this next generation when they come of age and join the market as independent consumer decision makers.

Ageing population and its travel patterns

While younger generations are bringing new behaviors to the market, the globally ageing population remains important for the travel industry too. With improved healthcare and longevity, more and more people remain active until later in life. With available time and disposable income on their hands, traveling is one of the most attractive ways for retirees to spend time. In addition to requiring specific experiences and supporting services (The Economist, 2017), the elderly also bring their own specific consumption patterns to the travel industry. Given the looser time restrictions they have, they are likely to spend more time on trips and to be less limited by seasonality and typical holiday periods. In pursuit of good weather many representatives of the older generation seek to be away from home for extended periods of a few months during colder or very hot seasons. In some cases their travels are determined by ownership of second homes but many simply seek to stay in a different place for an extended period of time while renting local space and living among locals.

Technology

Changing purchasing patterns

There is virtually no article or analysis reviewing trends in travel that does not highlight the big impact that technology has had on the tourism industry. From keyless access to hotel rooms and virtual reality technology that enhance the experience at accommodation facilities to chatbots that control customer service interactions, there are fast-spinning changes throughout the value chain. The main technology-related revolution that has occurred in the sector is the permanent marriage between the traveler and their mobile devices. Wearables and mobile phones are no longer merely facilitating the experience; they are integrated into it.

From a behavioral perspective technological developments have produced changes that represent both opportunities and challenges prompting travel service providers to think in new ways. The swirling changes in technology have lead to the formation of new patterns in the behavior of travelers. Equipped with mobile devices and wearables consumers seek to be in a 24/7 conversation with travel companies and to "converse seamlessly across the real and the virtual worlds" (European Travel Commission & UN World Tourism Organization, 2014, p.3). These new dynamics are leading to a more fundamental disruption—the dissolving of existing patterns of planning and consuming travel. Accustomed to online booking, the contemporary traveler is becoming increasingly independent of intermediaries in making travel plans. Mobile devices enable exploration and booking on-the-go, tempting travelers to plan less in advance and keep their options open (Nikolova, Asenov, & Lazarova, 2015). In the recent past the typical buying journey included spending time in front of the desktop or laptop during a lunch break, after the end of the workday or on a weekend in a typically calm environment allowing for mindful research and comparison of different options. In many ways this decision-making process was slow, conscious, logical, and based on considering the bigger picture, as well as the pros, and cons of the different available options, that is, very much a System 2 decision according to Kahneman's dual-system model (Kahneman, 2011) discussed in Chapter 1. With mobile devices in their hands, today more and more travelers make purchasing decisions on-the-go. Industry research from the last couple of years reveals that mobile is now the mainstream channel for booking travel and travel-related services (Sheivachman, 2017; WTM & Euromonitor International, 2015). This means that today's travelers are more and more inclined to choose and buy accommodation, food services or experiences while they are on-the-go—on the way to work, between meetings or while waiting for a friend on the street, and even when they are already in the destination. This means making purchasing decisions in a dynamic environment, in a state of mind that is elevated by the sights and sounds of the destination, and the excitement of being in travel mode. Under these circumstances, the decision-making process is faster, associative, less mindful, and driven by shortcuts rather than careful consideration of pros and cons, that is, very much a System 1 decision according to Kahneman's dual-system model (Kahneman, 2011).

This shift toward booking on-the-go or while already in the destination, is driven by the availability of mobile booking but is further strengthened by another significant trend: the rising demand for authentic experiences and eagerness to connect with the local character of places (Peak & Skift, 2014). In pursuit of a truly local experience travelers often explore and research before getting to the destination but leave the final choice of local provider or local excursion to the moment they are on the ground and can rely on some local hints and advice on the spot. Because mobile technology and on-the-go booking capabilities make them less locked to preliminary itineraries they are able to engage in unplanned and spontaneous experiences along the travel journey.

The rise of the traveler who enjoys flexibility and plans on-the-go is leading to two important changes for travel destinations and individual tourism service providers. First, travelers will continue to do some research and gather advance information about the destination they are planning to visit, but they are likely to leave plans flexible and make fewer booking decisions before their departure (Wang et al., 2014). Second, this will shift the competition for the attention of the customer and their decision to book, to the post-departure period and during the entire trip. These new decision-making and consumption patterns inevitably lead to the need for new approaches in designing and marketing offerings in the industry (Nikolova et al., 2015).

The more silent and less dependent traveler

Technology does not simply accompany the traveler on their journey; today it is intertwined with the actual experience (Mackay & Vogt, 2012; Wang et al., 2014). Always connected and equipped with numerous applications, today's travelers are more and more independent from local service providers in figuring out how to meet their needs and wants during trips (Gretzel, 2010). The tendency to find solutions and meet needs without seeking contact with service providers at the destination prompted Skift to describe today's traveler as "silent" (Ali, Clampet, Schaal, & Shankman, 2014).

On one side this technology-mediated independence means that destination service providers have less opportunity to connect with and understand the traveler with their expectations and demands. This also leads to the fact that many of the existing information and support services are fast becoming obsolete. This leads to lower engagement between the traveler and the place, as well as the traveler and local service providers.

On the other side, the increasing penetration of technology in the traveler experience provides opportunity for data collection and for the establishment of more digital touch points at which systematic information can be picked up. Whether through mobile devices, digital access solutions or mapping services destinations and service providers can obtain data that unlocks new level of understanding of traveler behavior and visitor flow patterns. Based on this they can design new solutions that enable the delivery of services that are relevant to today's travelers and to apply cutting edge visitor flow management tactics preventing overcrowding. The city of Amsterdam, one of the overtourism hot spots in Europe, has pioneered efforts to do precisely that—use technology and big data to enable real-time services designed to influence traveler decision-making and behavior (Ellwood, 2017).

Rise of digital detox

While technology offers new opportunities that can enhance traveler decision-making and their experience, and can improve the delivery of services or the management of traveler destinations, it also has a darker side. There is growing concern that contemporary lifestyle nurtures dependence on technology that can be harmful and that can highjack the actual experience at the destination. The habit to focus on the mobile screen is easily transferred from everyday life to travel life, which redirects attention away from the surrounding environment preventing travelers from obtaining a deep sense of place when experiencing the destination (Gretzel, 2010). A Facebook video that shows tourists on a gondola in Venice all staring at their smart phones completely ignorant of their surroundings, was actively shared by tourism professionals as the perfect illustration of this problem.

In addition to being a challenge, this shift toward less mindful experiences and disengagement with one's environment creates opportunities for the tourism industry. It is beginning to respond by offering experiences that enable travelers to unplug from their technology-dependent stressful realities and engage in activities that restore their mindfulness and well-being (van den Berg, Hartig, & Staats, 2007). Restorative holidays are just starting to appear on the market but as public concerns around the impacts of technology on well-being grow, there is likelihood that they will expand further. Service providers can adjust the design of offerings in ways that facilitates a more mindful experience of the destination that is not mediated by devices and that facilitates return to more human-friendly activities, better relationships and healthy experiences (see case on Factory Food-n-Dance at the end of the book for an example).

The 72 h Cabin in Western Sweden

A recent documentary produced by Visit Sweden presents an innovative experience available in Western Sweden that is designed especially for busy professionals whose daily lifes are defined by high levels of stress and dependance on technology. The 72-hour Cabin experience involves spending 3 full days in a glass cabin in the middle of nature unplugged from technology and civilization. The program is grounded on scientific research that confirms that raw contact with nature can have restorative effects and can improve one's physical and spiritual well-being within a relatively short period of time. As the documentary reports an experiment with a group of busy professionals living in stressful urban centers across the globe revealed that the 72-hour Cabin experience leads to much more than a perceived sense of rejuvenation. It

(Continued)

(Continued)

produces significant improvement of basic health indicators such as stress level, anxiety, blood pressure and heart beat.

Lublin & Klang, 2017

Climate change and sustainability

Climate change, the role of the industry and modifying weather patterns

Climate change as a theme has become regular on the agenda of the travel sector. Tourism is one of the industries that contribute significantly to global emissions and respectively to climate change. According to a targeted scientific study performed in 2005–2006 tourism was responsible for 5% of the global CO_2 emissions. 40% of these are attributed to air travel, 35% to car travel and other transportation, 21% are linked to accommodation, and 4% to activities (Daniel Scott et al., 2008). The same study projects that if the travel industry continues to operate without any change, its contribution to global CO_2 emissions will reach 7% by 2035.

In addition to being a contributor to climate change, tourism is highly dependent on it. The expected climate at a place is a key determinant of destination choice and actual weather conditions influence the traveler experience significantly (Scott & Lemieux, 2010).

The past years more and more regions are experiencing dramatic changes in weather patterns and natural disasters of untypical scale so regardless of whether their residents believe that climate change is real, they are certainly facing the need to adapt to new and frequently extreme weather realities. Just the summer of 2018 alone brought extreme heat waves to Japan, Canada, Western, and Northern Europe causing loss of human life, need for additional emergency care and other unusual measures. Southern Europe and the Southern parts of the United States fought deadly fires that took a lot of lives and caused significance damage (The Economist, 2018).

Changing weather patterns inevitably impact tourism, even if they do not produce dramatic natural disasters. This is even more so given the earlier discussed trend toward more flexible and relaxed planning enabling last-minute changes in destination choice or itinerary design (Scott & Lemieux, 2010). Analyses of the likely changes in travel demand triggered by expected weather fluctuations suggest that countries with colder weather may see sharp increases in domestic travel while destinations in warmer regions may face 20% decline in visitation (Bigano, Hamilton, & Tol, 2007).

Forward thinking winter sports communities have already began analyzing the implications of warmer winters and inconsistent snowing patterns (Burakowski & Magnusson, 2012; Hagenstad, Burakowski, & Hill, 2018).

Suffering from declining profitability a lot of winter resorts have started diversifying their offerings toward activities that are less dependent on snow and that expand into warmer seasons. Similarly regions that rely on warm weather and prime conditions for summer holidays may suffer from similar shocks if they see more rain and unstable weather during summer months.

Climate change, natural disasters, and environmental degradation

Climate change has been identified as the main reason for the changing strength, frequency and pattern of natural disasters across the world. Europe is seeing unusually powerful thunderstorms with heavy rains that cause floods and landslides. Winter and summer seasons have been accompanied by untypically strong cold and heat waves. Central America and the Caribbean, and the southern regions of the United States are suffering from more frequent and more powerful hurricanes explained with rising ocean water temperatures. These weather fluctuations and associated disasters are causing damage to many places that rely on tourism.

The growing number of natural disasters and the expanding geographical areas that are impacted by them are signal about the scale of the challenge and the need to seek solutions. Among the measures that can increase preparedness and lower risk for local residents and travelers are improving monitoring and weather forecast services, access to digital weather monitoring tools, as well as streamlining public information and warning services (Scott & Lemieux, 2010).

Natural disasters and climate change in general lead to degradation of natural resources, which exacerbates the negative impacts on the travel sector. Beach degradation, burned down forests, or destroyed natural areas translate to disappearing of assets that are at the core of destination attractiveness and to likely decline in traveler motivation to visit (Gössling, Scott, Hall, Ceron, & Dubois, 2012). This suggests that there is a risk that even if traveler demand adjusts to the induced by climate change different weather patterns, destinations will lose appeal simply because of disappearing tourism assets.

The aftermath of Hurricane Maria

In September 2017, Puerto Rico was severely hit by a category-5 hurricane. In addition to the loss of life and absolute disruption in the life of the island, it is suffering from inability to gain some restorative benefits from the important for the local economy tourism industry. Analysis of the damage of tourism assets and infrastructure reveal that Puerto Rico is likely to need more than a year to become tourism-ready. Months after the storm, electricity is still not restored on a third of the island, the majority of local small businesses are closed and 10,000 of them do not expect to be able to open again. Higher-end resorts have began renovation and rebuilding activities that will take an year to bring them back to market (Ekstein, 2017).

Behavioral perspectives to the changing system

A behavioral perspective to the realities of today's travel industry and the trends that will likely be shaping its future offers new dimensions of analysis and reveals new potential solutions. This section outlines some general behavioral themes that enrich the understanding of the current realities in the sector.

On growth and overtourism

One of the premises of traditional economic thinking is that if people have enough information they make the right choices. The decision-making failures that have led to the rising problem with overtourism and that continue to make its solving difficult, is a good illustration of the fact that this is not so. At the core of the overtourism problem is the violation of tourism planning and management principles that exist and have lived in introductory tourisms texts for at least a couple of decades (e.g., Bosselman, Peterson, & McCarthy, 1999).

As discussed in the earlier chapter lack of a systems thinking approach creates an unrealistic context for decision-making too. If behavioral thinking suggests that choices are an outcome of the combination between appropriate decision-making tactics and the particular decision-making context (Gigerenzer, Fiedler, & Olsson, 2012), then the lack of complete information explains the many mistakes of destination and business decision makers that continue to fuel sustainability and growth issues in the sector. The lack of a complete picture tempts the decision makers to focus on more immediate gains rather than the complex long-term scenarios requiring much effort to outline. This also becomes favorable context for a more powerful influence of present bias, that is, placing more weight on rewards that are possible now or in the nearer future rather than benefits, which can be expected to materialize within a longer period of time (O'Donoghue & Rabin, 1999). For a destination-level decision maker that may mean preference to enjoy the ability to report impressive growth in arrivals and spending of tourists next year versus the ability to claim pride in the successful preservation of the natural environment in 10 years (when they might not be even in office). For a local restaurant owner that may mean stronger focus on the shorter term potential for increased revenues from increased visitor traffic on the street rather than consideration of the benefit of keeping visitor flows at current levels to continue enjoying the small-town feel of the place 5 or 7 years from now.

Another behavioral mechanism that is activated in the lack of clear context is the poor ability of people to imagine the future, especially when it involves a complex process likely to be influenced by many different factors (O'Donoghue & Rabin, 2015; Thaler & Benartzi, 2004). This translates to inability of a local resident to imagine what might be the likely longer term effects of allowing cruise ships in the destination and how the waves of cruise passengers will alter the everyday social texture of the place within a few years. Similarly it may translate to the inability of a politician to imagine how the sudden increase of low-cost flights landing in the destination will impact infrastructure needs and require more public funds to cover higher maintenance costs. In many cases optimism bias (Sharot, 2012) can also play a role leading individuals to believe that the negative impacts that may be experienced by other destinations with similar growth rates will not unfold at their destination and that it will fare much better than negative examples.

The difficulty in estimating and describing in solid terms most of the social and environmental impacts from certain tourism management decisions adds to the behavioral complexity of controlling the sector's growth. The lack of ownership and in many cases the limited control over the utilization of tourism commons leads to discounting of the costs associated with their degradation or depletion.

An uncertain and unpredictable decision-making setting leads to bias-prone choices that are limited within the reality that is currently accessible to the decision maker. In that sense, satisficing (Simon, 1990) leads to decisions that are sufficient and satisfying within the trade-offs that can be identified at the current moment (i.e., a politician considering that allowing more low-cost flights from next year will translate to more arrivals and spending that can be reported as positive news but not considering some likely negative impacts such as overcrowding, overuse of public infrastructure, negative tourist-resident dynamics, etc.). In this sense, modifying the accessibility of likely growth scenarios that are triggered by changes in transport options (allowing or increasing cruise ships, allowing or increasing low-cost airline flights, etc.), unleashing private accommodation options (lack of regulation of peer-to-peer rentals) or launch of promotional efforts in new markets (China or India) can make decisions bound within a new reality. For example, technology-enabled modeling solutions that ensure a system approach and that can map likely impacts of potential tourism growth scenarios on the local physical space and social texture can make future outcomes much easier to imagine. This will enable decision makers, whether it is the national-level politician deciding on cruise ship policies or the local restaurant owner deciding whether to express public support for a large new development in town, to make decisions that are bound by a reality with much clearer trade-offs. Such solutions can also minimize the likelihood for inattentional blindness (Coyle, 2011) that prevents decision makers to account for phenomena even if it is in front of their eyes (e.g., failure to foresee the likely impact of the fast penetration of peer-to-peer accommodation services on the local place despite its obvious nature).

Another aspect that can contribute to a clearer decision-making context and elimination of a lot of the blind spots in understanding available tourism growth options is the advancement of valuation techniques for natural and cultural resources. Being able to estimate a value that will be extracted by a specific natural assets if it is preserved in its current condition makes it much easier to understand the cost of degradation or imporper use without maintanance. It also helps to frame the needed spending on maintanance of natural and cultural assets as a community investment rather than a comunity cost. Recent reports use tourism as basis of estimating the value of preserving animals species, for example, and suggest that a single elephant can generate $1.6 million in revenue during its entire life so killing it would mean losing this potential income (Blignaut, De Wit, & Barnes, 2008; The David Sheldrick Wildlife Trust, 2015). Similarly a report on the services generated by animals in Lapland region reveals that the annual value generated by them is over 15 Million Euro (Bohn, García-Rosell, & Äijälä, 2018).

The evolution of valuation techniques and the concept of ecosystem services discussed in the previous chapter have the potential to introduce new framing around decisions about the preservation or utilization of common pool resources making the decision context clearer and with tracable outcomes.

On climate change and responsibility toward the environment

One of the leading names in behavioral economics, Dan Ariely, states that "if we tried to manufacture an exemplary problem that would inspire general indifference, it would probably be [global warming]" (Ariely, 2010, p.383). He explains the inability of today's societies to respond to climate change in determined ways with several fundamental behavioral mechanisms. First, for many people climate change has not produced tangible changes in the realities of their everyday living as most of the current impacts are observed in distant regions or specific areas such as coastal zones. Second, neither CO_2 emissions that fuel global warming, nor climate change itself is observable so it offers easy opportunity for rejection and denial (Juvan, Ring, Leisch, & Dolnicar, 2016). Third, because the changes in weather patterns and living realities take time to unfold they are harder for us to feel. Our natural ability to adapt is not helping the matter either as when change is gradual our behavior adapts slowly along with it too. Fourth, the real negative outcomes from climate change are going to unfold in the distant future, which supresses the need to do something about it now.

In addition to these complicating factors, behavioral scientists have explored the mechanisms that explain the extreme polarization of opinions related to climate change. They found that because climate change is so politicized people's readiness to process scientific information on the topic is modified by their political views (Sunstein, Bobadilla-Suarez, Lazzaro, & Sharottt, 2016). If the scientific messages they hear align with the beliefs linked to the philosophy advanced by their political party, they are processed and lead to update of opinion. On the other hand, if the scientific facts that are being communicated go against the beliefs that are advanced by the political party, then exposure to them does not lead to change of behavior or update of their beliefs (Sunstein et al., 2016). This political bias explains the high level of polarization in society around the acceptance of climate change and suggests that there is need for de-biasing of attitudes. This is possible by shifting the emphasis from the politicized topic of whether climate change is induced by human activity to the observable scientific aspects of changing weather patterns and the objective need for more resilient infrastructure and behavior in our society (Nguyen, 2017).

One of the ways to change the behavior of contemporary people and society toward nature is to restore the human–nature relationship, which is broken by contemporary urban lifestyle (van den Berg et al., 2007). Contemporary lifestyle has disconnected people from nature, limited their understanding of how natural environments work and how they benefit one's physical and mental well-being. By promoting nature-based experiences the travel industry can facilitate a back-to-nature movement that restores the interaction between people and natural environment. Behavioral models for nature-based tourism reveal that travel experiences designed in ways that increase the mindful involvement with nature produce higher level of place attachment and commitment to conservation (Lee, 2011; Vaughan & Ardoin, 2014). Such behavior-based re-engagement with nature can increase sensitiveness toward ecosystem services and environmental processes, including changing weather patterns, breaking the association with the politicized climate change theme. It can stimulate more demand for interaction with nature, more responsible behavior and proactive efforts for building resilience in the context of dynamic climate patterns.

On technology and modified behavioral patterns

The technology-facilitated and mediated travel industry creates many situations in which System 1 decisions are prevalent. This means more and more choices made during the holiday planning phase and throughout the travel experience that are shortcut-driven, fast, affective, to some extend subconscious, and associative (Kahneman, 2011). The limited influence of System 2 processes involving control, effort and analysis increase the importance of context-based triggers and factors such as defaults, social norms, framing, and information salience. This has several implications for commercial success and sustainability that are relevant to both tourism destinations and service providers.

First, destination and experience design needs to align with System 1 processes rather than System 2. This means that promotional formats, including information presentation, selection of channels, and motivators should be more System 1 friendly than in the past (Nikolova et al., 2015). It also means that nudges and other behavioral tools will be much more relevant to stimulating traveler satisfaction but also facilitating desired behavior in the destination. Second, in specific situations and contexts, destinations and operators need to apply targeted mechanisms for mindful involvement of the traveler that activates System 2 processes. This may be needed to stimulate deeper and mindful experiences based on higher involvement with the place and the surrounding environment. It is needed also to ensure more responsible traveler behavior that fits with the social dynamics of the visited destination. Third, the industry has to use more behavioral tactics in destination and experience design to stimulate supply and demand dynamics that align with the principles of sustaiability and contribute to the overcoming of today's complex challenges such as overtoutrism.

With relevant behavior-smart approaches the travel industry can also address some of the bigger contemporary lifestyle problems such as increased stress levels, associated health problems, and deteriorating happiness levels (Helliwell, Layard, & Sachs, 2017). Through mindful engagement with the visited place that leads to self-actualization experiences, deeper involvement with nature that leads to rejuvenation and restoration, and experiences that facilitate increased sense of happiness (Zelenski & Nisbet, 2014) the travel industry can make a bigger impact in society at large and responsibly contribute to the addressing of some of humanity's contemporary problems.

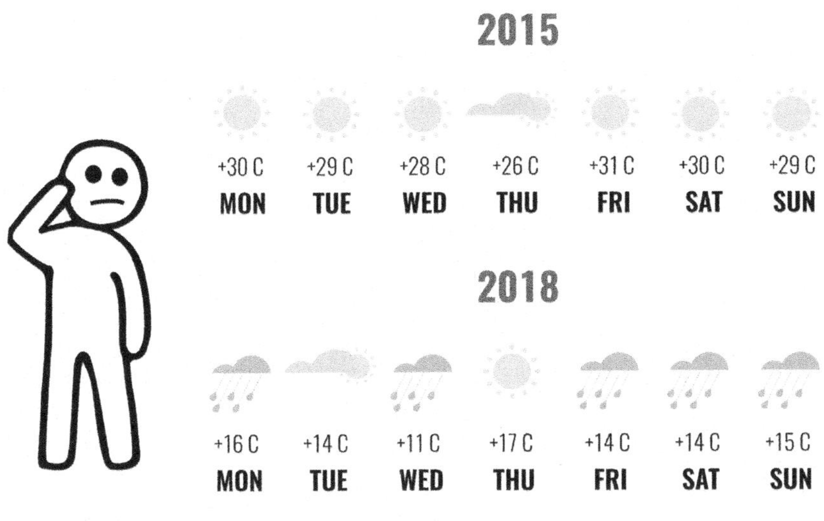

References

Airbnb. (2018). *Healthy travel and healthy destinations*. Retrieved from <http://www2.unwto.org/agora/some-points-domestic-tourism>.

Ali, R., Clampet, J., Schaal, D., & Shankman, S. (2014). *The 14 trends that will define travel in 2014. Skift Travel IQ*. Retrieved from <http://tmsfamilytravel.com/home/family-travel-conference-2017/>.

Ambrosie, L. M. (2015). *Sun & sea tourism: Fantasy and finance of the all-inclusive industry*. Cambridge Scholars Publishing.

Ariely, D. (2010). *The upside of Irrationality: The unexpected benefits of defying logic at work and at home*. London: HarperCollins Publishers.

Barton, C., Fromm, J., & Egan, C. (2012). *The millennial consumer: debunking stereotypes*. The Boston Consulting Group.

Becker, E. (2013). *Overbooked: The Exploding business of travel and tourism*. New York: Simon & Schuster.

Bigano, A., Hamilton, J. M., & Tol, R. S. J. (2007). The impact of climate change on domestic and international tourism: A simulation study. *The Integrated Assessment Journal*, *7*, 25–49, Retrieved from. Available from http://ssrn.com/abstract = 907454.

Blignaut, J. N., De Wit, M., & Barnes, J. (2008). The economic value of elephants. In R. J. Scholes, & K. G. Mennell (Eds.), *Elephant management: A scientifics assessment for South Africa*. Wits University Press, Retrieved from. Available from https://www.researchgate.net/publication/232700896.

Bohn, D., García-Rosell, J.-C., & Äijälä, M. (2018). *Animal-based tourism services in lapland*. Retrieved from <https://blogi.eoppimispalvelut.fi/elma/files/2018/01/Animal-based-Tourism-Services-in-Lapland_Report_2018.pdf>.

Bosselman, F., Peterson, C., & McCarthy, C. (1999). *Managing tourism growth: Issues and applications*. Washington DC: Island Press.

Bresson, G., & Logossah, K. (2011). Crowding-out effects of cruise tourism on stay-over tourism in the Caribbean: Non-parametric panel data evidence Crowding-out effects of cruise tourism on stay-over tourism within the Caribbean. A non parametric panel data evidence. *Tourism Economics*, *17*(1), 127–158. Available from https://doi.org/10.5367/te.2011.0028.

Burakowski, E., & Magnusson, M. (2012). *Climate impacts on the winter tourism economy in the United States*. Retrieved from <http://www.facebook.com/>.

Chien, P. M., & Ritchie, B. W. (2018). Understanding intergroup conflicts in tourism. *Annals of Tourism Researcg*, *72*, 177–179. Available from https://doi.org/10.1016/j.annals.2018.03.004.

Coyle, D. (2011). *The invisible hand meets the invisible gorilla: the economics and psychology of scarce attention*. Retrieved from <http://idei.fr/sites/default/files/medias/doc/conf/psy/2011/summary.pdf>.

ECSIP Consortium. (2015). *Study on the competitiveness of the recreational boating sector*.

Ekstein, N. (2017). In Puerto Rico Cruises Spark First Signs of a Tourism Recovery. *The Washington Post*.

Ellwood, M. (2017). How Amsterdam is solving its overtourism problem. *Condé Nast Traveler*. Retrieved from <https://www.cntraveler.com/story/how-amsterdam-is-solving-its-overtourism-problem>.

Epler Wood, M. (2017). *Sustainable tourism on a finite planet: Environmental, business and policy solutions*. New York: Routledge.

European Travel Commission., & UN World Tourism Organisation. (2014). *Handbook on e-marketing for tourism destination—Fully revised and extended version 3.0*. Madrid: UNWTO.

Gigerenzer, G., Fiedler, K., & Olsson, H. (2012). Rethinking cognitive biases as environmental consequences. In P. M. Todd, G. Gigerenzer, & A. B. C. Research Group (Eds.), *Ecological rationality: Intelligence in the world* (pp. 80–110).

Gössling, S., Scott, D., Hall, C. M., Ceron, J. P., & Dubois, G. (2012). Consumer behaviour and demand response of tourists to climate change. *Annals of Tourism Research*, *39*(1), 36–58. Available from https://doi.org/10.1016/j.annals.2011.11.002.

Gretzel, U. (2010). Travel in the network: Redirected gazes, ubiquitous connections and new frontiers. In M. Levina, & G. Kien (Eds.), *Post-global network and everyday life* (pp. 41–58). New York: Peter Lang. Retrieved from https://www.researchgate.net/publication/278409885.

Hagenstad, M., Burakowski, E., & Hill, R. (2018). *The economic contribution of winter sports in a changing climate*. Retrieved from <https://gzg764m8l73gtwxg366onn13-wpengine.netdna-ssl.com/wp-content/uploads/2018/02/POW_2018_economic_report-1.pdf>.

Helliwell, J., Layard, R., & Sachs, J. (2017). *World happiness report 2017*. New York: Sustainable Development Solutions Network. Retrieved from http://www.gluecksforschung.de/pdf-Dateien/World_Happiness_Report_2017.pdf#page = 10.

Juvan, E., Ring, A., Leisch, F., & Dolnicar, S. (2016). Tourist segments' justifications for behaving in an environmentally unsustainable way. *Journal of Sustainable Tourism*, *24*(11), 1506–1522.

Kahneman, D. (2011). *Thinking, fast and slow*. London: Penguin Books.

Law, C. (2017). Subsidy and fair competition. *Aeronautics and Aerospace Open Access Journal*, *1*(2), 48–51. Available from https://doi.org/10.15406/aaoaj.2017.01.00006.

Lee, T. H. (2011). How recreation involvement, place attachment and conservation commitment affect environmentally responsible behavior. *Journal of Sustainable Tourism*, *19*(7), 895–915. Available from https://doi.org/10.1080/09669582.2011.570345.

Lepoša, N. (2018). When sea becomes home. *Annals of Tourism Research*, *72*, 11–21. Available from https://doi.org/10.1016/j.annals.2018.06.001.

Leung, D., Law, R., Van Hoof, H., & Buhalis, D. (2013). Social media in tourism and hospitality: A literature review. *Journal of Travel & Tourism Marketing*, *30*, 3–22. Available from https://doi.org/10.1080/10548408.

Levels, P. (2015). *The future of digital nomads: How remote work will transform the world in the next 20 years*. Digital Nomads Festival. Retrieved from <https://levels.io/future-of-digital-nomads/>.

Lublin, P., & Klang, M. (2017). *The 72 hour cabin in Sweden documentary*. Visit Sweden. Retrieved from <https://visitsweden.com/72hcabin/>.

Mackay, K., & Vogt, C. (2012). Information technology in everyday and vacation contexts. *Annals of tourism research*, *39*(3), 1380–1401. Available from https://doi.org/10.1016/j.annals.2012.02.001.

Nguyen, N. (2017). *How political biases affect your perception of science (TEDxUniversityofRochester)*. TEDxUniversity of Rochester Retrieved from. Available from https://www.youtube.com/watch?v = SBU1-bE6iXI.

Nikolova, M. S., Asenov, J., & Lazarova, J. (2015). *From virtual goods to the real economy: Can psychological principles in the videogaming marketing increase sales in the new tourism market realities? TTRA-Europe conference*. Innsbruck: TTRA.

O'Donoghue, T., & Rabin, M. (1999). Doing it now or later. *The American Economic Review*, *89*(1), 103–124.

O'Donoghue, T., & Rabin, M. (2015). Present bias: lessons learned and to be learned. *American Economic Review: Papers & Proceedings*, *105*(5), 273–279. Available from https://doi.org/10.1257/aer.p20151085.

Peak, & Skift. (2014). *The rise of experiential travel*. New York. Retrieved from <http://skift.com/travel-trends/the-rise-of-experiential-travel/>.

Phocuswright. (2015). *Good travels: The philanthropic profile of the American Traveler* (Phocuswright White Paper No. September 2015). Retrieved from <http://static1.squarespace.com/static/54de6549e4b0541797820eb/t/560adce0e4b0c7c832b3e825/1443552480118/TC-Good-Travels-092915.pdf>.

RV Industry Association. (2018). *RV industry association annual report 2017*. Reston, VA. Retrieved from <https://www.rvia.org/system/files/media/file/RVIA_AnnualReport_Digital_FINAL.pdf>.

Scott, Daniel, Amelung, B., Becken, S., Ceron, J.-P., Gössling, S., Peeters, P., & Simpson, M. C. (2008). *Climate change and tourism—Responding to global challenges*. Madrid: UNWTO & UNEP. Available from https://doi.org/10.18111/9789284412341.

Scott, D., & Lemieux, C. (2010). Weather and climate information for tourism. *Procedia. Environmental Sciences*, *1*, 146–183. Available from https://doi.org/10.1016/j.proenv.2010.09.011.

Sharot, T. (2012). *The optimism bias: Why we're wired to look on the bright side*. London: Hachette UK.

Sheivachman, A. (2016). Iceland and the trials of the 21st Century Tourism. *SKift*.

Sheivachman, A. (2017). Mobile travel bookings will reach 40 percent of online sales in 2017. *Skift.Com*. Retrieved from <https://skift.com/2017/06/21/mobile-travel-bookings-to-reach-40-percent-of-online-sales-in-2017/>.

Simon, H. A. (1990). Bounded rationality. In J. Eatwell, M. Milgate, & P. Newman (Eds.), Utility and probability ((pp. 161–176). London: The New Palgrave. Palgrave Macmillan.

Sunstein, C. R., Bobadilla-Suarez, S., Lazzaro, S. C., & Sharottt, T. (2016). How people update beliefs about climate change: Good news and bad news. *Cornell Law Review*, *102*(6), 1431–1443, Retrieved from. Available from www.nber.org/papers/wl9244.pdf.

Thaler, R. H., & Benartzi, S. (2004). Save more tomorrow™: Using behavioral economics to increase employee saving. *Journal of Political Economy*, *112*(2), Retrieved from. Available from http://www.journals.uchicago.edu/doi/pdfplus/10.1086/380085.

The David Sheldrick Wildlife Trust. (2015). *Dear or alive? valuing an elephant*. Retrieved from <www.iworry.org>.

The Economist. (2017). *Special report: The economics of longevity*. Retrieved from <https://www.economist.com/node/21724879>.

The Economist. (2018). The world is losing the war against climate change—In the line of fire. *The Economist*, 1–6. Retrieved from https://www.economist.com/leaders/2018/08/02/the-world-is-losing-the-war-against-climate-change.

TMS Family Travel. (2017). *2017 TMS family travel conference & summit report*. Retrieved from <http://tmsfamilytravel.com/home/family-travel-conference-2017/>.

Tussyadiah, I. P., & Pesonen, J. (2016). Impacts of peer-to-peer accommodation use on travel patterns. *Journal of Travel Research*, *55*(8), 1022–1040. Available from https://doi.org/10.1177/0047287515608505.

UNWTO. (2018a). *UNWTO world tourism barometer (Jan 2018)*. Madrid. <https://doi.org/10.18111/wtobarometereng.2018.16.1.1>.

UNWTO. (2018b). *UNWTO world tourism barometer (June 2018)*. Madrid. <https://doi.org/10.18111/wtobarometereng.2018.16.1.3>.

van den Berg, A. E., Hartig, T., & Staats, H. (2007). Preference for nature in urbanized societies: Stress, restoration, and the pursuit of sustainability. *Journal of Social Issues*, *63*(1), 79–96. Available from https://doi.org/10.1111/j.1540-4560.2007.00497.x.

Vaughan, M., & Ardoin, N. (2014). The implications of differing tourist resident perceptions for community based resource management: A Hawaiian coastal resource area study. *Journal of Sustainable Tourism*, *22*(1), 50–68. Available from https://doi.org/10.1080/09669582.2013.802326.

Walker, B. (2018). *Crowded out: The story of overtourism*. UK: Responsible Travel Retrieved from. Available from https://www.responsibletravel.com/copy/overtourism.

Wang, D., Xiang, Z., & Fesenmaier, D. R. (2014). Adapting to the mobile world: A model of smartphone use. *Annals of Tourism Research, 48*, 11–26. Available from https://doi.org/10.1016/j.annals.2014.04.008.

WTM & Euromonitor International. (2015). *WTM global trends report*. London. <https://doi.org/10.1017/CBO9781107415324.004>.

WTTC. (2018). *Travel & tourism: economic impact 2018.*

Zelenski, J. M., & Nisbet, E. K. (2014). Happiness and feeling connected: The distinct role of nature relatedness. *Environment and Behavior, 46*(1), 3–23. Available from https://doi.org/10.1177/0013916512451901.

Chapter 4

Behavior-smart thinking for destinations

Chapter Outline

Introduction

Similar to broader socio-economic realities the tourism industry is facing "design challenges" (Ariely, 2015) that stem from the many incorrect assumptions about how people will behave and make decisions whether they are politicians, destination managers, private sector service providers or just tourists. It is assumed that tourism is based on collaboration involving the many stakeholders it touches but collaboration often drowns in competing personal interests and communication failures. Public institutions are assumed to be the stakeholder bringing long-term view and care for the interest of society, and especially its weakest segments, but political dynamics force public officials to think within election terms and place much more focus on the immediate gain rather than the long-term welfare of places and people. Businesses are assumed to be purely profit-driven and expected to make the best decision given the market conditions but in many cases the

Behavioral Economics for Tourism. DOI: https://doi.org/10.1016/B978-0-12-813808-3.00004-6

market is distorted and incentivizes unethical play. At the same time tourism offers a wealth of examples that demonstrate that businesses are motivated by more than just profit. Many private individuals and business people have been much more successful at caring for the wellbeing of nature and communities instead of responsible institutions.

And then there are travelers. Travelers are assumed to behave the way they should as long as they have the information about what is right and wrong. But that is not the case; traveler behavior often goes wrong even in cases when information is right in front of the eye.

All of these incorrect behavioral assumptions mix with the previously discussed trends shaping the present of the industry and explaining some of the monstrous challenges it faces. With the rise of giant crises triggered by these design failures it is clear that the tourism ecosystem needs a major redesign. This redesign needs to take into account the advancing knowledge about human behavior, and create an appropriate environment for the smart decision maker to independently arrive at the best possible decision (Altman, 2017) whether they are a tourism policy maker, destination marketer, tour operator, hotel owner, or traveler. Redesigning the tourism system, however, will take time and effort so there are two levels at which the application of behavior-smart thinking makes sense. First, the overall redesign of the tourism system needs to be more behavior-realistic and to offer an environment that enables effective decision-making that sustains smart growth. Thought leaders in the tourism industry should begin exploring possible ways in which the ecosystem can be bettered for the future and initiating dialog with innovators and influencers who can unlock such change. There should be efforts to explore and experiment on small scale with new models testing new assumptions and behavior-smart thinking. When successful, these small-scale experiments should be rolled out to more places and communities. When unsuccessful they should serve as source of further lessons learned and inform new trials.

Second, because a system redesign will take time and effort, we need some more immediate solutions. The tourism industry is at a crisis point and there is urgent need to incorporate behavior-smart elements that adjust behavioral failures now. This is why advancing behavioral thinking and applying choice architecture (nudging) can be the short- to mid-term approach in improving the sector's functioning.

The following sections outline potential directions for system redesign as well as opportunities for adopting a behavior-smart lens to challenges today.

Behavior-smart thinking for the future

A system redesign effort is needed but it should start with a discussion around the principles that the new system will adhere to and the failures it will avoid. One of the important principles should be behavior-realistic design. The following section outlines some of the changes that are needed to shape a decision-making environment making it more likely that stakeholders will steer the travel system in the right direction.

Frame sustainability as nonnegotiable

What is happening now?

The wrong framing of sustainability as a niche approach to tourism development corresponding to a narrow market segment of super environmentally conscious consumers, gives many decision makers an easy way out of the need to consider all dimensions of fueling growth in the tourism system. Many decision makers in the private sector and in the public sector justify the disregarding of negative impacts by claiming that they are pursuing a mass tourism strategy rather than a strategy that targets only the environmentally conscious client. This is irrational and wrong. Sustainability is a fundamental principle of developing and growing any business or initiative that wants to survive over time, and not simply a potential theme for a destination-marketing campaign. As such, sustainability should be a nonnegotiable principle in any tourism development effort and for any tourism destination at any stage of its growth lifecycle.

No business can survive in the long run without considering the costs along with the revenues, or without reinvesting in the essential assets that are at the core of the demand for its offerings. Disregarding the principles of sustainability is equivalent to doing precisely that. This is why the challenges that some of the most popular destinations today face can be traced to *sustainability ignorance*.

The even bigger problem with this is that because sustainability is still treated as optional, destinations that are facing growth pains continue to reject the need to restore balance in the system and destinations that are currently at early stages of their development lifecycle, excuse their sustainability ignorance with the need to grow.

Continuing to treat sustainability as one of the available choices in tourism development is a guarantee that the industry will continue expanding "the wrong way" damaging more places and communities rather than generating benefits for all stakeholders in the ecosystem.

What is the needed behavior-smart change?

There is need to change the social norm in the global industry and frame sustainability as a nonnegotiable principle of how tourism is done regardless of market focus, destination size, or lifecycle stage. A large-scale coastal area that has chosen to position itself as a mass-market beach destination needs to ensure that it balances the carrying capacity of the coastal region with the volume of incoming guests, and the impact that their likely behavior will have on the beach and infrastructure. The need to consider this balance is absolutely the same also for a small-scale protected area near a mountain lake looking to offer only highly specialized educational tourism programs. The difference is in the scale but the principle remains consistent.

Changing social norms takes time but it is essential as decisions that determine models of behavior, including when pursuing growth, are determined by perceptions of what is consistent with generally acceptable expectations.

Young destinations today consider excessive tourism growth and challenges with sustainability to be problems of their more mature peers. This is also wrong. Facilitated by some trends discussed earlier (technology and social media, peer economy, changing consumption patterns, etc.) overtourism can materialize in no time popping up in unexpecting and unprepared spots. This is why destinations of all size and maturity should acknowledge the risk, and use contemporary techniques to prepare against and prevent it.

Overtourism is nothing more than tourism that has developed in violation with the basics of tourism planning and sustainable growth. Therefore it can be avoided namely through smart analysis and relevant planning. The first thing that needs to happen is for everyone in the destination ecosystem to recognize that overtourism is a challenge that concerns stakeholders on all levels. Until most continue treating it as a "problem of others" they cannot begin addressing it. Once acknowledged overtourism can be tackled. Destination stakeholder networks should try to identify and map the potential threats that apply to them in order to identify ways to block risks while still growing tourism. They should also identify the gains that tourism generates and should look for ways to keep them while suppressing potential losses. Destination authorities can lead this dialog but a lot of the solutions will be driven by businesses so they need to be an active contributor to the dialog.

Travel to Tomorrow by Tourism Flanders

Tourism Flanders' initiative *Travel to Tomorrow* is a prime example of bold forward thinking initiated by a destination before it is overwhelmed by excessive growth. The goal of this strategy for the future is to go beyond existing norms and models in the industry and find innovative ways in which to "ensure there is a healthy balance between the interests of residents and visitors" as well as "honor and maintain the natural richness and historical authenticity of our destinations" as stated in the opening words of the document by Peter De Wilde, the leader of Visit Flanders.

To do that the initiative starts by identifying the core ingredients of desired travel experiences for tourists and the must-have elements of a healthy tourism industry for the destination and its resident. These two become the foundation of the desired future and basis for a series of development directions that break unnecessary norms and seek to find more positive forms of tourism ensuring that Flanders welcomes the future not as just another tourist destination but as *a flourishing community*.

In addition to the series of innovation-oriented approaches outlined in the strategy document, the initiative has set up small living labs to test new ideas and models for tourism that is net positive and leads to flourishing places.

Visit Flanders (2019)

Rethink measures of success

What is happening now?

As discussed in earlier chapters, one of the fundamental behavioral failures in the contemporary tourism industry is the acceptance of volume-based measures as leading performance indicators. The most commonly reported figures by destinations around the world are the number of arrivals that they see and the rate with which these arrivals are increasing. Number of visitors entering a destination is nothing more than an indicator of how many more people, in addition to the residents, are present on its territory. It is not a meaningful measure of whether and how tourism is impacting the place and its communities. Using number of visitors and even number of nights spent is limiting in that it also does not differentiate between the various types of visitors and more importantly between the different impacts they can have on a place. Essentially a tourist who enters the country with their recreational vehicle, brings their own food and spends very little locally during their seven-day trip through the country is counted the same as a visitor hiring a boutique local operator to take them on a seven-day tour around the country exploring local food by spending with local food service providers and staying at locally owned family hotels. While the economic impact that these two guests might have on the destination is very different they are treated as two equal counts in the total number of arrivals.

Success indicators are key because they determine the behavior and likely choices of key decision makers. When the measure of success is number of arrivals or number of heads in beds, then destination decision makers focus on actions that will grow the number of people coming to the destination regardless of what impact they have. As the story with Mr. Smith at the beginning of the book reveals the effort to produce high arrival numbers leads to tactics that are harmful for the destination and its stakeholders, especially in mid- to long-term.

Pursuing pure volume-based growth is what fuels the growing problem with overtourism as it encourages actions that are present-biased toward the immediate result of seeing more people coming to a destination. This focus on the now is accompanied by ignorance toward the long-term need to ensure that tourism generates enough revenues for the local economy to offset the costs of welcoming a growing number of visitors.

What is the needed behavior-smart change?

The behavioral solution is to stop encouraging decisions that lead to more and more arrivals without realistic consideration of the desired and undesired impacts of the presence of a growing number of travelers and their likely behaviors. There is need for destination-level decision makers to go back to the white board and reconfirm the goal of promoting tourism: generating economic benefits for the local economy, creating jobs and entrepreneurship opportunities, generating resources to support improvement for the quality of the physical environment, supplementing funds for conservation, etc. The ultimate goal for why a place is developing tourism should determine the measures of success and the likely positive and negative effects that come with that. This does not need to be complicated, especially in today's information realities, which offer multiple opportunities for information gathering and data collection. While modeling the full array of positive and negative impacts associated with the presence of travelers in the destination may be a complex task, extracting some basic estimates of costs and revenues should be possible with some collaborative efforts.

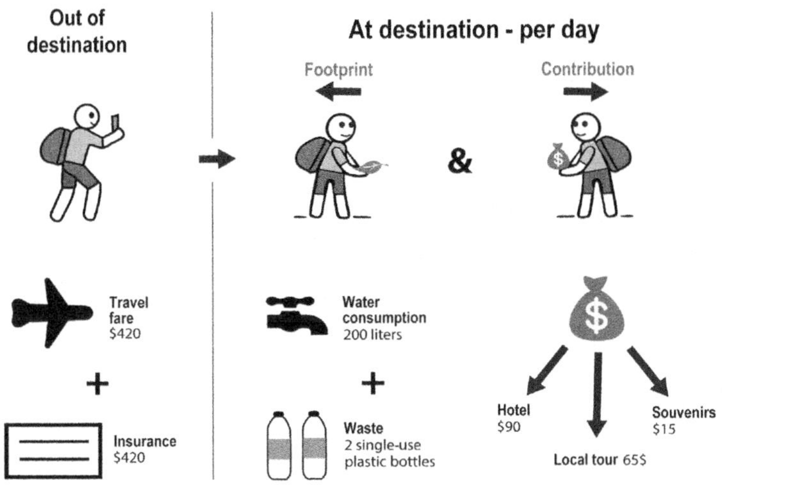

Deemphasizing volume as priority, and bringing cost and revenues in one equation will trigger new behavior in the tourism system. For example, if a destination accepts that its leading measure of success is the daily spending of each visitor directly in the destination, then destination-level decision makers will be encouraged to take steps that look to increase that spending. They will seek to incentivize industry players to design and deliver experiences motivating travelers to spend more on local food, local guiding services, local crafts items, etc. They will also see value in supporting local business development to ensure that there is a rich variety of locally produced offerings that are attractive and motivate travelers to spend more. If they decide to accelerate growth by using direct incentives for intermediaries who bring visitors to the destinations, it will make sense to tie these incentives not with simple counts but with local spending. Similarly if a destination finds most appropriate to encourage longer stays and takes length of stay of guests as a success measure, then decision makers will seek to incentivize offerings that lead to more time spent on the ground.

The discussions around the need to move away from volume-based measurement of tourism are ripe in the industry so more and more stakeholders understand it. However, counting arrivals is so deeply rooted in the system that making the transition is not that easy. Real change can be triggered by one or several bold and innovation-eager destinations that will take the risk of experimenting and adopting new approaches for measuring success. Once some successful practices and lessons learned become available in the global community, more and more destinations will explore the potential for transition and will change their ways. The hope that the industry will see some positive examples soon is supported by the fact that at the time of writing of this book there are several sizable initiatives led by leading industry institutions to develop new indicators for tracking tourism and its impacts. Some bold innovation-oriented destinations are also experimenting with breaking norms of destination planning and putting forward alternative ways of defining success (see illustration).

The Preservolution on the Faroe Islands

When it comes to breaking the norms of the tourism industry the Faroe Islands is one of the destinations at the very front. In early 2019 the tourism board announced that for one weekend it will close tourism attractions for tourists while welcoming volunteers wishing to help with maintenance and renovation activities. "Closing off" is an untypical tactic in the industry but in the context of the overheating industry, many tourism professionals saw this as an admirable and bold idea.

The Faroe Islands break norms also with their newest tourism strategy. There are many exciting elements of the document but one of the most significant is the statement of the three targets or measures of success:

- ✓ specific value of socio-economic revenues generated in the local economy (DKK 1.5 billion);
- ✓ agreement of visitors with the brand promise of being an unspoiled, unexplored, and unbelievable destination (90%);
- ✓ perception among local residents that tourism is net positive (> 80%).

This is a remarkable example of how focusing on different, nonvolume-based measures is possible. The focus on socio-economic value generated in the local economy incentivizes stakeholders to create opportunities for more spending and spending that stays in the economy generating desired social impacts. The focus on confirming the brand promise motivates stakeholders to align offerings with the promise made by marketing activities that reinforce the expectation of the traveler coming to be in touch with unspoiled nature, an unexplored place and an unbelievable destination. The prioritization of positive perceptions of local residents incentivizes all stakeholders to ensure that tourism never comes at the expense of the local community.

Visit Faroe Islands (2019)

As destinations seek to move to a new measure of success it is important to find an alternative that is not too complex. Sustainable tourism indicator systems have been out there for a number of years but all of them recommend long and complex sets of measures the execution of which is costly and effort-intensive. While it would be ideal if destinations around the world move toward systematic use of such comprehensive systems, it is behaviorally unrealistic to expect that this will happen, at least in the near future. Therefore there is need to replace current volume-based indicators (arrivals and nights spent) with alternative one or two tourism impact indicators such as spending per day or share of spending that stays in the destination, which might not capture the multifaceted impacts of tourism but will move the incentives from quantity to quality.

Enable systems thinking

What is happening now?

Another significant behavioral failure in the tourism sector is its artificial splitting into pieces, which are treated and managed independently without considering the implications that dynamics with one piece may trigger on another. This problem has two dimensions. First, there is strong bias toward the economic impacts of the sector (Northcote & Macbeth, 2006) and failure to account for effects on the social context and the natural environmental. Very often when towns or countries decide to invest in tourism promotion, they are led by the idea for economic prosperity without consideration of the fact that high numbers of visitors will also mean competitors for the same resources and space that are now available only to locals; or that increased tourism traffic will lead to deterioration of the quality of local environment.

The second dimension is that very often the costs and the benefits associated with a growing tourism sector do not live in the same equation. That means that while one player in the tourism system has the decision power to trigger growth and gain profit from it, other players can find themselves dealing with the costs of that growth without any ability to influence it.

The lack of embracement of systems thinking is explained with the complexity of the industry and is exacerbated by the fact that tourism seems to be underestimated as an economic sector. It is treated as a light and fun sector that does not require the same level of professionalism and seriousness as others. In the words of Elizabeth Becker: "The very idea of describing travel and tourism as a serious industry or business is an oxymoron to many people. The oil industry is serious. Finance is serious. Trade is serious. Manufacturing is serious. Foreign policy and economic policy are serious. Tourism is a frivolous pursuit: fun, sometimes educational in the lightest sense, often romantic, often exotic" Becker (2013), p.8.

This attitude fuels further resistance to acknowledging the complexity of the tourism ecosystem and consider all its impacts when making decisions about stimulating it.

The lack of holistic thinking in tourism is a significant challenge as it creates an ineffective decision-making setting. The distorted context and split in what should be a single equation simultaneously accounting for costs and benefits leads to decisions that do not capture system effects. For example, an airport authority motivated by the need to increase revenues may be pro active in pursuing agreements with more and more airlines, including low-cost carriers, to increase passenger traffic. More flights will translate to more revenues for the authority, which is a powerful incentive. At the same time this institution does not have to deal with where passengers go and what they do after they leave the territory of the airport. As a result local municipal authorities and local residents may suddenly find themselves dealing with an overwhelmed local infrastructure, water shortage issues, and overcrowding problem without any ability to influence the source of this growth. Another aspect of the same disconnect is that in its pursuit of increased passenger volumes the airport authority may decide to attract specifically low-cost airlines, which generate increased visitation by more value-oriented travelers. This produces positive results for the airport but changes the customer mix for local service providers. Local restaurants, crafts shops, and shopping areas begin seeing a decline in their sales because the crowd on the street consists of modest spenders producing a lower number of walk-in customers who spend within much lower limits.

What is the needed behavior-smart change?

There is need to accept as a norm in the industry the fact that tourism planning involves calculating potential revenues along with potential costs. This means applying tourism planning models that are grounded on a complete equation including both the gains and the costs to allow for choices leading to net positive tourism. The increasing sensitiveness toward the challenges associated with overtourism is making society at large more aware of the complexities of the industry. This momentum should be used to advance the understanding that if places want to gain the multiple benefits that tourism can generate they need to manage its growth. There should be no doubt by now that there are no shortcuts to planning and growing a destination—they require identifying the key potential benefits and possible negative impacts, and engaging multiple stakeholders beyond the ones directly benefitting from the sector. Destinations and stakeholders can make a choice as long as they are presented with the real options they have in terms of how much and what kind of tourism to develop.

In this context the redesigned approaches for tourism planning should overcome three main behavioral challenges. The first is the ability to see the full picture or to keep all benefits and costs of the tourism equation together. Second, tourism planning techniques should somehow go around the natural human inability to imagine the future, especially when it is extended over the years ahead and when it involves multiple dynamics. This will also help address the third challenge, which is the tendency of focusing on short-term gains rather than the one that can be expected in the future.

While the need to plan tourism and manage its growth is far from new, not many destinations have gone through a proper planning process that involved the development of different scenarios with mapped positive and negative impacts in their realistic scale. Part of the reason for that is that this is an intense, complicated, and time-intensive process with a lot of unknown variables. With the knowledge that the industry and science have today, however, there are real chances to optimize tourism planning and apply some techniques that are going to make unwise decisions less possible, secure a systems thinking approach and solve behavioral barriers associated with poor judgment.

One potential opportunity is to lean on technology and data solutions. With the advancing digitalization of societies and increasing number of data-generating touch-points during a traveler's experience, it is realistic to begin building standard holistic simulation models that reveal the full impact of tourism growth. They can enable destinations to produce different scenarios by manipulating different variables to understand how the rest of the system will be impacted (Doyle, 2018). Such modeling will make systems thinking possible because it will include all interconnections and interdependencies, and will fix the inability to predict a complex set of intertwined effects in a way that will make it less possible to focus on today and ignore tomorrow. They should make it possible, for example, to plug in the desired increase in arriving flights pursued by the local airport authority and see the effect that this will have on the entire system, including the local economy, public infrastructure, community spaces, the environment, etc. In her book on tourism sustainability Meghan Epler Wood talks about the need for an integrated impact measurement and monitoring solution that is based on agreed upon indicators. She suggest that leaning on geodesign (newer wave of geographic information system technology) combined with the ability to integrate live feeds of real-time data can make it possible to have "living maps of organic feedback loops to guide the management of tourism development" (Epler Wood, 2017, p.7). Such source of input and ability to track and predict growth dynamics can become an unbiased source of input for decisions made by governments, entrepreneurs, and community members. According to the author, a solution like this would most naturally be maintained by a consortium of universities that have the capability to manage and analyze data of such volume, and that can play the role of an unbiased source of objective knowledge.

While such models will be complex and will require large amounts of data as well as enormous calculation capabilities, they are possible. Chapter 2 revealed the Mauritius experience of developing a simulation exploring different scenarios that help make decisions accounting for all potential "side effects" of growing tourism in the destination. In the 1990s when the Mauritius project unfolded this took a significant amount of time and offline data processing. Automation and proliferation of data sources today can make the process much faster and much more precise. A notable proof for the power of such solutions is the *World3* model (see illustration) that is at the foundation of the series of progressive books modeling global sustainability scenarios authored by the late environmentalist Donnela Meadows and her colleagues: The Limits to Growth, Beyond the Limits and The Limits to Growth: the 30 year update (Meadows, Meadows, & Randers 1992; Meadows, Meadows, Randers, & Behrens 1972; Meadows, Randers, & Meadows 2005).

The World3 Simulation Model

World3 is a computer model simulating growth dynamics on the planet considering the interaction dynamics of a wide range of variables operationalizing the most important systems such as population (growth, life expectancy, etc.), food system (agriculture, food production, etc.), industry, nonrenewable resources, and pollution.

Based on the wide system of indicators and their relationships World3 is capable of producing scenarios of how the planet will turn out under different development dynamics. The authors of the model estimate that we have started "overshooting" our footprint over the carrying capacity of Earth since 1980 and in 1999 that overshot was around 20%.

The complexity and the scale of the World3 model make it hard to believe that it was initially created more than 40 years ago.

Advancing virtual reality technology is also a great opportunity to overcome current behavioral failures. Grounded on data-based models, existing scientific knowledge and practical experience, virtual reality technology can be adopted to visualize the outcomes that different scenarios of growth are likely to produce. The decision-making capability of all stakeholders in a tourism ecosystem will be transformed if it is possible to see how what is a wild beach today would look if the local airport starts accepting five more flights per week, if the port starts receiving one more cruise ship per day, and if the government authorizes the building of a new 300-room resort. Decision makers and local stakeholders will be able to see what infrastructure will need to be put in place to handle the larger number of beach goers and to determine whether this new reality is within the acceptable limits of change or whether the size of the investment required for the potential new infrastructure will yield a reasonable return and is acceptable to the society. Virtual reality technology directly impacts the ability to imagine future outcomes and visualize different complex processes in ways that are easily accessible to nonexperts (Voinov, Çöltekin, Chen, & Beydoun, 2018) or make visually accessible to a wider audience natural assets, which can be impacted by development but which are not visible to society in general. For example, it makes it possible to see how coral reefs are changing as a result of pollution or how development and human activity are impacting habitats in inaccessible high-mountain areas (Vercelloni et al., 2018).

Complex data-based and virtual reality-supported modeling can facilitate the process of determining the socially agreed upon limits of acceptable change that accompany tourism growth. If different stakeholders are able to see the potential change that will come with a 5% or 15% increase in arrivals, with emphasis on winter sports or emphasis on bird watching, they will be able to decide what is the ideal volume and type of growth that balances the socio-economic benefits of tourism with the desire to preserve the overall feel and socio-cultural texture of the destination.

Estimate nature and social impact

What is happening now?

One of the challenges of balancing costs and gains in tourism is the fact that nature, culture and the wellbeing of residents do not have a price. This makes it hard to build the complete cost-benefit equation and figure out in quantifiable terms whether a certain tourism development or its scale lead to a net positive result or not. When an impact cannot be compared against revenue and monetary gains, it becomes easy to ignore or undermine.

Today, many destinations suffer from inability to map and measure potential negative environmental and socio-cultural impacts. As discussed earlier in Chapter 2 some progress on valuing nature through the prism of tourism has been made but it has not trickled through the system and started influencing decision-making. Nature and natural assets are treated as free infinite resources that can be utilized for profit-generating recreational activities without any responsibility to maintain them or recover them. Outside of the rare cases when there is a formal setup outlining the terms of use (such as a concession mechanism) companies offering experiences out in nature are left to use their own judgment as to what is a reasonable balance between extracting benefits and recovering impact. The same applies to individuals who engage independently in nature-based recreational activities and whose behavior is guided by their own discretion. Even in cases when there are strict rules of behavior in managed protected areas, the control mechanisms are weak and mostly ineffective. For example, national parks and other protected areas are usually supervised by park rangers whose primary role is to ensure that behavior on the territory of the park is within the prescribed norms. According to the International Union for Conservation of Nature and Natural Resources the ideal ranger-area ratio is 1 per 5 square kilometers (Leung, Spenceley, Hvenegaard, & Buckley, 2018) but in reality this ratio is rarely achieved. And while the visible presence of a uniformed guard is known to have a desired effect on visitor behavior (Swearingen & Johnson, 1995), a single ranger cannot effectively monitor or ensure maximum compliance with rules in an area of a few kilometers. With the advance of technology more solutions are becoming possible. GPS technology tracking movement can increase the likelihood that people stay on trails rather than wander off (Bielański et al., 2018) but it is unlikely to influence other behavior that might be damaging to nature (such as picking wild flowers, disturbing wildlife, littering, etc.).

All of this, of course, applies to natural areas, which are proactively managed. Wilderness territories outside of any protection regime are even more vulnerable to the decisions and individual behavioral norms of every visitor or service provider offering nature-based activities. The perception that access to nature is a free right mixes poorly with lack of accountability and ultimately results in degradation, which is difficult to quantify and estimate in monetary terms. This is valid even for places where local residents have strong culture of respectful behavior toward nature and know how to enjoy it without leaving a trace behind. Visitors, however, might be coming from different socio-cultural realities and might not adhere to the same behavioral norms when it comes to nature. This means that tourists' misbehavior produces an extra cost on nature that is incomparable to the one attributable to locals and that remains unaccounted for. Examples for such dynamics are found in the Nordic region where the *freedom to roam* policy treats access to nature as every person's right. It means that people have the right to be in nature: to walk, cycle, ride, kayak, ski, and camp on any outdoors area with the exception of private gardens, the immediate vicinity of a private residence (70 m) or cultivated land. The right to be in nature also extends to private land as long as one is away from the dwelling home of the landowner (Swedish Environmental

Protection Agency, 2019). *Freedom to roam* is a constitutional right and part of the cultural heritage of the region shaping the outdoors culture of citizens of Nordic countries. Growing up with this principle means that people in the region have an excellent understanding of how to behave in nature in order to enjoy its recreational benefits but remain safe and respectful to the environment. In essence, freedom to roam has instilled a culture of treating nature as a source of recreational services, which are everyone's right but which come with the responsibility for maintaining nature as it is. In contrast, many of the tourists visiting the region, come from countries where the freedom to roam does not exist and where the outdoors culture is much less sophisticated. That produces a misbalance: on one side visitors claim their free right to be anywhere out in nature to benefit from its recreational services but on the other, they deviate from the responsibilities that come with that right: leaving natural areas as one found them. Increased flow of such tourists is putting significant pressure on nature in certain areas but also creates an economic problem: the freedom to be in nature means the right to enjoy its recreational services for free leading to no benefits for the local economy from tourism. At the same time increased visitation, damaging behavior, and waste directly impact the ability of locals to continue enjoying their outdoors as before. The lack of valuation of the recreational benefits of being out in nature and the costs of misbehaving outdoors make it impossible to quantify the lack of benefits and the likely losses occurring in this context.

Similarly recreational activities trigger undesired social impacts, which are just as difficult to control, as well as impossible to measure and include in cost-benefit analyses. Receiving more visitors in a destination translate to increased traffic on the streets and in public areas, which can cause significant nuisance (see illustration). The growing demand for authentic experiences fuels a desire to discover places on one's own and take on the off-the-beaten paths. On one side this can be positive as it helps to ensure that visitor flows are more spread out and there is less congestion in tourist hot spots. On the other side, however, this increases the risk of seeing quiet residential spots becoming Instagram celebrities and attracting excessive attention.

Instagram Nightmare on Rue Crémieux

Rue Crémieux is a small charming cobbled street located in the 12th arrondissement of Paris. In recent years it has become one of the most sought-after selfie locations in the city. Its popularity as a backdrop for Facebook and Instagram pictures is due to the colorfully painted residential buildings and nicely arranged flowerpots along the street. Rue Crémieux is closed for traffic, which creates a favorable environment for spending time without worry. The growing social media popularity of the street has unlocked the imagination of visitors who come up with all sorts of bizarre ways to photograph themselves on this famous

(*Continued*)

(Continued)

spot—from lying on the street and climbing on door fronts to doing yoga positions and flash mobs.

The celebrity status of their home street naturally produces increasing levels of nuisance for its residents. The constant flow of people outside of their doors and windows translates to constant noise and lack of privacy. Even though as public space the street should be accessible to citizens and visitors of Paris, residents have initiated a request to the mayor to seek the installation of gates that will limit access and restore peace on Rue Crémieux.

Quantifying the local residents' perception of being crowded out or estimating the cost of the sense of lost privacy is complicated. These are also hard to predict and imagine in advance making it hard to take into account when tourism development is in early stages and decisions are made about how much more growth is desired.

What is the needed behavior-smart change?

A future tourism system needs to account for environmental and social impacts in ways that allow their inclusion in the tourism equation. The discussed in Chapter 2 concept of defining and estimating the benefits that people obtain from natural ecosystems contributing to human wellbeing (TEEB, 2010), including goods, such as timber, fresh water, medicinal herbs, and services such as recreation, air purification, irrigation, etc. brings us closer to making this happen. Recent attempts to account for recreational benefits gained from nature are in the right direction but reveal that the solution is incomplete. Benefits can be estimated in cases when there are paid leisure services, that is, when a hotel commands certain prices because of its location near a costal area or when there is difference in the price of a room with a view to a natural landscape versus that of a room without a view; or when a kayak renting operation exists only because of the existence of a natural lake; or a tour operator is able to offer hiking adventures only because of the existence of a mountain with stunning landscapes (EC, OECD, UN, & World Bank, 2013). In these cases it is also possible to estimate the costs of making this ecosystem service possible, that is, public such as investment in visitor infrastructure within a natural area (development of hiking trails and observation points, installation of signage, etc.) or private such as investment in the development of a hotel or the purchase of kayaks for a renting operation.

The situation with unmanaged natural areas is different. There is currently no way to estimate the value of the esthetic enjoyment of beautiful landscapes while biking through rural Tuscany, the sense of rejuvenation after spending a few days exploring Patagonia in the summer or the sense of accomplishment after completing the Colorado trail in the Rocky Mountains.

The strength and meaning of these experiences varies greatly with the individual, which makes it hard to use perceptions as grounding point for any valuation effort too.

The situation is very similar with manmade and cultural assets. While the investment in maintaining an old town or a church is relatively clear, the value of the esthetic or personal growth benefits that they generate is hard to calculate. How valuable is the sense of getting lost through the streets of Bruges and the esthetic enjoyment derived from its charms? What is the value of the amazement experienced during the exploring of Sagrada Família?

A future tourism system needs to have the mechanisms that allow the estimation and potentially pricing of recreational and esthetic services derived from nature and culture. It must make it easy for destination stakeholders to compare different investment scenarios and consider the potential gains that will be generated from interaction with nature and culture, as well as the potential environmental and social costs. If the relationship between gains and losses is clearer, there will be much higher appreciation for ecosystem services and benefits from cultural experiences. The ability to easily recognize the gains in quantifiable ways will also lead to change in the framing of the resources needed to maintain assets from costs to investments. This in turn will change the attitude associated with budgeting for maintenance and will likely impact the amounts allocated toward nature and culture. Quantifiable gains will also modify the behavior of the users of nature and culture: service providers offering experiences around them as well as travelers themselves. Ultimately it may become possible to introduce pricing and appropriately charge for ecosystem and cultural services, which will lead to different level of appreciation. There should be care with that, however, because it is known that introducing a pay can also eliminate intangible barriers to undesired behavior and instill the sense that one has paid so they do not have to experience guilt or shame about norms of behavior. When people violate a rule or go against the acceptable norms of behavior, they experience a sense of guilt forcing them to minimize such deviations. If, however, they are asked to pay a fee for violating these norms, the guilt disappears as they feel they have paid for the violation and cleared their ethical record (Gneezy & Rustichini, 2000). This is why carbon offsetting programs based on asking travelers to pay a fee are a great way to raise funds for carbon offsetting programs but a poor way of keeping people sensitive to the need to behave in ways that limit carbon footprint and motivating systematic adherence to higher ethical norms when it comes to nature. Paying to offset the harm one has caused in reality erodes ethical barriers based on moral objections and reinforces harming nature as acceptable behavior (Ives & Bekessy, 2015). This is why there should be clear terms of the market "exchange" involving pay for use of ecosystem or cultural services outlining the acceptable behavior and framing payment as pay for the benefits rather than pay for offsetting harmful impacts.

Under these terms a system design that is based on quantifiable impacts on nature and culture can significantly change behavior toward them and influence the moral standards that guide it. As discussed in Chapter 1, behavioral thinking about moral is that it is shaped by the immediate external environment in the situation, in which the behavior is unfolding, combined with personal factors (Gigerenzer, 2011). In that sense a relevant redesign can have a significant impact on how players in the tourism system treat and consume nature and culture.

Make destination management possible

What is happening now?

As discussed at length in the second chapter current destination management practices are ineffective and need transformation. While tourism theory talks about destination management organizations as entities that plan and coordinate tourism development, in reality most destinations do not have the organizational infrastructure to support the needed functionality. Because different elements of the tourism ecosystem are influenced by different entities, the current system design makes a truly holistic and systematic approach to destination management impossible.

The rise of overtourism has increased awareness on the weaknesses of the current industry arrangements and the lack of proper basis for destination management. Part of the reasons for that is the difficulty in mapping all entities that touch on tourism in one way or another. For example, it is clear that transportation and infrastructure authorities deal with tourism but not always that agriculture, healthcare, or education authorities need to be involved in the dialog as well. The advancement of some modeling solutions discussed earlier will help to address that to some extent as the connectivity between tourism and other socio-economic sectors will become more obvious. Even without that it is clear that a shift in destination management setups is needed and future tourism systems needs a design centered around proper destination management.

What is the needed behavior-smart change?

Destination management will be possible if there are authorities responsible for tourism that play different roles and respectively have enhanced capacities to assume a leadership role. They need to provide the big-picture perspective to growth dynamics in the destination and be in live dialog with all institutions that influence the local tourism economy, for example, entities responsible for transportation and access, or authorities responsible for municipal areas and public infrastructure. They should also be able to influence decisions about education, food policies, and rural development.

Given the discussed in earlier chapters diversity of institutional models and organizational setups on destination level makes it hard to imagine how destination management will look like in a redesigned tourism system. Whatever the solution, to be behaviorally optimized, it needs to ensure several principles discussed in this section. First, there is need to instill sustainability as a nonnegotiable principle of doing tourism regardless of the scale or stage of tourism development. Second, there is need to ensure that tourism is not only framed as an ecosystem that cuts across or links to multiple sectors but is actually managed as one. Third, the possibility for short-term bias should be eliminated to ensure that decisions are made with a 5–10 year outlook considering growth dynamics within the ecosystem. The key mechanism that can ensure that is the shift toward different success measures that relate to the core goals of tourism development. Fourth, a future system design should make it possible to make decisions based on a complete tourism equation that accounts for both the gains from natural and socio-cultural assets, and the costs of using them. Proper accounting of economic, sociocultural, and environmental benefits and costs can really ensure that tourism is managed in ways that keep it net positive.

Behavior-smart thinking for now

While the bigger effort of redesigning the travel ecosystem and experimentation with new models that are more aligned with realistic behavior patterns will take time, there are plenty of behavior-smart fixes that can be applied in the short term. The following section outlines some destination-level solutions as illustrations.

New culture of travel

How to make this happen?

Many negative impacts in travel are triggered by uninformed behavior. Even though it is true that making information available alone will not lead to change in behavior, making specific and actionable information available in the right context and in the right format works. Simply asking travelers to be more responsible when they travel is unlikely to be effective as it is vague and unclear. Explaining how one's travel decisions matter and offering specific tips that they can easily understand and apply, can work.

There is an opportunity for programs that seek to enable the global traveler to be more responsible and to make choices that do not damage their experience but that limit negative impacts. These types of efforts need to make salient the outcomes that choices have for visited places. This can include making the connection between the single-use water bottle that a traveler holds in their hands, and a whale that was found killed by the significant amount of plastic in its stomach; or the difference that they can make for a local farmer by choosing from the menu a locally prepared meal with all-local ingredients versus well-known international classics cooked with imported products; or the support they are giving to a local entrepreneurial artist by making sure they buy a hand-made locally produced souvenir rather than a generic cheaper option imported from China. Making the link between the act and the consequence salient changes traveler behavior and can dramatically influence the footprint of their vacation (Stowell, 2018a).

Who can do this?

Improving the way travel is done is in everyone's interest so in that sense making an effort to educate travelers and help them to see the different impacts that their choices can lead to, should be a priority for international tourism organizations (trade associations, think-thanks, mission-driven entities, etc.), multilateral entities (UN World Tourism Organization, world travel & tourism council, etc.), industry influencers, destinations, companies, and other travelers. Simple tips can be included in destination campaigns or initiatives such as the Inspired by Iceland Academy for travelers offering fun educational tips that help future visitors behave in an environmentally friendly and culturally acceptable ways (see cases in the following chapter for more details).

Individual companies can also contribute to the awareness of travelers in many simple ways. Hotels, B&B, tour operators, and guides can provide their future clients with predeparture tips encouraging them, for example, to:

- Remind them to support efforts to maintain trips single-plastics by bringing their own reusable water bottle, camping cutlery for outdoor meals, coffee mug, and reusable straw;
- Encourage them to buy and bring filtration bottles or water purification devices, which they may be unaware of if their trip will take them to places where tap water is unreliable or clean water is unavailable;
- Give them specific guidance suggesting that they take a train from the airport to downtown to support the city efforts to cut down traffic and minimize air pollution.

Travel companies, service providers, and guides can influence traveler behavior also during their trip by providing educational information or weaving that in their interpretation. Informing tourists on a hiking tour that the route has been changed to avoid passing close to a habitat of bird species who are in the mating season, or explaining what kind of damage may be caused by people leaving the designated trails in a fragile natural area contributes to increased awareness and better traveling culture. Increasing familiarity with certification systems and impact management tools is also part of the education that individual companies can use. Many responsible travel service providers invest in obtaining certification that acknowledges that they operate in a sustainable manner but fail to ensure that all of their clients understand that. Once they are aware of the meaning and significance of a sustainability certification system, travelers are more likely to look for it when they are choosing a travel company to support their next holiday. Similarly informing guests of the carbon footprint of their trips and individual activities can help to educate them about the difference that transportation or lodging options can make, and can make it easier to plan holidays with carbon footprint in mind. Carbon footprint tracking solutions such as CARMACAL make that possible and easy to do. Read more about how a similar solution for the restaurant industry helps customers consider climate footprint in their choice.

Travelers themselves can help influence peers too. Those who are aware of ways to enjoy vacationing with minimal footprint can share that via social media the same way they post selfies from prominent locations. If more people saw their friends holding reusable water bottles on their holiday pictures, more people will consider traveling with one themselves.

Widespread efforts by different industry stakeholders to increase the impact awareness of travelers can make a big difference. They can lead to more clients who are better informed about the choices they make and can slowly transform some behaviors into social norms that are picked up by newcomers. A great example of behavior-smart public education that has contributed to a changed attitude toward food and cooking is the work done by celebrity chef Jamie Oliver (see illustration).

Jamie Oliver's Food Revolution

In the last decade celebrity chefs have gained special recognition in society. Many of them fueled a change in food culture and restored appreciation for preparing food at home. One of the biggest names among celebrity chefs who have impacted contemporary food culture is Jamie Oliver whose efforts to combat poor eating habits have been admirable.

Jamie's movement—the Food Revolution—took many dimensions, including advocacy for taxing sugar, regulation of junk food advertising, transformation in

(*Continued*)

(Continued)

student cafeteria menus, cooking classes for children from underprivileged communities, etc. In addition to many of his high-level efforts Jamie Oliver's work offers some behavior-smart tactics seeking to kill the most common barriers that we know lead to unhealthy eating choices. Here is a list of examples of how this has worked:

Behavioral problem	Behavior-smart solution
Eating or feeding children with junk food and sugar due to lack of awareness of the harms	Accessible public education content explaining in simple terms why sugar and junk food are harmful, especially for children
Eating processed or fast food because cooking is difficult	Featuring easy to follow recipes with step-by-step cooking instructions that can easily be followed by people with no cooking experience in different formats: TV shows, books, apps
Eating processed or fast food due to lack of time	Launching *15-Minute Meals* and *30-Minute Meals* TV series and book series offering step-by-step guidance on preparing daily healthy home-cooked meals for a short amount of time
Not buying fresh foods and cooking at home due to the perception that healthy products are expensive	Launching *Save with Jamie*—TV shows and book with budget meals that are healthy but include only affordable ingredients
Not cooking at home because it is complicated and requires special shopping habits	Launching *5-Ingredients: Quick and Easy Food*—a TV series and a book that offers a step-by-step guide to preparing home-cooked meals with only five ingredients

Behavioral segmentation

How to make this happen?

Segmentation and targeting are fundamental elements of any marketing effort, in any industry. In the context of tourism segmentation helps destinations and companies to recognize the different groups of consumers who are out there and to identify the ones that are the likely best match to their offerings. Based on that they target the select groups by promising benefits (value proposition) that position them as an attractive choice among all alternatives available on the market.

The most common ways of doing segmentation are based on demographics (nationality, education, gender, age, occupation, etc.) and psychographics (values, attitudes, lifestyle, interests, etc.). Despite the obvious value of considering psychographics many destinations and even individual companies base their marketing efforts on trying to reach everybody or on casting a net over loosely defined mega segments defined by nationality. The problem with that is that marketing to "the German traveler" or "the Chinese traveler" means marketing to a wide variety of travelers who like many different things and travel in many different ways but who happen to be from one and the same country. You can receive from one and the same country a guest who is curious about the place, looks to immerse themselves in the local culture and who is willing to spend on exciting experiences, and a guest who does not care much about whether they are in Prague or Berlin, and who is not eager to make an effort to align with local cultural norms. Nationality does not matter, what matters is behavior. This is why in contemporary realities the best way of ensuring a focused and effective match between a destination offering and traveler profiles is segmenting on the basis of behavior.

Applying behavioral segmentation is not difficult and involves asking oneself a set of basic questions about the likely ways in which different traveler groups will behave if they are to visit the destination, for example:

- How do they purchase their trip? (package through a large operator, specialized operator or individual planning, etc.)
- How do they arrive? (air, road, rail, etc.)
- What activities do they engage in? (sunbathing on the beach, biking through the country, going to wineries, etc.)
- How long do they stay? (1 day, 3–4 days, 5 or more days, etc.)
- How much they spend in the country per day? (5–10 Euro outside of their package, 20–50 Euro, 60 or more Euro, etc.)
- What is their motivation for visiting? (exploring local culture, enjoying local food, cheap summer holiday, visiting friends and family, etc.)

The answers of these questions enable the behavioral profiling of each potential segment that can be targeted allowing for identification of the best match with local assets, experiences, and socio-cultural norms. For example, if the destination lacks sophisticated road networks and visitor infrastructure around major sites but has a vibrant local culture and culinary traditions, it may want to target travelers who are interested in exploring living culture by going to local markets and taking small-group culinary classes, and biking to a nearby small unpolished farm to learn about local farming practices. This behavior pattern will align much more with the destination offerings than that of a guest who is used to visiting well serviced and conveniently socialized classical cultural sites, and who expects to move from one location to another by riding a convenient large coach on highways.

Below is a summarized example of applying a behavioral lens to describe all existing segments traveling to a country in order to identify the ones that match best the state of local infrastructure, available experiences, and supporting services. Although demographic data comes up as part of the detailed profiling of the different groups, it is much less relevant in the description and factors that influence the prioritization of target groups.

Table example for behavioral segmentation brief

Segment	Charter tourists	European short break tourists	Classical regional tourists	Organized active tourists
Source Region	Western Europe	Western and Central Europe	Europe/Asia/ surrounding countries	Europe/North America
How do they purchase?	All inclusive package with charter flight	Arrive on low-cost airline to capital city	Package including two or three countries in region visited with a coach bus	Package with small specialized tour operator
How do they arrive?	Air	Air (low cost)	Road/by coach	Air
What do they do?	Stay in all inclusive resort, may take one or two excursions outside of property	Explore capital city and immediate surroundings on their own; might take a one-day excursion to the beach	Go around the main historical and cultural site	Hike/bike around the country and explore living culture
How long do they stay?	7 days	Weekend or long weekend (2–4 days)	2–3 days in country	7–12 days
How much do they spend?	15 Euro per day (outside of package paid to tour operator)	180 Euro per day (includes lodging, food and attraction fees)	15 Euro per day (for one meal that is not included in their package paid to TO + some souvenirs)	80–100 Euro per day (on local food, crafts and souvenirs)
What is their motivation?	Low price summer holiday	Visiting and off-the-beaten path place, low-cost food, lodging and airfare	Exploring culture and history of region	Exploring an interesting culture and new destination; being active and in contact with beautiful nature

Adapted based on World Bank. (2016b). Market Analysis of Tourism Along Western and Eastern Circuits and Central Corridor in FYR Macedonia for the Local and Regional Competitiveness Project (LRCP). Skopje. Retrieved from <http://lrcp.mk/tourism-market-analysis/>.

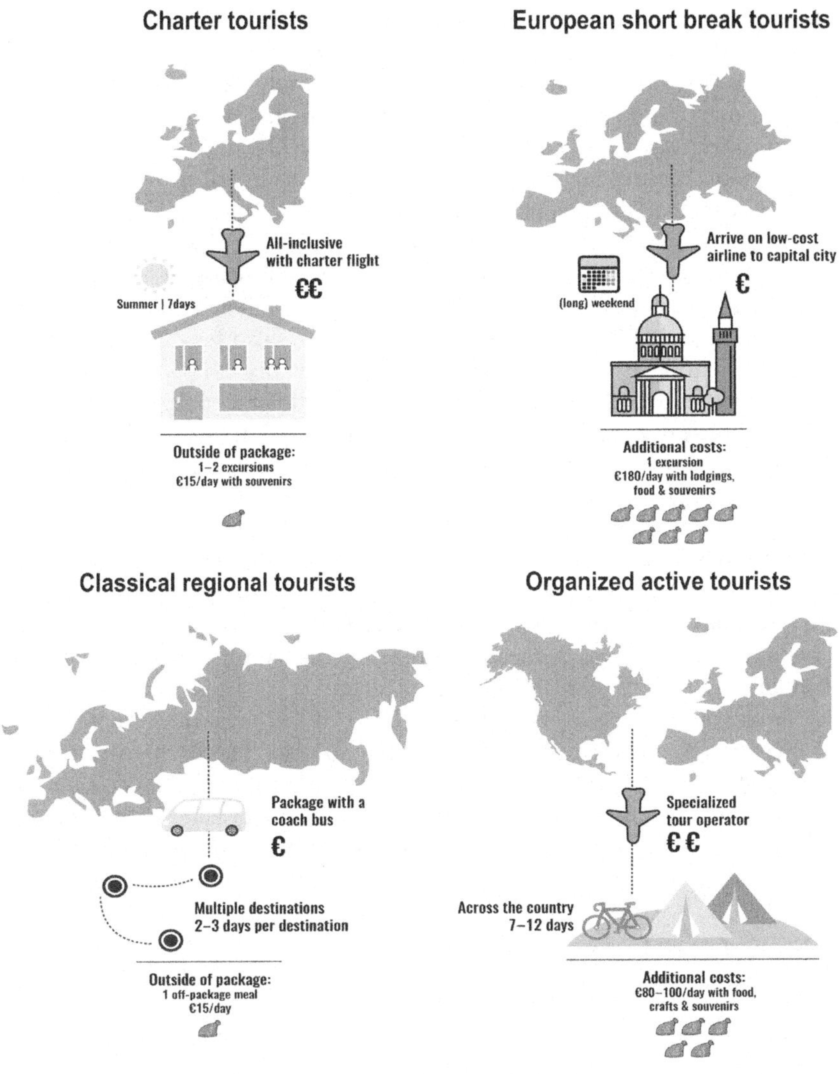

Who can do this?

It is most logical that behavioral segmentation happens on destination level as destination-marketing efforts influence the type of audience that will arrive at entry points. Many of the service providers do not do outreach to markets and seek to provide service to the guests who are already in the place. In that sense the business of local restaurants, local crafts and souvenir shops, local attractions depends on whether the type of guest who has been attracted by destination-marketing campaigns is interested in their product or service, and is willing to pay their price. So when considering segments destination-level decision makers should not only think about which traveler segments will like the nearby beach but also who among them are likely to explore the local old town and buy gifts for family and friends from the many charming but pricy crafts shops selling high-quality hand-made items.

Companies, however, have a role to play too. First, if the destination-level decision makers are not doing a good job at identifying segments on the basis of their likely behavior and target travelers who are likely to break local socio-cultural norms, local stakeholders can initiate dialog with destination decision makers and seek to correct that. Second, many of the local suppliers of traveler experiences do their own market outreach and promote the destination to global markets. These companies can also benefit from behavioral segmentation by thinking what kind of behavior aligns best with the experiences they offer, including whether they will be comfortable with the available infrastructure and type of services (small transportation vehicle traveling on narrow roads rather than highways), whether they will care about professional standards and quality (professional certification, safety procedures), and whether they will have the preparedness to engage in the offered activities (appropriate outfit and gear or the physical culture to endure a hike). If a provider of kayaking trips receives guests who do not come with the right gear and outfit for water-based activities, and who are ready to easily switch to a cheaper competitor despite the fact that they do not hold any safety certification, then there is a behavioral mismatch between the targeted travelers and the offering of the kayaking company.

Behavioral segmentation secures a more focused approach to attracting visitors, which in the day and age of excessive tourism, is of great value. A destination that has formulated the behavioral model that suits its portfolio of experiences, economic goals, and socio-cultural norms is in a position to target very specific groups and balance costs and gains much more successfully.

Established social norms

How to make this happen?

Tourism involves exploring new cultures and social norms. For the traveler visiting a new place involves trying to understand the differences between its socio-cultural texture and that at their home. For the host, welcoming tourists means trying to meet their expectations and deliver a good service without violating the cultural expectations of the guest. In this balance both sides learn about each other and enrich their perspective on the world while staying true to their cultural identity. Throughout the industry, however, this cultural exchange has not been balanced and many destinations, and service provider have undermined their own identity in effort to feel more welcoming to visitors. Instead of offering traditional local food providers seek to offer cuisine that is similar to what the guests might eat at home. Instead of ensuring that visitors understand and adhere to local behavioral norms, hosts agree to bend their own customs. Giving in on food traditions is one example and even though it is associated with the impact that tourism can have on the local economy, it might not be that damaging. Giving in on respect for local socio-cultural norms, however, can produce direct harm. There are too many places where residents experience discomfort due to the fact that visitors behave the way they want disregarding local culture and social norms. To a large extent this is fueled by the promoted philosophy that travel is a right so the visitor has the right to be in this place and act as is comfortable for them instead of the hosts. This is wrong. Travel is not a right, it is a privilege (Stowell, 2018b) that comes with responsibility and appreciation for the opportunity to be in someone else's home. It is the role of the destinations and host companies to change the framing and ensure that guests experience their stay through that lens.

Destinations should be much more proactive in maintaining their cultural identity and in setting norms about what is acceptable behavior that is in line with local expectations. They should be proactive in making the traveler aware before or upon arrival about what are some of the fundamental rules of behavior they are expected to abide by. These rules should consider local norms as well as local resources that might require special care.

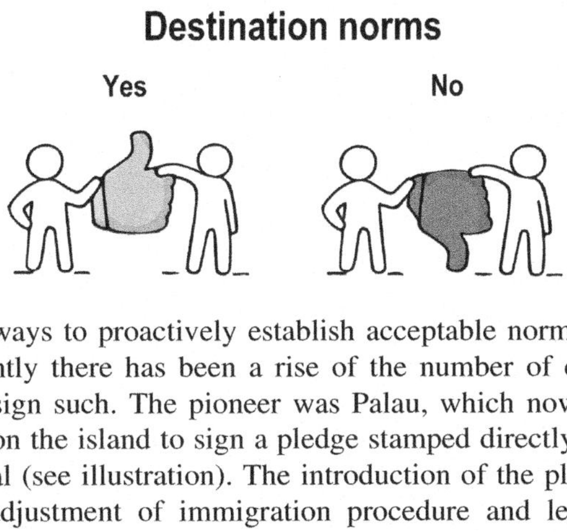

One of the ways to proactively establish acceptable norms of behavior is a pledge. Recently there has been a rise of the number of destinations that ask visitors to sign such. The pioneer was Palau, which now requires every visitor landing on the island to sign a pledge stamped directly into their passport upon arrival (see illustration). The introduction of the pledge in this format involved adjustment of immigration procedure and legislation. Many other destinations are following Palau's example and asking travelers to commit to certain rules that they will follow during their stay. In most cases, however, they are voluntary.

While pledges are a great tool for establishing norms of behavior, they cannot be a solution on their own. Palau's pledge is one element of an entire program designed to influence how tourists will behave. Awareness materials, including a required video played for the passengers of all airplanes landing into Palau and a passport insert makes sure that tourists are informed about the expected rules of behavior and understand the rationale behind them. This makes it harder to ignore and disregard. Signage around the island in the same visual style as seen on the awareness materials reminds tourists about the do's and don'ts during the stay and informs them about the fines they will have to pay in case of violation. Special accreditation for collaborating tour operators is also part of the program to ensure that local service providers are promoters of the norms as well. All of these elements working together strengthens the effectiveness of the pledge and ensures change of behavior. The fact that tourist sign in their passport during the formal immigration process triggers a different sense of commitment than if this is a voluntary pledge on the destination's website or on a flying sheet of paper. The proactive awareness, especially the video shown onboard airplanes and the passport insert, ensure that guests will be informed and aware of the expectations during their stay. The signs installed at places where the respective undesired behavior is likely to take place (e.g., signs reminding that tourism and stepping on corals damages them installed along beaches) ensure that the rules remain salient in the tourists' minds in the right moment and keep the sense of commitment alive.

Destinations that have tried to repeat the experience of Palau have done that with partial success because pledges alone cannot change behavior sustainably. A pledge can work only if it is part of an entire program that nudge travelers throughout their stay. The effectiveness of pledges or guidelines also depends on their timing. If this is done when there are signs that travelers are starting to have a negative impact but things are within some limits, a pledge can help steer things in the right direction through embraced social norms. However, in places where behavior has long surpassed local norms and is to some extent out of control, a pledge will not have the power to do anything, especially if it is voluntary and introduced without any other behavioral tactics.

Another note of warning is that pledges work because they are new and still unusual for travelers. But as more and more destinations seek to apply them, the sense that pledges are something common will make tourists less sensitive to them and will prompt them to accept them automatically without internalizing. This is why it is important for destinations to take a more integrated approach toward instilling social norms, and to constantly innovate to ensure that their efforts really impact behavior.

Who can do this?

Establishing acceptable norms of behavior is a role that destinations should adopt and carry out as part of the increasing understanding that tourism boards (or similar structures) should do much more to be managers rather than mere marketers of places. Local service providers who can channel information to their clients, of course, must support their effort. For example, whether a tourism authority has decided to use a pledge or a set of guidelines to educate tourists and influence behavior, it should ensure that they are made available through all possible channels to ensure all arriving guests are reached. For island destinations such as Palau this is fairly easy as the only means of arrival is air and an in-flight video helps reach everybody. For larger destinations where people arrive by air, road, rail, or water this might be much harder and this is where local service providers can help. It does not matter whether it is a hotel, an Airbnb host, tour operator, or individual guide, they can contribute by ensuring that guests receive the pledge or code of conduct as part of the booking process. Making reminders by placing rules or parts of them at the homestay or every hotel room, printing them on maps that are given to tourists, and simply mentioning them during interactions can all strengthen the effectiveness for everyone's sake.

The Palau Pledge

Palau was the first country to launch a tourist pledge. The pledge is stamped at immigration check on the visitor's passport upon arrival and must be signed on the spot. The roll out of the program required amending legislation to incorporate this as a required step in the immigration process.

The text of the pledge was developed with local children and is on behalf of the youth of Palau. Below is the text of the pledge:

(Continued)

(Continued)

Children of Palau,
I take this pledge,
as your guest,
to preserve and protect
your beautiful and unique
island home.
I vow to tread lightly
act kindly and
explore mindfully.
I shall not take
what is not given.
I shall not harm
what does not harm me.
The only footprints
I shall leave are those
that will wash away.

…………………………………

(signature)
Visit Palau (2019)

An important note on social norms is that destinations should be just as proactive in establishing rules of behavior for local service providers as with travelers. It is companies serving visitors that are in direct interactions with them and can play the main role in making them aware of local rules of behavior. If a destination seeks to establish the avoidance of single-use plastics as a social norm it can include it in a pledge or code of conduct, and of course in its promotional materials that are visibly presented for travelers everywhere, including at local hotels, restaurants, attractions, etc. The local hotels that will be hosting travelers or the tour operators that will offer the activities they engage in, can build on that by sending prearrival tips encouraging the use of reusable water bottles or by gifting one upon arrival. Restaurants and food service providers can be encouraged to serve water in mugs by default. Similarly if the destination finds it important to establish norms of behavior at important cultural or natural attractions, local companies should be expected to include such language in brochures, maps, or other information materials they share with clients. They should make sure that guidelines and tips are displayed in visible places and are easy for travelers to see and understand. Local service providers should also be encouraged to talk to their guests about that and remind them when they are leaving in the morning for their day of exploration or when they are seeking information about particular sites. Such proactive efforts to establish and adhere to norms can ensure that visitors behave in desired ways but they will also strengthen the daily commitment to norms of local service providers (see illustration).

The Svabald Community Guidelines

Svalbard is a Norwegian archipelago located between the country's mainland and the North Pole. It is the northernmost inhabited area in Norway.

Svalbald is a relatively young tourism destination but its attractiveness as a place offering a true Arctic experience is growing. Tourism is new for the place and has become a vehicle for alternative economic growth seen as viable replacement of the coal mining industry, which has become economically unviable. As part of the transition from mining to tourism local authorities realize that there is need to prepare the local community for receiving guests and to ensure that guests are ready to visit the area. This gives birth to the idea to develop and popularize the Svabald Community Guidelines.

Svabald is one of the first destinations to develop and popularize community guidelines as a way of formulating and introducing norms of behavior. While the primary focus is of course on the future visitors of the archipelago, the process of developing these has an important behavioral effect on the local tourism stakeholders as well. The initiative involves active discussion groups among local community members that aim to distill what is important to know about Svalbald and what makes it different from other places. The process leads to the formulation of 11 points that synthesize the important issues and considerations from local community perspective:

1. For your own safety, do not leave town without polar bear protection.
2. Chat with locals but ask before photographing, and please respect privacy and do not take pictures of children at kindergartens or school.
3. Enjoy a walk through town, but please walk on the left side of the road if there are no sidewalks.
4. The Svalbard reindeer, grouse, and birds can be seen around town. Enjoy our wildlife at a safe distance, remember that birds and other animals are not to be disturbed.
5. Dogs in the dog yards are a common sight in Longyearbyen, please do not feed, touch or disturb the dogs by getting too close to them for photographs.
6. We have many beautiful flowers, enjoy the sight but do not pick them.
7. Help us respect our history, please leave old cultural remains alone. Law protects all traces of humans from before 1946.
8. You are welcome to photograph parked snowmobiles, but please do not touch them.
9. The use of drones is prohibited in Longyearbyen less than 5 km from Longyearbyen airport.
10. Help us keep beautiful Svalbard clean. Use our garbage bins and leave no traces behind.
11. Shop locally! You are welcome to buy our locally made products, but we do not have a tradition for bargaining.

(*Continued*)

(Continued)

The participatory discussions in essence nurture a stronger sense of commitment to these issues within the community. Today community guidelines are embraced by all and shared by everyone who is part of the tourism value chain. In addition to the local tourism authorities they are displayed on the websites of service providers, at local tourism facilities (hotels, B&Bs, restaurants, etc.), and screens in cruise ships, at the local airport, and hotel lobbies. Community members talk about them and refer to them in their conversations with guests.

The process of developing and promoting the community guidelines in Svalbald is a great example for effective setting of social norms that guide the behavior of visitors but also that of local stakeholders.

Kornfeldt (2019)

It is true that destination authorities currently have no power to influence the behavior of local service providers through regulations but they can exert influence through voluntary tools such as asking local businesses to sign a pledge, providing guidelines, or offering recommended improvements in service design (see illustration). The behavior of local service providers is a crucial source of influence for tourists, many of whom arrive in a destination expecting that there might be some differences in social norms so they are prepared to adjust. If they notice that their guide uses a reusable water bottle and talks about water stops on the way, they will ensure they reuse the bottle they have in their hands, even if they have made the mistake to buy a single-use plastic one. If they see that guides keep their cigarette butts in hand until they are near a bin rather than drop on the street or hiking trail, they follow the example. Similarly if the hotel reception by default provides every guest with a special bag for collecting their waste during the hike they are about to embark on, this will be perceived as the norm.

Examples for voluntary tools for local companies

Voluntary tools for establishing clear social norms for local tourism businesses can be effective because companies operating in the destination have a vested interest in making sure tourists behave respectfully and mindfully. Below are some examples of different tools and options in which they can be applied for local service providers encouraging them to adopt (and promote) minimal use of single-use plastics and zero littering as social norms:

Tool	Examples
Pledge/code of conduct	Sample code/pledge principles: • I commit to avoiding single-use plastic options in every instance, in which there is a better option

(Continued)

(Continued)

	• I commit to proactively encouraging my guests to bring and use reusable bottles for drinks • I commit to serving food and drink only in reusable serveware • I commit to ensuring that travelers on my tours are aware of the rules of conduct at cultural sites and in nature • I commit to ensuring that all my guests are aware of our destination's *leave no trace behind* policy
Operational guidelines and tips	• Send preliminary tips for future guests encouraging them to bring reusable water bottles and cutlery for outdoor meals • Enable guests who do not have their own reusable bottles and cutlery to easily find a place to buy before embarking on their tours • Design itineraries with water refill stops • Provide guests with bags for their trash before every nature-based experience and ensure that they dispose of the bag in the appropriate places at the end of the trip • Clearly display recycling instructions around bins on your property/at your attraction
Guidelines for recommended design improvements	• Install water fountains or water taps in or near common areas • Install a water dispenser in an easily accessible common place • Install large reusable dispensers for soap, shampoo, and other toiletries
Manuals	• Manual with step-by-step guidelines for behavior-smart tactics for discouraging clients from using single-use plastics • Manual with step-by-step tips for behavior-smart tools for applying a zero-waste tolerance
Grants	Small grant programs supporting desired design or operational changes requiring investment: • Grant for small hotels, B&Bs and other accommodation providers for installation of permanent dispensers for soap, shampoo, and other toiletries

(*Continued*)

(Continued)

	• Grant for accommodations, attractions, and other tourism service facilities for installation of water fountains • Grant for introduction of recycling bins for separate collection of plastics in all rooms of accommodation properties • Grant for signage with antilittering tips for visitors

Finally while tourism authorities, especially on regional and local level, have limited ability to influence big international players who are part of the destination ecosystem, they can activate processes for policy adjustment that can help. For example, a local and even national tourism board can help to set social norms that discourage local accommodation facilities from offering toiletries in single-use plastic packages. This however, is unlikely to change the practice of international brand hotels that are present in the destination unless they are restricted by local regulations. Destination authorities can initiate dialog with policy authorities and lobby for the introduction of regulations that prohibit the use of toiletries in single-use plastic packaging on the destination's territory. Properties will have no other way but find a new way of making these available for their guests—either in innovative nonplastic packaging or in larger reusable dispensers. While there are complaints that larger dispensers are not perceived as luxury and are therefore not appropriate for high-end brands, there should be an alternative and it will be found only if the existing option is no longer possible. Until exceptions are available, there will never be motivation to explore viable alternatives.

Cruise companies are another example of an ecosystem stakeholder that currently cannot be influenced by tourism authorities and requires the involvement of higher-level institutions. Destination management organizations can activate a dialog toward introducing desired (or required) norms of behavior for them as well. If the rest of the players in the ecosystem find it relevant to enable access to their destination only for cruise companies that align with destination norms, then tourism authorities should initiate policy amendments that guarantee that. For example, if a destination has committed to the elimination of single-use plastics, cruise companies should be required to make sure that none of their guests can buy onboard and bring from the ship single-use plastic bottles; or if destination stakeholders have accepted as a norm that every tourism service or product is net positive for the local community, then cruise companies should commit to ensuring that every excursion offered to their passengers follows that principle.

The most common objection for large cruise and hospitality operators when faced with attempt to regulate them toward being more responsible is that the cost of such changes is too large, and would lead to more expensive offerings. More expensive offerings, they claim, would make travel exclusive and inaccessible to larger audiences (Becker, 2018). This argument is nonsense for two reasons. First, the unwillingness to accept the cost of shifting to more responsible practices does not make the cost disappear; it is merely avoided by the cruise company and transferred to the destination by sustaining the harmful social or environmental impacts. Destinations should proactively reject that deal. Second, the most contemporary theories for innovation suggest that true innovation happens under conditions of constraint (Boyd & Goldenberg, 2013). That means that if cruise companies are put under a situation of constraint, they are much likelier to produce innovations that help them stay in business and enjoy profit while being much more sustainable. If more and more destinations reject access to cruises unless they adhere to destination norms, ultimately large cruise operators will find ways to change and continue doing business. Until they find ways out, nothing motivates them to change their ways.

Experiences versus trips

How to make this happen?

One of the changes that can be made now toward overcoming some of the behavioral barriers in today's destination management practices is to adopt an experience economy perspective. Framing the offering of the destination as an experience rather than a trip, visit, or stay changes the perspective and the ability to influence it. This lens makes it much easier to see and understand what are the different elements contributing to the overall experience. This is very logical from demand perspective for two reasons. First, for the customer the offering in the tourism market exchange is the experience in its entirety. Despite its multiday nature in the mind of the traveler the entire trip with all its components is perceived as one single experience extended over time rather than a collage of episodes that are stitched together (Nikolova, 2009). In that sense, if a destination is eager to be customer-oriented and perform well in the eyes of its clients, it needs to take their consumption perspective. Second, even thought the intuitive perspective is that the market interaction between the supplier (the destination and its network of service providers) and the customer ends when the customer leaves the place to return home, the postreturn phase is very important from a behavioral points of view. This is the stage when all events are reflected upon and the final positive or negative long-term satisfaction is formed. It is this retrospective evaluation that becomes the basis of the stories that visitors will be sharing with friends and family, and that will shape their memories about the experience. Because word of mouth is tremendously important for future demand the retrospective evaluation of travel experience by past visitors should be treated as an important asset for tourism places (Nikolova, 2009). To some extend retrospective evaluation becomes more important than the experience itself because behavior outcomes (future purchase decisions, word of mouth, etc.) occur when travelers are outside of the destination setting and are driven by the memories for experienced positive or negative events rather than the original events themselves (Ariely & Zauberman, 2000).

One approach toward understanding the elements and dynamics of the experience that shapes the value for the traveler, is applying an experience value chain (Hawkins & Nikolova, 2005). This is a tool that is constructed around the five main phases of the travel experience (Clawson & Knetsch, 2011): anticipation phase, travel to the site, on-site activities, return travel, and a recollection phase. An experience value chain leads to the main questions about what happens at each phase and identifies the moments that constitute the string of events shaping the outcome in its entirety. It is an effective tool in helping identify areas of strength and areas of weakness throughout the string of moments so that the overall performance is strengthened (Nikolova, 2009). An example for a template with questions for each phase enabling experience value chain analysis is presented below.

Experience value chain analysis template

Anticipation	Travel to	Onsite experiences	Travel back	Recollection
How do they think of the destination? How do they find information for the destination? How do they book? How do they research before leaving? How do they buy trips (package or not)?	Means of travel to destination? Entry point to destination (land/air and location)? Do they need visa (is it obtained pretrip or on the spot)?	How long do they stay? Where do they stay (locations)? What type of accommodations do they use? How do they move around? (transportation, biking, etc.) What activities do they engage in? (How do they book them, i.e., Viator or local supplier) What attractions do they visit?	Means of travel back? Exit point from destination (land/air and location)	What souvenirs/ gifts do they back? What feedback/ memories do they share with friends/ family? Where do they share feedback/ memories (online, social media, word of mouth)? Likelihood to return (curiosity to come back) or to encourage friends/ family to visit?

(Continued)

(Continued)

Anticipation	Travel to	Onsite experiences	Travel back	Recollection
		Where and what do they eat (as part of package or not)? Are they guided/ unguided and independent/group? How much do they spend locally? On what?		

Adapted from World Bank. (2016a). *Development Plans for Tourism Along Western and Eastern Circuits and Central Corridor in FYR Macedonia for the Local and Regional Competitiveness Project (LRCP).* Skopje.

The application of a value chain approach using the template above is based on using the key moments and key questions to construct what would be an ideal traveler experience in the respective destination and for a particular traveler segment. This serves as the benchmark against which the current experience is compared allowing for easy identification of problem areas. An example of how this may look is presented in the following illustration that compares the ideal experience flow of visiting a country ABC for an independent active tourist and the current experience they will like have in the destination.

Travel experience

Experience value chain analysis for independent active tourists

Anticipation phase

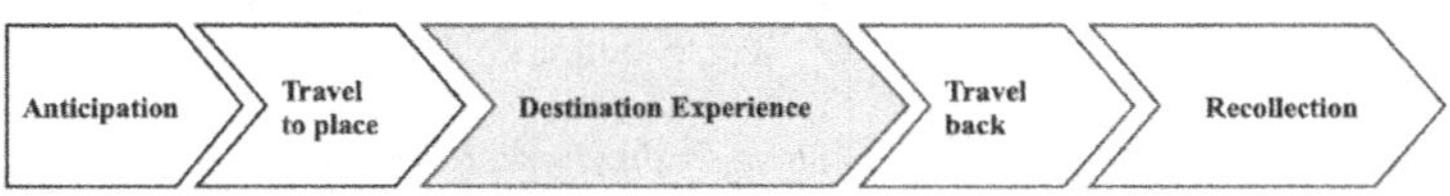

Ideal experience

How do they think of ABC?

- Read an article in specialized outdoors media such as National Geographic

Current experience

How do they think of ABC?

- There are very few materials published in travel media on ABC and they are not

Traveler, Wanderlust magazine, Outdoors magazine, Lonely Planet, some travel blogs such as Everything-Everywhere, Traveling Jackie and others; in many cases they see it posted in Facebook or when they go to the website for a leisure read;
- See friends post in social media about their recent travels in ABC;

How do they find information for ABC?
- Check online travel portal for ABC as well as Facebook, Instagram, Tumblr and Youtube, as well as in the travel blogs and forums they follow.
- Ask friends or colleagues in their network about hints and tips

How do they book?
- They book on their own everything separately through Booking.com, Airbnb, and Viator. They check out ratings and traveler feedback in TripAdvisor, Airbnb, Booking, Viator, and forums.
- They also refer to guidebooks such as Lonely Planet, Bradt, etc.

How do they research before leaving?
- They buy/download guidebook (Lonely Planet, Bradt, etc.)
- Research articles in travel media and travel blogs on ABC
- General online research for places they are visiting

How do they buy trips (package or not)?
- They book everything independently based on peer reviews in online platforms or recommendations from travel bloggers and sometimes personal friends.

regular to ensure visibility over time. Some publications on ABC have been published in outdoors travel media.
- Information on ABC shared by people is limited as there are still few travelers with this profile that have visited yet. There is limited authentic traveler content that is channeled through the national-level social media channels.
- Current media coverage on ABC is not positive and is more likely to provoke associations with risk and danger than interest in visiting. Nothing much is being done to offset that.

How do they find information for ABC?
- ABC currently has two portals, none of which comes up among the first results of most logical searches; ABC Timeless is by far the better travel website but it does not appear in general search results; ABC does not have an official page in Facebook and there is a Youtube channel called *Welcome to ABC*, which has nothing to do with tourism. There is limited organic customer content on national social media channels.
- Article searches produce some hits on travel articles on ABC.

How do they book?
- Many service providers in and around the main cities in ABC are present on Booking.com, Tripadvisor, and Viator but few outside of the two centers. Many providers have recently joined online platforms and do not have any ratings and feedback (especially in Viator). A number of service providers and experiences are not searchable or bookable online.
- The majority of hotels and service providers are not very active with their Booking and Tripadvisor profiles and rarely respond to customer comments.
- Few articles are available upon online search but more are expected in the near future.

How do they research before leaving?
- Bradt has standalone guides for ABC and its capital city, Lonely Planet has chapters on ABC in its guides on Europe and Eastern Europe; there is no Rough Guide on ABC

- Few cities and locations have their own travel websites but useful travel information on places in ABC is available on the national portals and on the websites of some local adventure operators who come high up on searches

How do they buy trips (package or not)?

- They buy online but do not have access to everything they hear is available as experience. They have very limited information about and options to book places and activities outside of Skopje and Ohrid.

Travel to phase

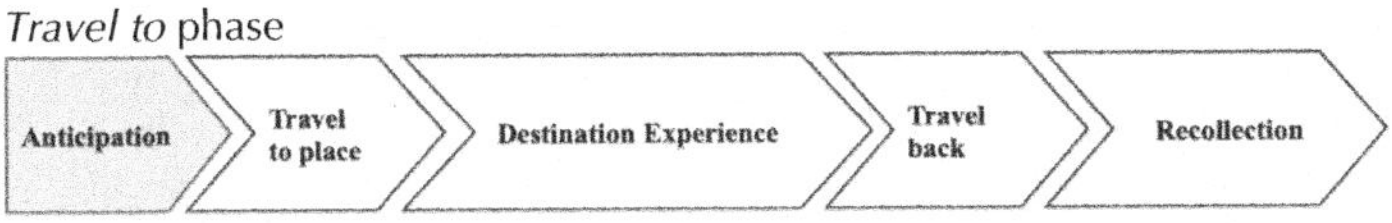

Ideal experience

Means of travel to ABC?

- They travel by plane from home to ABC, ideally direct

Entry point in ABC?

- Skopje by air

Do they need visa?

- No need for visa for citizens of EU, US, Canada

Current experience

Means of travel to ABC?

- They travel by plane from home to ABCa. There are direct connections between the capital city and main European markets. Lack of direct flights significantly decreases interest in considering ABC.

Entry point in ABC?

- Skopje by air

Do they need visa?

- No need for visa for citizens of EU, US, Canada

Destination experience phase

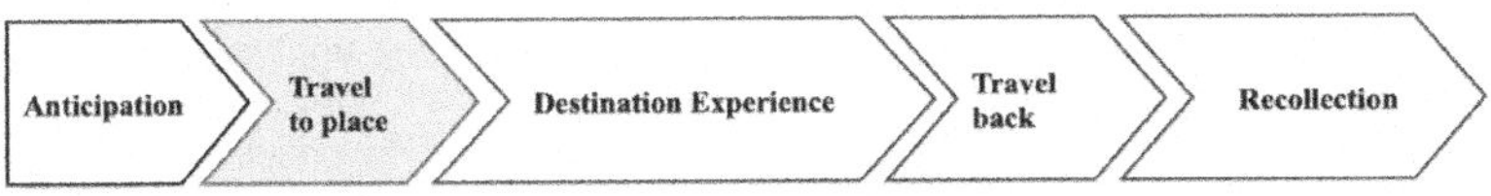

Ideal experience

How long do they stay?

- They usually would like to spend in destinations between 4 and 10 days depending on the richness of available things to do. The crossing of borders and covering of more than one country is interesting if they are able to stay long enough. They are fine with spending the entire time just in ABC and maybe doing a quick daytrip to neighboring countries for additional excitement if staying for five or more days.

Where do they stay (locations)?

Current experience

How long do they stay?

- They stay only 7 days in and combined the trip with Bulgaria to fill 15 days. According to their operator ABC has potential for a lot more than is included in the itinerary but the level of the facilities, the infrastructure, and the service is still not at an acceptable level.

Where do they stay (locations)?

- They cover the capital city and surrounding area, spend a day in the wine region and go to the National Park for a day or two, they go to the coast for

- They spend their time in Skopje and Kumanovo, Prilep and Krusevo, Bitola and Pelister National Park, Prespa lake, Ohrid lake and the surroundings, Mt Bistra, Galichnik and Mavrovo, Tetovo and Popova shapka.

What type of accommodations do they use?

- Any kind of accommodation between a private Airbnb apartment (in Skopje), small family-owned B&B to a nice four-star boutique property. Regardless of size and number of stars accommodation places are ideally clean, have reliable water/electricity/ heat, have their own character, offer beds that are comfortable, offer good service and address arising needs with readiness, and of course offer good local food (at property or in the area).

How do they move around?

- They move around with private transfers, which they book through local providers or local taxi drivers available via Uber, Viator, or relevant travel forums.
- In some cases when they decide to hike from one location to another, they may ask the accommodation provider to arrange transportation for their luggage so they do not have to carry it with them on the hike.

What activities do they engage in? (How they book them, i.e., Viator?)

- Being outdoors is the most important driver of itinerary planning but it is very exciting for them to combine hiking with enjoying beautiful landscapes, visiting churches and other interesting sites, as well as experiencing rural areas. They always enjoy doing wine tours so they take a wine making and tasting tour in the Tikvesh area, which involves walking through the vineyards and enjoying an outside picnic. They booked the tour through Viator.
- While hiking they like to stop in mountainous villages and farms to learn about living traditional lifestyle.
- Other activities they enjoy include farmer markets tours, living traditions experiences, culinary and farming demonstrations, local crafts

two days, and return to the capital (or possibly proceed to neighboring countries). They cover key spots that they find information about. They consider going to Western National Park but with limited time, they leave it out.

What type of accommodations do they use?

- They use various accomodations during their trip varying from private Airbnb apartment, small two-star to four-star facilities. The quality and the rating vary widely so they choose places that seem to have strong ratings by other travelers. Availability of a good place to stay is a key factor in the itinerary design. Many of the properties have some charm and are clean but the beds are not very comfortable and sometimes there are problems with water temperature or room heating. They frequently lack relevant services (parking for bikes, laundry service, vegetarian menu options, etc.).
- English language skills are very poor, which creates problems. Service quality is inconsistent although it is obvious that the reason for that is lack of service training and understanding of customer needs rather than lack of willingness to learn.

How do they move around?

- They move around with private transfers that they book through Viator or contacts they have obtained from friends or peers in forums. They were unpleasantly surprised with the driving style and had to ask some of the drivers to slow down and pay attention to traffic rules.

What activities do they engage in? (How they book them, i.e., Viator?)

- They plan their outdoor experiences based on traveler forums. Based on recommendations from others, they connect with local mountaineering clubs to ask for recommendation as there is very limited official information online and the one that is available is in Macedonian.
- They book all their activities independently through online channels: Airbnb, Booking, Viator, etc. Peer feedback and rating are leading factors

demonstrations, etc. They usually book these on Viator.

What attractions do they visit?

- The most important attractions such as the castle in the capital city, the Blue canyon, etc. are must-see but in addition to that they truly enjoy the off-the-beaten path local places that are distinctive for ABC and that hold interesting stories. Visiting living and preserved villages with interesting traditions, spending time on farms and in rural areas, engaging in traditional farming or living traditions (i.e., forest berry collection, rakia making), spending a night at a monastery or traditional rural home, going to a traditional festival (aivar or rakia festival), etc. are all things that end up being more important for the creation of memories and building their satisfaction with trips.

Where and what do they eat (package or not)?

- Eating local food is something that they enjoy tremendously and is part of the core experience of immersing themselves in the destination. Local ingredients and freshly made meals are extremely important. Eating can be at traditional local restaurants with excellent reputation as well as local farms or rural homes. Interpretation around food is very important and they frequently ask about ingredients and local products that are used. Information about ingredients is also very important to meet some dietary limitations that some of the friends that they travel with have.
- They choose where to eat based on research on TripAdvisor or recommendations friends, peers in forums, or locals they meet during their travels. If they like any of the local food or wine, they will buy some to take home for the traditional local dinner with friends they plan to as usual after their trips.

Are they guided/unguided and independent/group?

for their decision but the fact that many providers have recently started using the platforms leads to very few peer ratings (especially in Viator).

- They have heard about some cool crafts, culinary, and cultural traditions but are unable to find information in English and in Viator. They ask some locals that they meet during their trips.

What attractions do they visit?

- Most of their time seems to be spent in the most developed tourists areas, as most of the available offerings through the channels they use are concentrated there. They find out about other interesting things to do as they travel but they are unable to stay longer to cover them. The most enjoyable part of their trips ends up being spending a night at the traditional rural home in a small southern village learning about rural life and culinary traditions, and eating authentic local food, as well as hiking to through High-Peak National Park to reach the stunning nearby lake. They wished to spend more time in rural areas and experiencing local rural, farming and culinary traditions that they learned about from locals during their trip but there were not that many options to do that outside of the culinary demonstration in the traditional rural home.
- They enjoyed hiking but poor marking and lack of maps or guides for independent travelers made it almost impossible to do that on their own without taking a local mountaineering guide.
- The garbage in some of the areas they visited, including natural areas was shocking to them and to some extend ruined the experience of being out in nature.

Where and what do they eat (package or not)?

- Although the flavor and good quality of the food in ABC is a positive surprise for them, there are definite opportunities for improvement. The breakfast at one of the hotels they stayed at was one of the disappointments where focus was placed

- They travel independently and hire guides only for specific activities if there is extra value in that.

How much do they spend?

- The total amount they spend (without airfare) is 550 Euro per person for a five-day trip and included lodging, private transportation, one-day excursions, and souvenirs they purchased....

on having a classical continental breakfast rather than serving a small set of traditional breakfast items. Some of the traditional restaurants they ate at offered some good meals but also some disappointing ones. There was little information on the food traditions and some of the servers were not capable of explaining the dishes in English.

Are they guided/unguided and independent/group?

- They travel independently and hire guides only for specific activities if there is extra value in that. They prefer to hike without a guide but the lack of any guides or services that support independent travel combined with poor and missing marking, made this necessary. The guide ended up giving them some interesting information and stories so it ended up being a good thing.

*How much do they spend?*Total price or the ABC trip (without airfare) is 400 Euro, which is an attractively low price for a trip of this length and is at the lower for this kind of trip. They wanted to spend a bit more and include some additional items but the options were limited and they ended up not doing that. They also had very limited opportunity to spend on local culinary or other souvenirs: they bought some local wine and local aivar but not much else. ...

Adapted on the basis of World Bank. (2016a). *Development Plans for Tourism Along Western and Eastern Circuits and Central Corridor in FYR Macedonia for the Local and Regional Competitiveness Project (LRCP)*. Skopje.

An experience value chain approach makes the importance of collaboration within a destination very obvious because it becomes clear that every service or product along the experiential journey contributes to one whole. Taking an experience perspective to decision-making entails considering the connectivity between all elements and stakeholders that influence the offering consumed by the traveler. It facilitates a system-thinking frame at destination level and among different players along the value chain. An experience-driven approach to planning and managing tourism would entail the application of experience tracking tools that audit the traveler experience identifying gaps and failures that must be addressed through proper interventions (Nikolova, Bakker, Nevill, Metz, & Popovik, 2017).

The behaviorally optimized destination

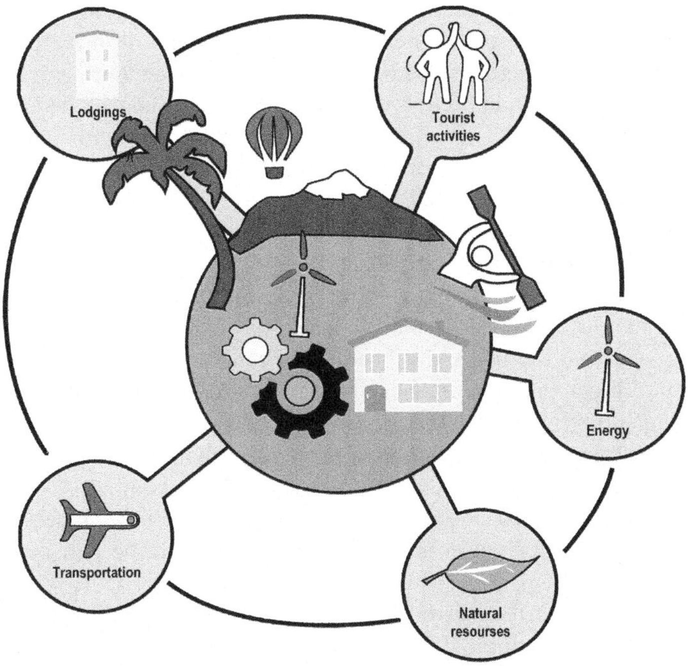

With the advanced knowledge about human behavior and the weaknesses in many assumption that have informed institutional and business models until now, there is opportunity for human-centered optimization. A behaviorally optimized destination is a destination that in its design and its operations is aligned with realistic assumptions about human behavior. Its design should de-bias the decision making on all levels, from policy maker and destination manager to the small service provider and the traveler who is there as a customer.

Equipped with new knowledge and in an environment marked by serious crises provoked by the current failures in the state of the travel industry, destinations have an opportunity to reform their own role in the travel ecosystem and to enable decision-making that shifts the balance of impacts toward a net positive outcome. Naturally some changes will take time and need more work but others are a matter of applying some existing and proven choice architecture techniques that can produce immediate improvements.

In the long run destination-level decision-making should be grounded on sustainability as a nonnegotiable principle to which there is no alternative. If sustainability is framed as the only way of doing tourism, the behavior of decision makers, and users will go along as there will be no alternative. This, of course, will be linked to the changed industry norms about how tourism is measured and what are the widely accepted measures of success emphasizing the benefits generated first and foremost for the local hosts. The new agreement on what constitutes successful tourism within the destination will make it more proactive in setting norms of behavior that companies and guests are expected to adhere to. What is accepted and unaccepted as behavior will be at the core of how a destination collaborates with international and local companies operating on its territory, and the policies that influence the entire ecosystem. This will also shape its marketing strategy as the behavior-smart destination will use behavior as the main approach to segmentation and targeting seeking much better alignment between the experience it offers and the travel consumption style of pursued markets.

One of the keys toward de-biasing decision making on destination level is making sure that the costs and benefits of tourism are in one equation. A systems-thinking approach is what is needed in order to truly capture the full array of impacts triggered by tourism growth and to outline potential growth scenarios. The more important change in mindset that is needed, however, is the valuation of resources that are treated as tourism commons. Nature and culture, and the recreational, esthetic, educational, and spiritual services they offer need to be properly accounted for so that they can be part of the tourism equation.

Managing through the prism of the experience rather than individual elements is another behavioral shift that will make decision-making more positive and effective from the perspective of the traveler and their satisfaction. Experience-based thinking makes the need for more proactive management and coordination throughout the value chain very obvious as well.

Behavior optimization for destinations is not the ultimate solution to today's challenges in the travel challenges but it certainly offers an opportunity to limit, if not eliminate, the potential for many of the systematic failures. As some of the cases at the end of this book reveal, using choice architecture to influence likely behavior and make it more natural for people to engage in sustainable behavior during their travels, can produce tremendous impacts with minimum investments. In that sense being a behaviorally optimized destination is reasonable from a purely economic perspective too.

References

Altman, M. (2017). Rational inefficiency: Smart thinking, bounded rationality and the scientific basis for economic failure and success. In M. Altman (Ed.), *Handbook of behavioral economics and smart decision making* (pp. 11–42). Northampton: Edward Elgar Publishing.

Ariely, D. (2015). Behavioral economics: An exercise in design and humility. In S. Samson (Ed.), *The behavioral economics guide 2015 (with an introduction by Dan Ariely)* (pp. v–x). , Retrieved from. Available from www.behavioraleconomics.com.

Ariely, D., & Zauberman, G. (2000). On the making of an experience: The effects of breaking and combining experiences on their overall evaluation. *Journal of Behavioral Decision Making*, *13*, 219–232, Retrieved from. Available from http://citeseerx.ist.psu.edu/viewdoc/download?doi = 10.1.1.20.2051&rep = rep1&type = pdf.

Becker, E. (2013). *Overbooked: The exploding business of travel and tourism*. New York: Simon & Schuster.

Becker, E. (2018). Personal communication with Elizabeth Becker, author of Overbooked (31 May 2018).

Bielański, M., Taczanowska, K., Muhar, A., Adamski, P., González, L.-M., & Witkowski, Z. (2018). Application of GPS tracking for monitoring spatially unconstrained outdoor recreational activities in protected areas—A case study of ski touring in the Tatra National Park, Poland. *Applied Geography*, *96*, 51–65. Available from https://doi.org/10.1016/j.apgeog.2018.05.008.

Boyd, D., & Goldenberg, J. (2013). *Inside the box: A proven system of creativity for breakthrough results*. New York: Simon and Schuster.

Clawson, M., & Knetsch, J. L. (2011). Economics of outdoor recreation. Economics of outdoor recreation (2nd ed.). New York: Earthscan. <https://doi.org/10.4324/9781315064215>.

Doyle, C. (2018). Personal communications with Chris Doyle, Executive Director at the Adventure Travel Trade Association (June 2018).

EC, OECD, UN, & World Bank. *System of environmental-economic accounting 2012: Experimental ecosystem accounting*. (2013). Retrieved from <https://unstats.un.org/unsd/envaccounting/eea_white_cover.pdf>.

Epler Wood, M. (2017). *Sustainable tourism on a finite planet: Environmental, business and policy solutions*. New York: Routledge.

Gigerenzer, G. (2011). Moral satisficing: Rethinking moral behavior as bounded rationality. In G. Gigerenzer, R. Hertwig, & T. Pachur (Eds.), *Heuristics: The foundations of adaptive behavior* (pp. 203–221). New York: Oxford University Press.

Gneezy, U., & Rustichini, A. (2000). A fine is a price. *The Journal of Legal Studies*, *29*(1), 1–17, Retrieved from. Available from https://rady.ucsd.edu/faculty/directory/gneezy/pub/docs/fine.pdf.

Hawkins, D. E., & Nikolova, M. S. (2005). A value chain approach to tourism destination knowledge management. In *International conference on knowledge applications for competitive destinations, UNWTO education council general assembly conference*. Dakar, Senegal.

Ives, C. D., & Bekessy, S. A. (2015). The ethics of offsetting nature. *Frontiers in Ecology and the Environment*, *13*(10), 568–573. Available from https://doi.org/10.1890/150021.

Kornfeldt, E. B. (2019). Personal Communication with Eva-Britt Kornfeld, Manager Svalbard Cruise Network at Visit Svalbard (24 April 2019).

Leung, Y.-F., Spenceley, A., Hvenegaard, G., & Buckley, R. (2018). *Tourism and visitor management in protected areas: Guidelines for sustainability*. Gland, Switzerland. Retrieved from <www.iucn.org/pa_guidelines>.

Meadows, D. H., Meadows, D. L., & Randers, J. (1992). Beyond the limits: Confronting global collapse, envisioning a sustainable future *(1st ed.)*. Vermont: Chelsea Green Publishing.

Meadows, D. H., Meadows, D. L., Randers, J., & Behrens, W. W. (1972). *The limits to growth*. Washington, DC: Potomac Associates.

Meadows, D. H., Randers, J., & Meadows, D. (2005). *Limits to growth: The 30-year update*. London: Earthscan.

Nikolova, M. S. (2009). *Brand effects on retrospective evaluations of past consumption experiences*. The George Washington University.

Nikolova, M. S., Bakker, M., Nevill, H., Metz, M., & Popovik, G. (2017). Applying a visitor experience value chain for destination market performance assessment. In *ATLAS annual conference 2017: Destinations past, present and future* (p. 39). Viana do Castelo, Portugal. Retrieved from <http://www.atlas-euro.org/LinkClick.aspx?fileticket = nGjtRwuJTOA%3D&tabid = 263&language = en-US>.

Northcote, J., & Macbeth, J. (2006). Conceptualizing yield: Sustainable tourism management. *Annals of Tourism Research*, *33*(1)), 199–220, Retrieved from. Available from http://researchrepository.murdoch.edu.au/3492.

Stowell, S. (2018a). Change the world. . .take a vacation. TEDxBend. Retrieved from <https://youtu.be/0Lud6xAWN_c>.

Stowell, S. (2018b). *Forward (losing keynote speech at the 2018 Adventure Travel World Summit October 18, 2018, Montecatini Terme, Italy)*. Montecatini Terme: Adventure Travel Trade Association (ATTA).

Swearingen, T. C., & Johnson, D. R. (1995). Visitors' responses to uniformed park employees. *Journal of Park and Recreation Administration*, *13*(1), 73–85.

Swedish Environmental Protection Agency. (2019). *This is the Right of Public Access*. Stockholm: Swedish Environmental Protection Agency. Retrieved from <http://www.swedishepa.se/Environmental-objectives-and-cooperation/Swedish-environmental-work/Work-areas/This-is-the-Right-of-Public-Access/#>.

TEEB. (2010). In P. Kumar (Ed.), *The economics of ecosystems and biodiversity ecological and economic foundations*. London and Washington, DC: Earthscan. Retrieved from <http://doc.teebweb.org/wp-content/uploads/StudyandReports/Reports/EcologicalandEconomicFoundations/TEEBEcologicalandEconomicFoundationsreport/TEEBFoundations.pdf>.

Vercelloni, J., Clifford, S., Caley, M. J., Pearse, A. R., Brown, R., James, A., & Peterson, E. E. (2018). Using virtual reality to estimate aesthetic values of coral reefs. *Royal Society Open Science*, *5*, 1–10. Available from https://doi.org/10.1098/rsos.172226.

Visit Faroe Islands. (2019). *Join the preservolution: A sustainable tourism development strategy for the Faroe Islands towards 2025*. Tórshavn.

Visit Flanders. (2019). *Travel to tomorrow: Innovators are designing the future*. VISITFLANDERS, Brussels.

Visit Palau. (2019). Palau pledge. Retrieved from <https://palaupledge.com/> Accessed 18.04.2019.

Voinov, A., Çöltekin, A., Chen, M., & Beydoun, G. (2018). Virtual geographic environments in socio-environmental modeling: A fancy distraction or a key to communication? *International Journal of Digital Earth*, *11*(4), 408–419. Available from https://doi.org/10.1080/17538947.2017.1365961.

World Bank. (2016a). *Development Plans for Tourism Along Western and Eastern Circuits and Central Corridor in FYR Macedonia for the Local and Regional Competitiveness Project (LRCP)*. Skopje.

World Bank. (2016b). *Market Analysis of Tourism Along Western and Eastern Circuits and Central Corridor in FYR Macedonia for the Local and Regional Competitiveness Project (LRCP)*. Skopje. Retrieved from <http://lrcp.mk/tourism-market-analysis/>.

Chapter 5

Behavior-smart thinking for tourism companies

Chapter outline

Introduction

The solution lies in the principle of shared value, which involves creating economic value in a way that also creates value for society by addressing its needs and challenges. Businesses must reconnect company success with social progress. Shared value is not social responsibility, philanthropy, or even sustainability, but a new way to achieve economic success. It is not on the margin of what companies do but at the center. We believe that it can give rise to the next major transformation of business thinking.

Michael E. Porter and Mark R. Kramer, Creating Shared Value.

Behavior and shared value

A changing market reality requires change in the behavior of all market players. From a behavioral point of view there are three main directions in which change makes sense particularly for service providers. First, given the changing behavior and consumption patterns of the traveler discussed in Chapter 4, Behavior-Smart Thinking for Destinations, travel companies will benefit from aligning the design of their marketing and product development efforts to the ways the consumer makes decisions and behaves. Second, in

Behavioral Economics for Tourism. DOI: https://doi.org/10.1016/B978-0-12-813808-3.00005-8

line with the need for the entire travel ecosystem to operate in ways that lead to more benefits and less negative impacts, every company should be seeking ways to streamline its operations toward minimizing negative impacts and maximizing benefits for itself and the entire ecosystem. Third, the industry as a whole has the opportunity to demonstrate reverse responsibility, that is, responsibility to society by using its powers to contribute to the alleviation of some more global societal challenges of our contemporary realities.

Earlier in this book a discussion around the changing behavior of the traveler highlighted the influence of technology and other socioeconomic factors on decision-making and consumption patterns. In a fast-paced market reality where attention is becoming a scarce commodity travelers have become much faster decision makers. Even though choosing a holiday is a multifaceted decision with a lot of choice steps, today's buyer applies many more shortcuts and is much more frequently in the impatient System 1 mode than the rational and the carefully weighting System 2 mode (Kahneman, 2011). This means that the information that is perceptually captured during the buying journey and the ingredients that produce the buying decision are different from the ones in the past. Respectively, the presenting of promotional information and details that aid the buying decision should be different and align with new choice formation processes.

It is already clear that the tourism system cannot continue operating the way it has been running until now. As discussed in the previous chapter, destinations are beginning to be and need to continue being much more proactive in setting norms about what behavior is acceptable on their territory and what is not. These norms will apply to travelers visiting the destinations but also to the tourism companies that operate within them. Service providers will be increasingly expected to consider the footprint of their business and to adjust operations in which they minimize the negative impacts on the local place and community while maximizing the positive.

Behavioral economics offers a wide variety of solutions that can help tourism companies make such adjustments on the basis of designs that realistically align with how people decide and consume. Some of the cases at the end of this book are inspiring illustrations for how this can work.

Finally as an industry tourism holds potential for bigger impact on society and alleviation of some of its contemporary ailments. The increasing dynamic and pressure that characterize the life of the contemporary person produce a lot of negative impacts on well-being. Falling happiness rates, growing cultural intolerance, deteriorating health, and disconnect from nature are among the main sources of the problems that accompany contemporary lifestyle. Travel has the power and tools to influence many of them in a positive way. Development in this direction would be in harmony with the contemporary thinking about *shared valu*e advanced by Michael Porter and his collaborators (Porter & Kramer, 2011) calling for rethinking of the intersection of society and business performance toward putting societal needs at the core of the strategic thinking of companies, not the periphery.

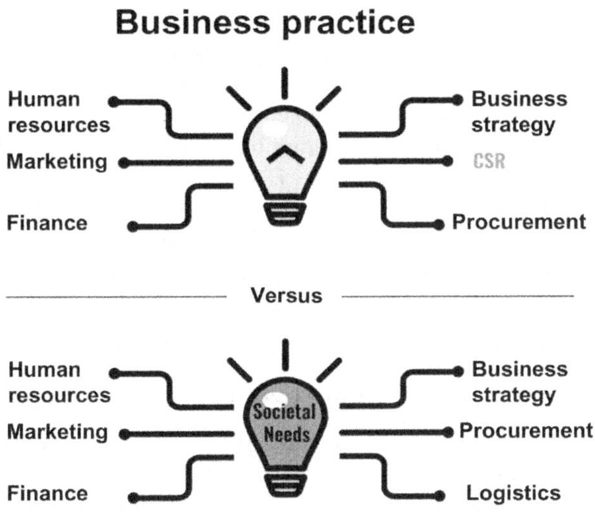

Travel as human right. . .or responsibility

Article 24 of the Universal Declaration of Human Rights states that "Everyone has the right to rest and leisure, including reasonable limitation of working hours and periodic holidays with pay." In the summer of 2010 international media widely covered the statement by Antonio Tajani, the then European Union commissioner for enterprise and industry, that the EU will treat vacationing as a human right and will design a program that guarantees holidays for the socially disadvantaged (Miller, 2010).

Framing holiday travel as a right aligns with the idea that societies and policies should aim to increase the overall well-being of societies, not only their material success. Vacationing impacts happiness (Nawijn, 2011) so guaranteeing it as a human right is a way to guarantee higher levels of well-being. Travel also produces other desired benefits for individuals and, respectively, societies such as higher level of cultural competence and tolerance (Stone & Petrick, 2013).

As discussed in earlier chapters of the text, travel comes at a cost for the visited destinations. For that reasons the right to go on holiday should be carefully measured against the negative impacts that tourism can have both on host communities and the environment (Eriksson, Noble, Pattullo, & Barnett, 2009). Framing travel as a human right leads to sense of entitlement and eliminates the need to be responsible to the places and hosts one visit. In that sense the promoted thinking about travel as a right combined with its increasingly low-cost (accelerated by the advance of low-cost airlines and price competition) pushes down the level of involvement with the experience and produces undesired behavior of disrespect and disengagement. If travelers perceive their visit to a destination as their right to be there, they feel entitled to behaving the way they want without regard for the local social norms and cultural specifics or potential damaging impacts that they may have on the place.

As discussed in the previous chapter destinations must be much more proactive in setting the behavioral norms that they are comfortable with and choosing the type of travelers to host. Local service providers and tourism businesses also have a responsibility in translating destination norms into principles guiding their operations and product designs. Since they are the ones who interact with the traveler, they have the power to ensure that travelers are aware of norms and adhere to them.

Aligning with the 21st century traveler

The two main factors that disrupt the buying behavior in the context of travel are the growing accessibility of mobile and wearable technologies along with the scarcity of time associated with contemporary living (Nikolova, Asenov, & Lazarova, 2015). Pressured by the lack of time and tempted by the ability to browse at any moment, today's traveler makes many more decisions on the go while their attention is split between different stimuli from the surrounding environment and pressures from other pending tasks. This activates a System 1 mode of decision-making, which is associated with avoiding lengthy rational analysis of options and choosing on the basis of quick shortcuts.

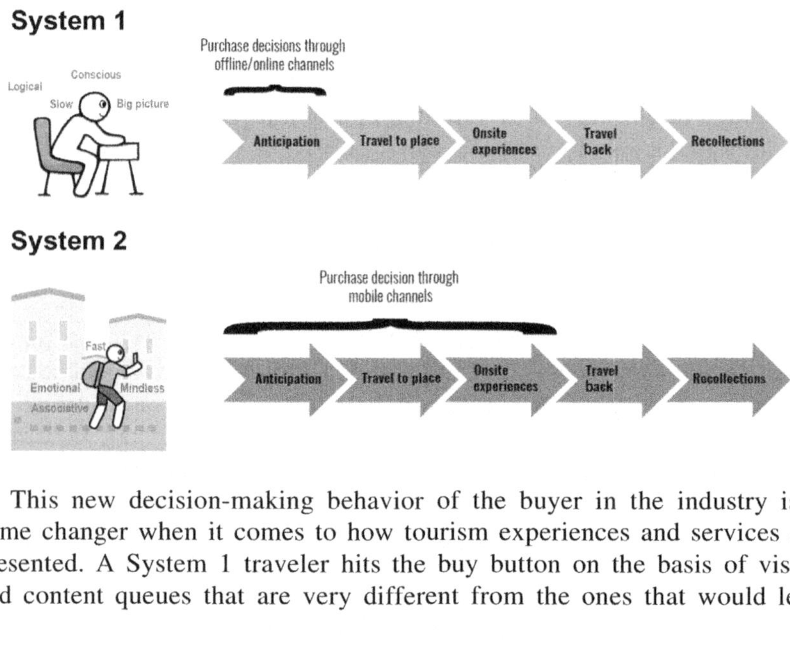

This new decision-making behavior of the buyer in the industry is a game changer when it comes to how tourism experiences and services are presented. A System 1 traveler hits the buy button on the basis of visual and content queues that are very different from the ones that would lead

System 2 to a buying decision. This new behavioral profile of today's traveler requires new communication and service design tactics. They need to be aligned with the shortcut-driven decision-making mode and the reality that the customer is less involved and less mindful. This means that how information is presented and organized, how messages and pricing information are framed, and how content is sequenced can have significant impact on the response of the consumer and the likelihood for engagement or purchase.

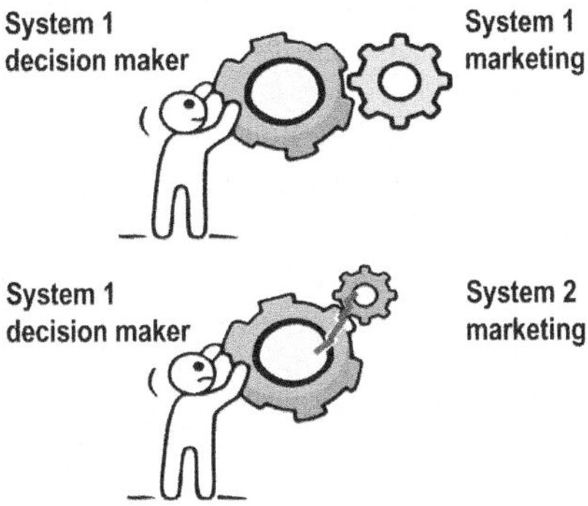

Facilitating choice making

One of the most relevant behavioral approaches to aligning with today's consumer is simplifying and facilitating choice. The constant information overload, the permanent need to choose and the availability of too many options screaming from different communication channels tempt decision makers to opt for *satisficing* (Simon, 1990), a decision-making strategy that relies on shortcuts rather than a *maximizing* decision-making strategy requiring analysis of all pros and cons. There are several ways in which tourism businesses or destinations can structure promotional and information content to align with the *satisficing* decision maker. A set of choice simplification tactics are proposed by Sheena Iengar, author of one of the most prominent books on consumer choice "The Art of Choosing." In her work she identifies four keys to making consumer choice easier: *simplifying choice* by limiting available options, *categorizing and organizing* choices in sets, *enabling easier imagination* and understanding of the offered choice, and *facilitating gradual movement through the decision-making journey* (Iyengar, 2010). This means several things. First, presenting the traveler with a smaller set of packages or activities rather than an overwhelming set of options increases the likelihood that they will purchase. A wider selection of options may engage them to browse longer but overwhelm them and ultimately make it easier for them to leave the decision open.

Given the complexity of the tourism offering, it is understandable that destinations, experience or service providers manage complex portfolios of offerings. This means that they cannot cut down choices to just a few to make it easier for the traveler. In such cases a relevant tactic is to organize available options in categories and choice sets that break the overall buying decision into smaller and simpler steps. For example, if a tour operator offers travel packages that involve active outdoors experiences across different regions around the world, their portfolio may well include twenty or thirty different programs. Instead of having the traveler browse through the entire list, the operator might organize them in a way that simplifies the process and moves the decision maker through a journey of making choices one by one from simpler to more complex ones. The first step might be asking the traveler to choose whether they want to explore a coastal area, urban area, or a mountainous region. Once that choice is made, they are presented with a small set of geographic options—Europe, Asia, or Latin American. After choosing the region, the traveler can be invited to select the types of outdoor activities they want: biking and/or hiking, kayaking, pedaling, etc. Applying choice architecture that relies on steps and choice sets simplifies the decision-making journey and exposes the decision maker to small sets within which choosing is fairly straightforward. This is a technique that is widely used in complex purchase situations, which are likely to unfold in online context, for example, buying a car.

Another tactic that facilitates decision-making and is especially relevant to the travel industry is concretization that makes it easier for the traveler to imagine and understand the offerings they are presented with (Iyengar, 2010). Given the intangible nature of the tourism product and the inability to test or taste the experience in advance, helping travelers to picture the destination or holiday activities, is essential. Relying on contemporary technology this means incorporating visuals and video content that makes it easy to envision oneself in the respective place. Using imagery with other travelers engaged in the promoted experience or in the respective place strengthens the sense of relevance.

Using categories

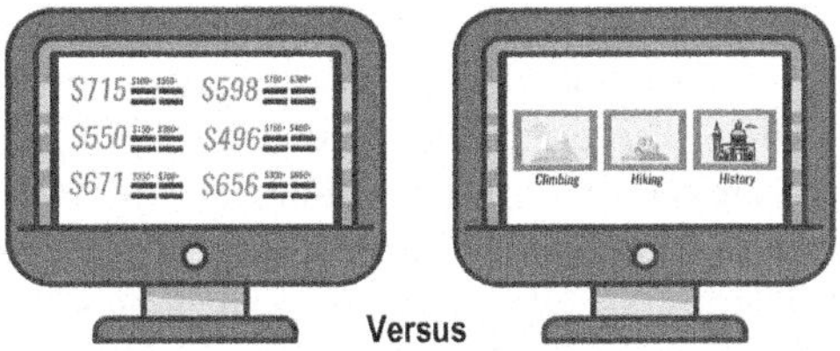

Organize your portfolio using natural (Easy to understand) categories. offer a small set of options within each category.

Make it easy to imagine

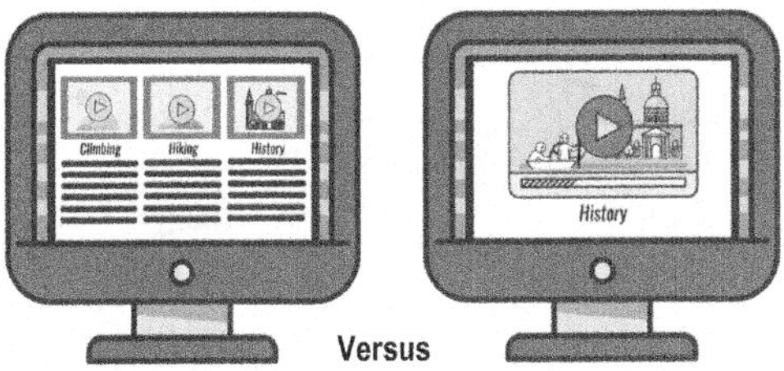

Incorporate videos. Use the similar characters in visuals.

Condition for complexity

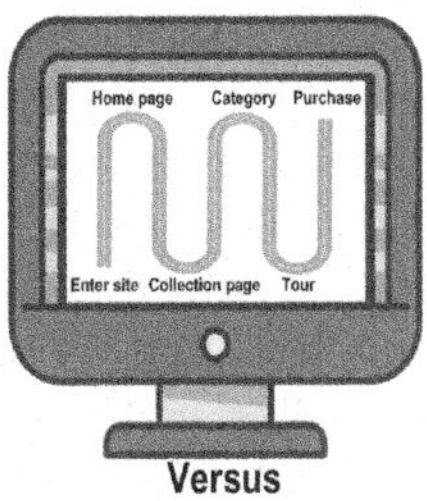

Facilitate gradual movement through the decision-making journey

Because of the intangible and complex nature of the tourism product, and the fact that it is to be consumed in the future, its purchase is considered as relatively high risk (Dholakia, 2001). This, combined with the increasing dynamic in which travelers make holiday choices, has given rise to tactics that stimulate a positive buying decision and nudge the buyer to complete the buying journey sooner rather than later. Among the more popular nudges that produce increased intention to purchase in the context of travel offers are *focus on the gain* (placing stronger emphasis on the benefits of the potential offer), *including a time-limited offer* (providing additional benefit that is available only for a short period of time), and *applying social conformity* (highlighting the option that is most preferred by other buyers) (Nikolova et al., 2015). These are also among the most widely used techniques by the leading digital platforms that dominate the industry today. Their application translates to design and formulations that influence the perception of the buyer by triggering specific psychological effects. Focus on the gain, for example, seeks to put stronger emphasis on the benefits of the presented offering to overcome loss aversion, which is the natural human tendency to pay more attention to potential losses rather than potential gains. The format of the promotional information and the framing used in the description of the experience should seek to draw attention to the benefits of the offering instead of its price that buyers treat as a loss (Carmon & Ariely, 2000).

Foucs on the gain

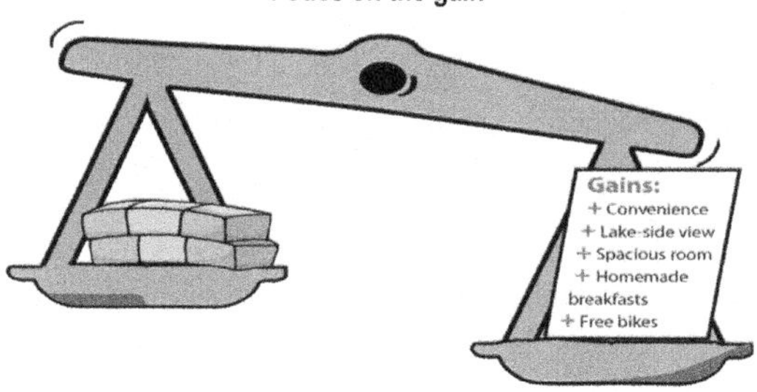

Including a time limitation within which the offer is available activates emotional decision drivers (Cialdini, 2007) and accelerates the purchase decision (Aggarwal &Vaidyanathan, 2003). In their most typical format time-limited offers present the buyer with an attractive additional incentive that is available to them only if they complete the buying journey within a certain period of time. This could include an attractive discount or free gift or an additional service included in the package for the same price. This is a widely used technique by a lot of the online platforms, including in travel, which apply it to overcome the challenge with incomplete purchase journeys.

Time limited offer

Applying a social conformity nudge to offers involves presenting information about the choices of others as a shortcut leading the targeted buyer to express preference for them as well. This might mean highlighting the option on offer that is selected by the majority of the buyers or informing the decision maker about the option that is most frequently purchased by members of the same segment (Cialdini & Goldstein, 2004). Social conformity effects limit the sense of risk and increase the likelihood for decision in cases when the buyer has limited information or is uncertain about the differences between the different options. Social conformity tactics are also regularly used in online purchase context and are popular among online travel mediators who offer experiences and packages that are difficult to compare. They are usually applied through formulations such as "our most popular package," "the most preferred option," or "our best-selling trip." More recently digital platforms seek to combine desired effects through statements that pop up while a buyer is exploring hotels, for example, informing them that a certain number of other buyers are also looking at the same option. Such information, presented in the specific moment, seeks to trigger social conformity effects by assuring the buyer that the option they are considering is popular among others as well. At the same time the statements also seeks to add time pressure by suggesting that the others who are looking might buy first and leave the buyer without the opportunity of doing so.

Social conformity

Another technique nudging buyers toward completing the buying journey by choosing a particular option is using offer design that triggers a *decoy effect*. This happens when an offer is based on two available options, option A and option B, but is redesigned to include a third option (option B-1), which is very similar to option B but is slightly inferior (Ariely, 2009). For example, option A might be a 3-day package for a rural farm holiday with breakfast, dinner and transportation while option B is a 3-day package for a mountain retreat with breakfast, dinner and transportation. Option B-1 also presents a 3-day mountain retreat with breakfast and dinner but without transportation. Even though option B-1 is essentially an irrelevant option that no buyer would select from this particular choice set, it influences how the two actual alternatives are perceived and dramatically shifts the choice balance in favor of Option B. Because the decoy option is similar to one of the main options but is inferior, it enhances the attractiveness of the similar main option and leads most buyers to selecting it (Simonson & Tversky, 1992).

Decoy effects

2 Options		3 Options (Decoy effect)		
3-Day mountain retreat	**3-Day rural family holiday**	**3-Day mountain retreat**	**3-Day mountain retreat**	**3-Day rural family holiday**
breakfast	*breakfast*	*breakfast*	*breakfast*	*breakfast*
dinner	*dinner*	*dinner*	*dinner*	*dinner*
transportation	*transportation*	*transportation*		*transportation*
51%	**49%**	**78%**	**0%**	**22%**

The several mechanisms presented here are just some of the possible choice architecture tactics that can facilitate the traveler decision-making process. Given socioeconomic dynamics and consumer behavior trends, buyers will continue to be more and more overwhelmed by time scarcity, too much information and too many choices. To align with these realities service providers and entrepreneurs need to realign the design of their promotional activities and content, and benefit from behavior-smart tactics that will make it easier for travelers to complete the decision-making journey.

Presenting price information

There is no doubt that price is an essential element of promotional content and a key factor determining purchase decision outcomes. Strategic thinking about pricing has evolved significantly from the early neoclassical economic models and today it is significantly influenced by behavioral thinking (Cheng & Monroe, 2013). In the context of a busy dynamic marketplace dominated by on-the-go decisions, seemingly simple changes in price information can have significant impact on the way price is perceived and the impact that that has on the purchase decision (Asenov, Lazarova, & Nikolova, 2016). Among the factors that can have profound impact on price perception are availability of price information, ease of understanding, price relativity, and order of presentation.

One of the most important behavior-smart principles for presenting price information is to make it easy to understand and easy to process. If price is not available or easy to find, this triggers a sense of suspicion and frustration (Romani, 2006) or leads the buyer to assume that the price tag might be too high for them (Lynch & Ariely, 2000). Especially if they are considering an alternative, the price of which is easily accessible, buyers are likely to walk away from options where price information is missing.

In addition to being accessible and visible, price information needs to be easy to understand. For example, many destinations and tourism service providers present their prices in their local currency instead of popular currencies that most travelers are used to. In reality, if the buyer is not familiar with the local currency, price information is meaningless to them. Moreover, the face value of the currency can trigger further negative effect: higher denomination currencies create the misleading sense that the price is too high and ultimately suppress readiness to buy (Lowe, Barnes, & Rugimbana, 2012). Therefore in travel context, it makes sense to present prices in currencies that are likely to be understood by travelers.

Price is an important signal that shapes expectations about quality, especially when it comes to intangible experiential products, such as a trip or a holiday (Zeithaml, 1988). However, price is meaningful as signal when it is compared with something else that puts it in perspective. Price relativity is especially important when it is impossible to estimate the value of the product or service of interest, and so comparing its price tag to that of a similar offering becomes the mechanism that leads to judgment (Ariely, 2017). In the context of tourism offerings are often very hard to compare to each other because of the great variability in the elements included in the experience, the destination characteristics, the season, the regulations, etc. A 1-day tour of local farmers markets in town A can cost 180 Euro because it includes a privately guided tour, a short educational lecture on local spices and herbs, private tasting of traditionally made local pastries and a bread-making demonstration at a traditional bakery. A 1-day tour of local markets in town B can cost only 45 Euro because it is self-guided, includes simple browsing through the local markets and only one visit at a traditional local pastry shop. Given the difficulty of figuring out the value of offerings in tourism and the natural inclination to compare value to other things, it makes sense to accompany price information with a carefully considered basis for comparison. For example, a half-day traditional culinary class in Tuscany can cost 90 Euro. The potential buyer considering this program might look at the price and compare it to 45-Euro farm tour experienced last year during a holiday in Spain, in which case the current offer might seem a bit high. On the other hand, the buyer might compare the price to the 95-Euro dinner at a London restaurant during a weekend getaway earlier this Spring, in which case the culinary tour appears as good value for money. Which of the comparison comes up in the consumer's mind is beyond the control of the seller but comparison-smart information provided along with price can influence the process. For example, the half-day traditional culinary class in Tuscany can be presented with the price tag of 90 Euro along with a description such as "for the price of one dinner at an average restaurant in London you will taste a selection of the most popular Tuscan meals and will learn how to prepare two of our most favorite recipes." By providing the basis for the comparison the seller can influence buyer perceptions and increase the relative sense of value for money.

Price relativity

One of the aspects that are not always considered is the sequence in which price and the description of the experience are presented. The reality is that whether buyers see first the price and then the product description or vice versa influences the decision-making process by shifting the focus toward the functional aspects or toward the pleasure-related aspects of the offer. This is because the first information to which the decision maker is exposed leads to the activation of different areas of the brain shaping the pattern leading to the final choice (Karmarkar, Shiv, & Knutson, 2015). In travel context this means that if a holiday offer is designed to start with a description of the trip emphasizing its experiential characteristics and is followed by the price at the end, decision-making is shaped by pleasure-related (hedonic) considerations; if the offer begins with the price at the top followed by the holiday description, decision-making will be driven by the functional characteristics (Asenov et al., 2016). This suggests that offers that are based on a functional cost-benefit advantage (Thaler, 1999) will benefit from a design that begins with the price tag and is followed by the description of the trip. On the other hand, offers that not seek to compete on price but on the experiential value that they offer, would be more effective if they start with a description of the trip and present price at the end.

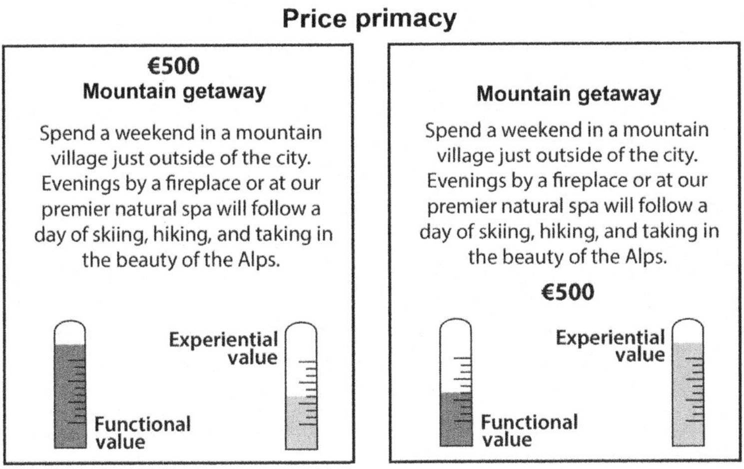

In the last decade pricing strategies have increasingly become influenced by psychology insights from behavioral sciences that explain how price format and presentation may lead to different perceptions, and lead to different decision-making outcomes. In addition to the tactics illustrated here, behavior-smart pricing can be aligned with the many known psychological mechanisms of factors such as whether the price ends with the number 99 versus round numbers (Kleinsasser & Wagner, 2011), the use of commas or dots in price information (Coulter, Choi, & Monroe, 2012), structuring price as an all-inclusive or partitioned price (showing base price, taxes, add-ons, fees, etc.) (Greenleaf, Johnson, Morwitz, & Shalev, 2016), presenting price in different color (Puccinelli, Chandrashekaran, Grewal, & Suri, 2013), order of presenting original versus discounted price during promotions (Biswas, Bhowmick, Guha, & Grewal, 2013), framing of bundle pricing (Bagchi & Davis, 2012), etc. The navigation of all known psychological effects associated with price information requires time and alignment with the specific decision-making specifics of different providers. In any case the leading principle in behaviorally informed pricing should be to ensure that price is as transparent and easy to process as possible because buyers are most likely to choose an option with a clear and easy to understand price even if it ends up being more expensive than the alternative with a more complicated price tag (Homburg, Totzek, & Krämer, 2014).

Experience—experiential design

There is no question that at the core of the product in leisure travel is the experience. Being a behavior-smart business means also being experience-smart, that is, designing and delivering offerings using the principles of experiential consumption.

Experiential consumption became focus of strategic thinking for many contemporary companies and organizations after in the late 1990s Joseph Pine and James Gilmore officially welcomed us to the experience economy (Pine & Gilmore, 1998). In their prominent book, *The Experience Economy*, Pine and Gilmore introduce the notion that consumers desire experiences while businesses respond by designing and promoting services and goods in ways that engage the customer, and create a memorable event (Pine & Gilmore, 1999). Experiential consumption involves the engagement of consumer senses, emotions and imagination in a way that creates meaning for them. An important characteristic of experience-smart business thinking is that it spans beyond the very instant of consumer–product interaction and includes the decision-making process at the preconsumption phase, as well as the reflection during the postconsumption phase (Carmon & Ariely, 2000).

For travel service providers, being experience-smart means several things. They can use the principles of experiential consumption to design itineraries or to plan the stay of their guests, they can apply an experiential lens when they evaluate the performance of their offerings, and they can take an experience-smart approach to planning investments for expanding or upgrading offerings.

Designing experiences

Designing travel offerings with the experience in mind means accounting for psychological factors and experiential benefits that accompany the experience of the traveler. The important starting point in this perspective is to recognize that the big difference between delivering a tourism service and facilitating an experience is in that the first is *presented to* the traveler while the second is *cocreated with* the participation of the traveler (Pine & Gilmore, 1999). Because experiences are cocreated with the consumer, they are highly individual and depend on personal specifics and the specifics of the given moment within the surrounding context. Therefore experience-smart service providers strive to create the best possible setting to *facilitate* a favorable experience. The setting is de facto an experiencescape where the experience is shaped by the physical characteristics of the environment, the other participants in the situation, and the quality of the service delivery (O'Dell, 2005).

For example, the traveler experience at a hotel includes the first impressions of the consumer when they reach the entrance and take a look at the building, feel the carpet they walk on when they make their first steps into the lobby, see the light and the décor in the common area, notice the selection of flowers or fruits at the reception desk and the lobby, feel the scents or smells, and hear the music or the noise. Even before they have entered the first interaction with a staff member at the hotel, travelers' senses have captured impressions that shape their first expectations toward their stay. The first encounter with the hotel staff, as well as the other hotel guests that are present in the common areas will influence this first episode of the hotel stay, which becomes an important element in the overall experience journey of the guest.

Senses

As mentioned earlier, experience-smart thinking means accounting for the preconsumption and the postconsumption episodes (Carmon & Ariely, 2000). In travel context this includes considering the pretrip planning phase and the posttrip reflection phase (Clawson & Knetsch, 2011) and understanding that they can have important impact on the overall experience and the formation of the final evaluation of the guest. For example, the moment of choosing the hotel and reviewing its website, or its page on the online booking platform trigger certain expectations and engage the imagination of the traveler who visualizes the trip and the hotel stay. Similarly upon return the traveler reflects on their trip and shares pictures, memories and impressions with friends and relatives, which influences the overall experience and more importantly, the evaluation of this experience that remains in the traveler's memories over time (Nikolova, 2009). This suggests that when travel service providers use techniques that shape or influence the experience of their guests, they need to start with the touch points at the time of the booking. Think about the experience that a new guest is likely to have when they first land on their website or their social media page, or when they call by phone to make an inquiry. The same applies to the postconsumption phase when a small souvenir or an exceptional photo can be the basis of a memory that the traveler shares with close ones. For example, a small provider of 1-day nature-based adventures can smartly identify interesting locations where the specific surroundings or the way the sunlight penetrates through the trees create an impressive backdrop for a photo. The exceptional nature of the picture would ensure that it makes it in the set of photos that are shared with friends in the posttrip phase and would significantly increase the word of mouth referrals that the small company will receive.

A behavior-smart approach to experiential thinking involves understanding that actually the most important experiential asset for a service provider is the memories that stay with the traveler rather than the experience itself. This is because the behavioral outcomes, that is, whether travelers will make a recommendation to friends or will return in the future, depend on what they remember about the experience rather than the experience itself (Kahneman, Wakker, & Sarin, 1997). What the traveler remembers retrospectively will not be an exact recollection of all events included in the original consumption experience but a "collage" of key instants from that experience, which the customer retrieves in the current moment. Given the discussed earlier individual nature of experiences, it is hard to make a precise forecast of how a traveler will remember a past trip and what episodes will make it into the collage of remembered moments but the most recognized factors that determine what is retrieved later are the peak-end rule, the trend of the experience and the meaning of the experience (Ariely, Kahneman, & Loewenstein, 2000). The peak-and-end rule suggests that the most influential moments that determine the remembered experience are the peak moment and the end moment in the string of episodes that form the entire experience. While the contribution of the final episode to the end evaluation of the experience can vary (Tully & Meyvis, 2016), especially in the context of complex experiences such as multiday trips, the weight of the peak moment is defining (Nikolova, 2009). This suggests that service providers have the opportunity to influence the value that the traveler will associate with a past trip by facilitating moments that can become powerful and memorable peak moments (see the following illustration).

What episodes represent a peak moment in a trip?

The peak moment is the moment in the entire travel experience when the intensity reaches highest levels. Peaks can be instants of being in a state of delight or the most intense moment of experiencing an unpleasant event like pain or loss. The following are the statements of travelers who were asked to describe the peak moments of a past trip to Mexico (Nikolova, 2009):

Positive peak moments:

- It was awesome to see the sun rise and set on the mountains. I loved it and cherished every moment of it.
- We visited an ecological park and saw native wildlife.
- We went fishing in a small panga boat and I caught a couple of small fish. It was exciting being in the middle of all that water in a tiny boat.
- Standing at the top of a pyramid at the Aztec ruins.
- Visiting the ruins of Tulum and looking over the cliffs to the sea.
- Enjoying the best authentic Mexican cuisine ever during my 2nd evening
- Swimming with dolphins along with our children and grandchildren.

(*Continued*)

(Continued)

- During our boat trip through the wetlands a pelican landed on the boat and we fed him with our hands.
- The peak moment of my travel experience to Mexico came after a long hike reaching the Aztec ruins that I saw for the first time in my life.
- Learning history in Acapulco from an experienced guide.
- Being able to walk around the city on the last day and soak in the atmosphere, eating authentic Mexican foods.
- I was horseback riding through the jungle.
- Negative Peak Moments:
- I had heart attack and had to be evacuated by air.
- We were involved in a traffic accident.
- Our money and belongings were stolen from the beach.
- We were survivors of a hurricane that unexpectedly hit the area during our holiday.
- We had a very poor experience at the hotel on the first day and this destroyed our entire stay.
- I became ill from eating something in a restaurant on the second evening and was not in good shape for the rest of the trip.

Peak Experiences

Another mechanism that impacts the favorability of remembered past experiences is the trend of the episode series. Research has shown that trend and sequence of events impacts the total evaluation producing the so called "preference for happy endings" (Ariely & Zauberman, 2003). For example, two series of three events—one positive, one negative, and one neutral—may lead to different retrospective evaluations depending on the sequence and the overall trend. To illustrate with a simple travel example, let us take a 1-day trip sequence, including bus ride to a local cultural attraction, the visit of the attraction and an afternoon rest at the nearby beach. Possible values are just positive [+], negative [−], and neutral [n]. In the first scenario, the traveler enjoys the bus ride because of the beautiful scenery along the way [+], finds the cultural attraction okay [n] and does not enjoy the rest at the beach [−] because it is too crowded [+ , n, −]. In the second scenario, the bus ride is bumpy and unpleasant [−], the cultural attraction visit is okay [n] but the afternoon rest at the beach is nice and relaxing [+] thus producing the following sequence: [−, n, +]. The two scenarios essential contain the same string of event values but in different sequences and with different trends. According to theoretical suggestions, despite the similarities, the second sequence will evoke more positive global evaluation because of the improving trend suggesting that in case of service failure in the earlier part of the travel experience, service providers still have a chance to make customers happy if they make an effort to gradually improve the rest of the stay. This positive trend effect can be illustrated as follows:

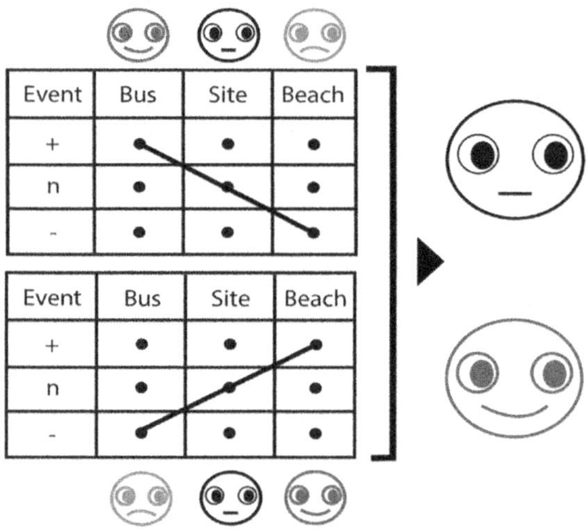

In addition to peak moment and the trend of the experience, the remembered experience is shaped by the meaning associated with the events. This means that a specific past holiday may be more clearly remembered than others because this was the trip during which a couple got engaged, or the one during which a family member had a biking accident (Ariely et al., 2000). Meaning relates to the very personal way in which an individual reflects on themselves within the world around them in a particular moment. Peak-and-end moments carry the "privileged status" in the memories of the traveler because they often carry more personal meaning than other moments (Fredrickson, 2000). For example, the dinner during the final evening of a week-long holiday of a family is likely more special as they will reflect on the past days and share thoughts about what they enjoyed least and most. This will make this final night more emotional and meaningful than previous dinners.

The advances of scientific research exploring the mechanisms of human memory in the last two decades have revealed that what people remember about past moments is influenced not only by meaning and the contextual factors at the moment of the experience but also by events that unfold after the experience has passed (Cowley, 2007). In travel context this means that a positive recall of a past trip or hotel stay triggered by an advertisement, a photograph or a story shared by a travel companion can impact the memory about the trip and increase its positive evaluation (Nikolova, 2009). For example, let us imagine that a traveler has enjoyed a pleasant holiday in Mexico several years ago and has evaluated their Mexico experience on a 7-point scale as 5.5. If they are exposed to an emotional advertisement promoting Mexico as travel destination that showcases some of the places that the traveler visited, the exciting experience of watching the video and remembering the highlights from the trip will bias their memory. As result, if asked to evaluate their experience after watching the promotional video, they are likely to give it a higher score, for example, 6 or even 6.5 (Nikolova & Hassan, 2013).

Evaluating experiences

Some of the discussed here principles that influence how people experience settings and events offer valuable insights that can help travel service providers influence the design of the experiencescapes (O'Dell, 2005) they create to facilitate desired experiences for their guests. Using knowledge about how human perceptions work, what are the ingredients that make moments meaningful and what factors trigger positive emotions can enable entrepreneurs in the travel industry to take experience design to another level and increase the value for both the traveler and themselves.

One approach that can be used to understand the experiential performance of spaces and activities is to use experiential measures for customer feedback. Academic literature offers many complex theory-grounded scales for measuring experiential value but some of the more streamlined ones can easily be transferred into practice and used as tools for identifying strengths and weaknesses in experiential performance. For example, a relatively simple approach is to evaluate experience episodes on all sense-based dimensions: touch, taste, smell, sight, and sound (Meacci & Liberatore, 2015) as described in the following illustration. This can be achieved with a simple paper or electronic form where guests can indicate how they evaluate their experience along each sense on a basic scale of 1–7 or 1–10.

Using a simple sense-basis scale to evaluate experiences

In a research piece presented at a conference on experiential tourism Luca Meacci and Giovanni Liberatore demonstrate the application of sense-based evaluation to a culinary experience. They suggest that measuring the

(Continued)

(Continued)

effectiveness of the experience according to each of the five senses allows the identification of weaker points that can be strengthened to increase engagement and the experiential value the traveler gains at the end. The specific experience that the authors use as illustration is a culinary experience where touch is associated with the feel of the dough that guests knead with their own hands, smell is associated with the smell of the cooking sauce, sound is linked to the stories shared by the chef during the activity, sight is linked to the setting of the authentic traditional kitchen and taste is associated with tasting the self-made tagliatelle at the end of the cooking class. The authors suggest that the average of all sense-based values produces the experiential value achieved by the activity.

Meacci and Liberatore (2015)

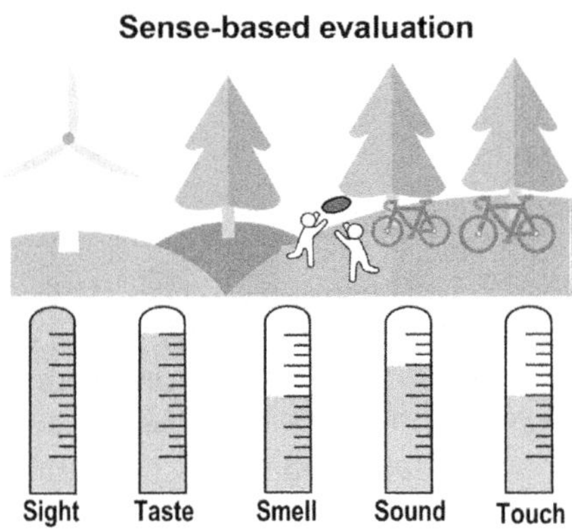

Another approach to evaluating experiences is applying the categorization of Pine and Gilmore (Pine & Gilmore, 1998) who suggest that experiences can be evaluated based on two dimensions: level of consumer involvement and level of immersion, and thus categorized as entertaining, educational, escapist and aesthetic. Entertaining experiences absorb the attention of the consumer but are more passive in terms of cocreation (e.g., watching a move, being at a concert, watching theater, and being at a classical group guided cultural tour). Educational experiences are engaging and involve the active participation of the consumer whose attention is absorbed in the learning process (taking a swimming lesson, learning to play a violin, and learning a new dance). Escapist experiences combine active participation with full immersion of the consumer (being an actor in play and kayaking on a stunning mountainous lake). Experiences that are immersive but involve little participation from the consumer are aesthetic (enjoying a piece of art in a museum and enjoying a beautiful landscape from a nature observation point).

A third approach to evaluating the experiential value of travel episodes or entire trips is to lean on the proposition of Kevin Voss and colleagues that there are five dimensions that form the total value of an experience: whether it is fun, exciting, delightful thrilling, and enjoyable (Voss, Spangenberg, & Grohmann, 2003). An evaluation of each of these dimensions produces a total evaluation of the overall experience.

Five dimensions of experiences

	1	2	3	4	5	6	7	
Not fun				4				Fun
Dull			3					Interesting
Not delightful							7	Delightful
Not thrilling	1							Thrilling
Not enjoyable						6		Enjoyable

Average experiential score
4.2

	1	2	3	4	5	6	7	
Not fun							7	Fun
Dull							7	Interesting
Not delightful						6		Delightful
Not thrilling						6		Thrilling
Not enjoyable							7	Enjoyable

Average experiential score
6.6

Investing in experiences

Experience-smart service providers would apply an experiential lens to investment decisions as well. This would involve investing in the physical elements that shape the setting or the tangible elements of the experiencescape, as well as in training, which strengthens the soft skills of experience facilitators such as guides or staff members that interact with the guest.

One of the aspects that can guide decisions about investment in physical setting relates to the perceptual signals that the setting sends to the guest. For example, if the owner of a small hotel has evaluated the experience of guests on the basis of the five-sense scale, they may have found out that guests were overall happy with their experience but that the insufficient light in the lobby made a poor first impression or that guests are satisfied with the cleanliness of the rooms but that the cleaning detergent leaves a strong scent that they find intrusive. Such findings can lead to practical investments such as installing additional lights or changing cleaning detergents that might not be large but can significantly impact the experiential value for the traveler.

The physical setting of accommodation, food and other hospitality service providers can have an impactful effect on the thematic context of the experience. Elements in the interior and exterior design can incorporate cues that enhance the setting and expected type of the experience. For example, the nature-based getaway experience would be nicely enhanced by a hotel décor that includes natural materials such as wood and stone, and walls that are decorated with stunning photos of nature. Similarly a wine tasting experience will be enhanced if the tasting areas are in an actual cellar or an area that is designed as one. Physical design of hospitality facilities can also be based on a story-based theme that enhances the experience of guests by stimulating the sense of entertainment, engaging the fantasy of guests, and increase the feeling of joy (Mossberg, 2008). This is especially relevant to areas, which are identified with particular historical events, legends, local stories, or specific traditions.

Experience-smart investments are even more important in intangible elements such as the skills and behavior of staff members. This relates to all members of the service providing teams that directly interact with guests but most importantly to the ones, such as guides, who have the power to facilitate an impactful immersive experience that can become a peak episode. As discussed earlier, experiences are highly individual but they can be facilitated to a high extent by the guide or interpreter who accompanies the guest. Through their behavior guides can ensure that guests are mindfully present in place and time, and are disconnected from their daily realities in ways that allows them to safely and effectively engage with the leisure experience (Carù & Cova, 2006). The type of information the guide provides, their communication style, their ability to facilitate social interactions and the quality of their interpretation stories can break or make an experience by preventing or facilitating immersion (Hansen & Mossberg, 2017). For example, let us imagine a guide picking up a small group for a half-day discovery walk through the traditional bazaars in an old town. If the guide is experience-savvy upon meeting the guests s/he will take time to provide them with some background on what they will see today preparing the group for the theme, and triggering curiosity and expectation. This introduction would include also safety information and specific instructions if higher risk is expected or safety equipment is needed at any time during the tour. During the experience the guide would use storytelling to interpret what the group will see at the bazaars. These stories can reveal interesting facts about local farming traditions or ways in which local fruits and vegetables are weaved in culinary practices; or they can demonstrate how local spices are produced and used in typical local meals, etc. In addition to using interpretative stories experience-smart guides facilitate social interaction within the group even when the guests do not know each other from before. In that sense, a guide able to transform a tour into an immersive experience that produces peak episodes needs to combine three levels of skills: safety management and instruction (when guests need to be instructed about how to behave or how to use a piece of equipment such as a kayak or bike for example), ability to facilitate the mindful engagement of guests and encourage social interaction among them, and ability to transform knowledge into stories and performative acts (Hansen & Mossberg, 2017). Even though these skills seem to be most needed and expected for guides or group leaders, it makes sense to invest in training along them for all team members who interact with guests. For example, front desk staff members at a nature-based resort can welcome guests in ways that invites them into the theme of being out in nature by giving them some information about how they can enjoy the natural surroundings and offering safety information. Other members of the hotel staff, such as host and servers at the restaurant or managers of the bike renting office can complement the thematic experience by sharing stories or more interesting information about the natural surroundings. This way the entire team of the hotel turns into a group of storytellers who paint the theme and create a story in which the guest is a coauthor and participant.

New norms of doing business

As discussed in a previous chapter the global tourism system has reached a point of failure requiring redesign of many of its elements and adjustment of the principles of operation of different industry stakeholders. The dramatic processes unfolding in many destinations struggling with overtourism or sustainability crises demonstrate the dire consequences of ignoring the balance of visible and invisible impacts produced by tourism (Epler Wood, Milstein, & Ahamed-Broadhurst, 2019). As discussed in earlier chapters this reality calls for new norms of behavior not only by travelers but by destinations and service providers.

In line with the shared value theory advanced by Michael Porter and Mark Kramer (Porter & Kramer, 2011) tourism enterprises need to align their business models and principles of operations to a positive cycle harmonizing company with local destination and community prosperity. This transition to shared value as a regular business norm in tourism would mean treating sustainability as nonnegotiable business principle that opens new opportunities for creating value rather than impeding market success. It would also mean that the design of products, services, and operational processes will incorporate responsibility as an inseparable element.

Nonnegotiable sustainability as business principle

There is no question that traveler behavior needs to be influenced to see significant lowering of the harmful impacts generated by tourism in many places. The widely accepted approach is that what is needed is education – raising the awareness of travelers about sustainability issues, informing them about the right thing to do, educating them about the importance of their actions, etc. While educating the traveler is a noble mission worth support, it cannot be a solution that will reach all 1.5 billion international tourists crossing the world today.

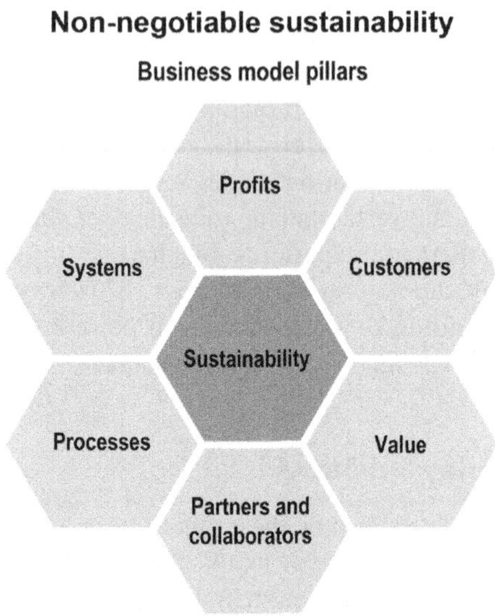

The behavior-smart approach to making sustainability nonnegotiable and putting it at the core of the business model can be translated to making sustainability performance a key measure of success for the business and for its employees (see case on Virgin Atlantic at the end of the book). It should also trigger adjustment of the design of products and services to eliminate nonsustainable options or at the very least to make the sustainable option the default.

One of the great challenges with moving to sustainable operations is that often entrepreneurs firmly believe that this is the right way of doing business but they do not know how to do it and where to start. This is at the core the intention–action gap leading many stakeholders to find it hard to undertake steps toward sustainability. The appeal of continuing to operate the same way as now rather than switching to a different way of doing business, also known as status quo bias, is another barrier for entrepreneurs. One solution to these behavioral obstacles is sustainability certification systems. Even though most of these have been originally created to benefit the customer by signaling that an operator adheres to certain standards, they are increasingly being used by businesses to operationalize sustainability through the specific steps and benchmarks that the programs involve. Examples for such established certification systems are the ones that help companies align operations to the Global Sustainable Tourism Criteria (such as Control Union, Travelife, and Vireo Srl) and to sustainability principles in general (such as B Corp) by offering an extensive processes of responding to long lists of criteria. Their great advantage is that they provide a clear framework that breaks down the big concept of sustainability into understandable steps and address the "where to start?" problem. The challenge, especially for smaller businesses, is that the completion of the certification process takes time and resources, leading many to postpone the initiation of the steps even if they are convinced in its value and importance.

Sustainability-driven design

Most contemporary car companies take safety very seriously and incorporate numerous features that discourage or prevent the driver from engaging in risky behavior. These include a wide range of solutions from active sound and light signals that alert the driver about risks on the road to automated breaks that kick-in when the person behind the wheel fails to react. These contemporary car safety solutions seek to cover more and more instances when behavioral failures, such as distraction or poor judgment, lead to undesired consequences like injuries or loss of life.

Just like the safety features of new car models nudge drivers to stay within the street lane, maintain appropriate distance, stop the car if calculations suggest risk of accidents, etc. travel service providers can incorporate in the design of services and products nudges that minimize the risk of sustainable behavior failures. This includes eliminating unsustainable options wherever that is possible, making sustainable options the default options, using design tools, and soft approaches that encourage desired behavior.

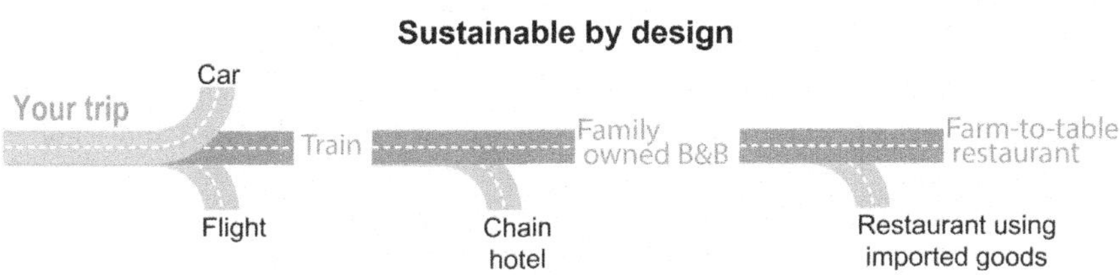

While the classical libertarian paternalism at the core of behavioral economics assumes that decision architecture should steer people's choices toward the most beneficial option without eliminating freedom of choice (Sunstein & Thaler, 2003), some of the choices that are currently left to the traveler produce risks that in the long run are unacceptable for society and especially for the host destination. Therefore the design of behavior-smart services and products in travel may have to include elimination of options based on the need to avoid choices and costs violating sustainability principles. The options that travel service providers can eliminate can vary greatly in scope and ambition. The elimination can be executed by adjusting product or service design in a way that adds value. For example, a tour company can eliminate the option of buying water or another drink in a single use plastic bottle by asking travelers to bring reusable bottles in advance or by gifting a reusable bottle at the start of the tour. A hotel or a restaurant can eliminate the option of not eating locally by not offering meals, which need imported ingredients and by changing its menu based on seasonal availability of local products. If the menu describes meals in an appealing way emphasizing the local flavors, what might originally seem as limitation will be turned into source of value.

Another powerful behavioral approach that can produce significant impact in the footprint of tourism businesses is the use of defaults. Even if service providers decide to leave their customers with the freedom to choose between more sustainable and less sustainable options, the sustainable options should be the default. One of the simplest examples of how this should work in the travel industry is towel changing at hotels. Currently the most common practice is to display a sign requesting that the hotel guest reuses their towel because the default is that the towel is changed every day. In essence this design leaves the choice between the responsible option and the less responsible option to the guest. If the guest cares to be responsible, they have to proactively make an effort to pursue the more sustainable option, that is, hang their towels in a specific way to not have them changed. In reality, guests are not stewards of the destination so leaving them, rather than the hosts, with the power to decide whether to behave responsibly or not, is not optimal. In most cases travelers are at the destination for a short period of time that does not allow them to connect with it in ways that can shape their behavior and choices. It is also known that while on holiday, people release many behavioral controls that would otherwise guide their actions in regular day-to-day realities (Miller, Rathouse, Scarles, Holmes, & Tribe, 2010). That combines with the fact that most often people actually do not care much about their towels so they do not make the effort to make a proactive choice and simply go with the default option without thinking about it. In that sense, the more appropriate design would be to switch the default option to not changing towels every day so if guests do not do anything, their towels will be left for reuse. If, however, travelers really need or want a change, they need to make the effort to choose the nondefault option and request change of towels. While this sounds like a simplistic example, it is a brilliant illustration of the power of behavior-smart solutions in the context of travel. If all accommodation providers in a region or country destination adopt a simple switch to this towel-changing default, the cumulative environmental impact linked to the lower use of chemicals, optimized water, and electricity consumption can be quite significant. It can be even bigger if a similar default switch is applied to room cleaning. In the Nordics many hotel companies have introduced the option for a room cleaning opt-out as an environmental measure. Its impact can be even more powerful if not cleaning rooms every day is the default option and guests need to proactively request the service if they really want it daily. Such default-based design modifications, especially when applied by a critical share of the travel service providers within a destination, can be very impactful in optimizing the footprint of the local industry. They are also very powerful in terms of changing social norms within the industry ecosystem and sending a clear signal to travelers about the norms of behavior expected from them. In summary, the footprint of service providers can be significantly strengthened if they use designs that minimize the effort required by the traveler to act responsibly, rewards or incentivize desired behavior and refer to social norms (Villarino & Font, 2014).

Soft behavior-smart approaches such as providing the right type of information in the precise context to make an issue or norm salient can also be quite effective. In many cases travelers are simply unaware of local sustainability issues and needs so they do not consider them when making consumption decisions. Making travelers aware has two aspects. The first is providing the information about a problem that requires limitation or specific behavior such as water shortage, problematic energy supply, lack of recycling facilities, etc. The second is locating the message in place and time so that it reaches the guest in the most relevant moment when they are likely to be engaging in the behavior of interest. For example, if the traveler needs to be made aware that the local community suffers from water shortage and that guests are asked to avoid water waste, this message should appear, respectively, in the bathrooms and washing facilities of accommodation and food service facilities. Hotels and resorts that take proactive steps toward lowering food waste inform guests and give them tips by placing signs at the breakfast buffet. This ensures that guests are made aware of the problem at a moment when they can actually do something about it.

Providing information

An optimal approach to putting sustainability at the core of operations is to weave it in the design of facilities, products and services. Energy-saving and water-saving solutions such as automatic electricity switches and faucets in facility design are nothing new. They essentially eliminate the need for the guest to decide how to consume water and energy by automating the process. More advanced solutions build on this principle and include nudges when automation is not possible. This includes the installation of visible meters near showers that show water consumption and as result can lead users to consume over 20% less water (Tasic et al., 2012). Another more sophisticated solution is the installation of shower heads that use light signals to indicate when the user reaches water consumption milestones (every 10 L) and that turn red when the water consumption passes the volume used by the average shower taker. Experiments with such smart shower heads reveal that they can easily produce water savings of more than 20% (Burkel, 2019).

Similar principle can be used in product and service design. There is an increasing number of examples in the travel industry of how this can work. For example, the itinerary for a nature-based tour might include the planting of a tree that supports a local reforestation program or a plogging experience (see the following illustration) that combines being active in nature with collecting litter. If multiple activity providers in a destination include such components in the design of offered experiences, then the cumulative impact that will be generated will be significant, especially if there is coordination and all activities address a specific locally important issue.

The birth of plogging

Plogging is a new form of leisure activity that combines jogging with trash collection. The idea was initiated in 2016 by Erik Ahlström who moved to Stockholm after living in a remote natural area in Northern Sweden. Ahlström was shocked at the amount of trash that could be seen in natural areas and came up with a solution that offered the wellness benefits of being active with the environmental benefits of extracting litter from nature. The sense of doing good and the gamification element of hunting and collecting pieces of trash has fueled the popularity of plogging, and today there are plogging clubs and regular plogging events in many countries around the world.

Over many years, just like with destinations, tourism businesses have adhered to segmentation-based thinking in their attitude toward sustainability excusing themselves from much effort with the belief that responsible consumption is something demanded by a small segment of traveler that is not their target. The current state of the industry suggests that this approach has produced a failure requiring fundamental change. A much more logical approach is the product development approach, which weaves sustainability principles in the design and marketing of travel products and services. This is the path that can ultimately mainstream sustainability (Font & Mccabe, 2017) and ensure that every service provider in the sector accepts it as a non-negotiable principle.

Reverse responsibility

Today, in the context of the climate crisis and excessive growth in tourism, much focus is placed on the responsibility of travelers in managing their footprint. As argued earlier in this chapter, service providers and entrepreneurs working in tourism should be proactive as well and apply behaviorally informed solutions to accelerate the shift toward the desired traveler behavior. But the travel industry has the potential to do good at a scale that is well beyond its limits. It can make an impact that goes beyond its own sustainability and addresses some of the biggest challenges that contemporary societies face. Among the areas in which the tourism sector can give back are happiness and well-being, restoration of the human–nature relationship, cross-cultural tolerance, and understanding.

Travel as a happiness industry

Among the biggest challenges of today's contemporary societies are the low level of happiness, triggered mainly by poor work-life balance, troubling interpersonal relationships, and extraordinary levels of stress (Helliwell, Layard, & Sachs, 2019). Contemporary lifestyle is most often associated with fast-paced professional dynamics that consume most of the energy and time of people. Ambition, financial needs, and social expectations add weight to the importance of work in daily life motivating people to sacrifice personal and family time, as well as time for relaxation and well-being. In many otherwise progressive societies, taking time for a proper long holiday or taking time off to spend more time with family are considered as behaviors that are inconsistent with real career ambitions. Contemporary social norms often add to the sense of pressure preventing people to pursue work-life balance even when they feel the need to.

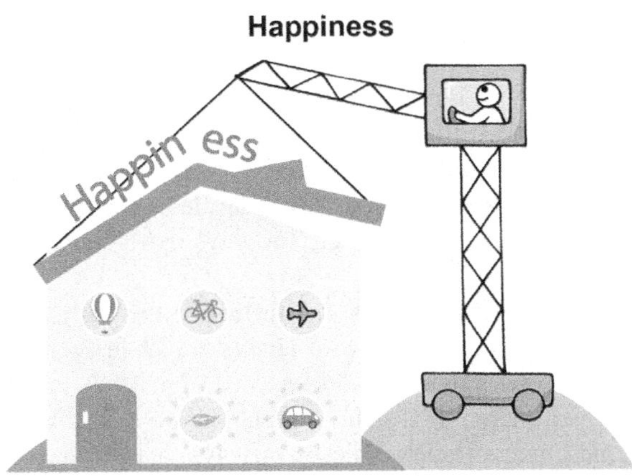

Somewhat associated with work-life balance and fueled by lifestyle trends is the fact that significant shares of people in contemporary societies experience unsatisfying interpersonal relationship. This may include poor family relationships between generations, the two parents, or between parents and children.

While the ultimate solutions to some of these contemporary challenges will most likely take time and require a combination of approaches, the travel industry holds powers to make a contribution to the battle against them. Companies operating in the industry have the opportunity to mindfully strengthen the happiness effects of traveling when designing their products and services, and when delivering their offerings. They can do that by ensuring that guests are mindfully present and engaged with the destination, that they are less dependent on technology and that the design of the experience prioritizes happiness effects.

Travel is linked to well-being in multiple ways—from enjoying an opportunity to relax and feel pleasure to enjoying an experience that enriches the self through learning or transformative activities such as pilgrimage (Kay Smith & Diekmann, 2017). Tourism experiences affect the overall sense for quality of life so more frequent and longer vacations make people more likely to describe themselves as happy and content with life overall as well as its dimensions such as leisure life, social dynamics, family and marital relationships, work, spiritual well-being, and others (Uysal, Sirgy, Woo, & Kim, 2016). However, all of this is true only when the traveler is mindfully present at the destination and really experiences the trip in ways that disconnect them from daily realities. Even though contemporary lifestyle has made the boundaries between travel and daily realms less distinct, the ability to disconnect and mindfully experience the trip is essential for restorative effects. One of the key factors influencing this dynamic is technology. As discussed in earlier chapters technology has transformed the way tourism works and has disrupted behavioral patterns in both supply and demand. While many of the impacts of technology are positive, there are many that are less desired, including the fact that mobile and wearable devices have increased distraction and alienation preventing the traveler from engaging with the experiencescape. John Tribe and Mucha Mkono coin the term *e-lienation* to describe the cumulative negative effects that technology can have on the traveler experience. These include deviation from social norms, self-estrangement, isolation, anxiety, etc. in ways that block the benefits of a leisure trip (Tribe & Mkono, 2017).

Behavior-smart service providers can influence the ability of travelers to extract stronger well-being effects from leisure travel in two ways. The first is to incorporate product, service, and space designs that increase mindfulness and maximize happiness. This might involve applying experience design tactics that engage traveler senses in ways that elevate their emotions and trigger their imagination. For example, an itinerary for a 1-day urban adventure can include walking through a charming small street or passing by lush city gardens specifically to ensure that travelers experience and enjoy the area through all of their senses (see cases at the end of this book).

Design solutions can also limit activities that have damaging impact on the experience such as distraction with wearable technology. The demand for rejuvenating holidays has fueled the growth of a specialized segment of digital detox offerings. While this specialized niche will most likely continue to grow but still remain highly specialized, mainstream operators can borrow from it elements that help design engaging and restorative environments that are digital-free. For example, resorts areas can set up technology-free spaces or limit the use of technology in certain areas; travel itineraries can include activities that by design require that travelers use their human senses to interact with the surroundings instead of technology.

The second approach to influencing the ability of travelers to extract stronger well-being effects from travel experiences is to make targeted effort to ensure their mindful presence and deeper engagement during their holiday. A big role here falls on guides and group leaders, or other service providers who facilitate the traveler experience. To be successful they need a combination of storytelling, social, and educator skills that enable experience cocreation and deeper involvement in the present moment and place (Hansen & Mossberg, 2017). This highlights the importance of targeted capacity building to ensure that service providers have the knowledge and skills that allow them to facilitate deeper immersion and stronger well-being effects during travel activities.

Travel has the power to make people happy. If more travel service providers take on this as a mission, the tourism industry can become a force for bettering the state of human well-being. Through behavior-smart designs and solutions service providers can put happiness at the core of the experience they present, and fulfill a big responsibility to our contemporary societies.

Back to nature

Another area in which travel service providers can give back to society is the human–nature relationship. Contemporary living has disconnected people from nature. The average living space in today's urban area is far from natural landscapes; lifestyle dynamics tend to limit interaction with nature in many ways. Even though in recent years many contemporary cities are looking to move to the development of public spaces and buildings designed with natural green elements, there is a long way to go before the everyday living environment restores the human–nature relationship.

Travel experiences can address this so the tourism industry has a responsibility to give back by proactively facilitating a back-to-nature culture among more traveling audiences, not just the specialized segments pursuing outdoor holidays. This is important for two reasons. The first relates to the earlier discussion about physical and psychological well-being. Nature has strong rejuvenation and restorative effects, and the lack of green space in everyday environment is linked to some of the most destructive phenomena accompanying contemporary living, such as psychological disorders and poor physical health (Tost, Champagne, & Meyer-Lindenberg, 2015). In this context travel is an opportunity to close the gap between nature and everyday living by weaving in more mindful interactions with nature across all holiday forms. This is possible if natural environment is emphasized as element of the traveler experience even when it is not a primary motivator. For example, the transportation from one point to another can be made more exciting and experiential if travelers are engaged in mindful appreciation of the natural landscapes along the road rather than killing time by looking at their phones or newspaper. With some interpretation and information about surrounding nature, it can suddenly become a more prominent element in an otherwise low-value episode of an itinerary. Nature-smart service providers can also make targeted effort to include more activities that offer interaction with nature. Even a classical sun and sea holiday can be enhanced with an activity that offers interaction with marine environment in ways that emphasizes the beauty of coastal landscapes and richness of marine biodiversity.

The second reason why it is important for the travel industry to facilitate a back-to-nature culture among more traveling audiences relates to the sustainability and climate crisis that humanity is facing. The disconnect from nature has produced ignorance about how nature works and how it can be impacted by harmful activities. In many ways people act in environmentally unfriendly ways not because of evil intentions but because they are unaware about the negative impacts of their choices. Less contact with nature leads to less appreciation and lower interest in preservation too (Lee, 2011). This is why travel entrepreneurs and service providers can help transform popular attitudes and behavior toward the environment by facilitating back-to-nature processes. This can be achieved by increasing the activities involving interaction with nature across holidays and itineraries. For operators that already offer nature-based activities such as hiking, biking, or kayaking, this may mean making an even bigger emphasis on natural environment in their experiences by adding interpretative information that educates tourists about ecosystems and biodiversity, and ensures that they appreciate them more mindfully. For service providers who have no interaction with nature there is always the opportunity to add something small that exposes guests to the local natural wealth. For example, classical sun-and-sand or winter resorts only have to offer some well-presented information about the surrounding nature or offer some exciting add-on activities that motivate guests to appreciate the sun-and-sand or the winter landscapes in a different way. Incorporating interaction with nature should be possible even for classical urban hotels whose focus is on serving business or city break travelers. Tactics for such facilities can include presenting guests with recommendations for a walk to the nearby park with some interesting information about bird species that can be spotted or for a half-day trip to the outskirts of the city to enjoy a beautiful lake or a well-preserved forest. If more and more service providers accept the reverse responsibility to always make nature an element in any kind of offering, the cumulative impact on human–nature interaction will be massive. The scale of such an initiative can be especially large if it is picked up by some of the digital platforms that have the biggest reach on today's tourism market. What if every booking of accommodation or experience automatically comes with two interesting facts about local nature and some propositions for exciting ways to discover it?

A discussion in Chapter 3, Tourism of the (Near) Future: Growing, Faster, On-The-Go, highlighted an image problem of the tourism industry. Despite its complexities and linkages to many other key global sectors, it is not taken as seriously as other industries by many (Becker, 2013). Maybe because of that, even entrepreneurs and business decision makers in the sector are not as serious and bold in their thinking about the impact that they can have. The heat around overtourism, the climate crisis and other sustainability threats, has definitely began changing the general awareness and sense of responsibility of businesses in the sector. At this time, however, these concerns are mostly limited to the impacts related to tourism itself—the need to sustain attractions and assets so they can last longer, the need to leave higher share of profits in the local economy, the importance of sourcing local food, etc. It would be great if in the near future more entrepreneurs in tourism start thinking beyond the limits of the sector and find inspiration to contribute to the solving of some global societal problems that can make the world a better place to live for all.

Conclusion

Insights from behavioral sciences have begun penetrating knowledge in many socioeconomic domains shaping strategic thinking and solution design. Entrepreneurs and business leaders in the travel industry can benefit greatly from that trend both in optimizing the success of their commercial operations and the effectiveness of their footprint management. A behavior-smart travel company is a company that applies insights about human behavior as a perspective it applies to both strategy and operations. It uses behavioral thinking in designing its products and services, in pricing and promoting them, as well as in their delivery. It also uses behavioral techniques to manage its operations and employees.

Behaviorally optimized business thinking inevitably translates into better commercial performance because it aligns the design of supply solutions with actual demand dynamics. Being realistic about the context in which targeted consumers are likely to make choices allows for smart placement of promotional content. Understanding the actual decision journey that leads buyers to a purchase makes it possible to craft effective messages and pricing information. The key to unlocking the power of the traveler experience, which is at the core of the tourism offering, is in understanding how to attract one's attention, engage their imagination, provoke emotions, and create memories. In essence, a behaviorally optimized travel service provider is one that is commercially more successful.

Behavioral tools are powerful in helping businesses react to today's realities in the travel industry by improving the footprint of their operations and contributing to the sustainability of the destinations where they operate. Today's global tourism marketplace is already seeing success stories of companies whose business models are built on the premise that sustainability is nonnegotiable (see cases at the end of the book for example). Hopefully these will be multiplying in the future by benefitting from behavior-smart thinking. The majority of the service providers, however, need to make adjustments that optimize their sustainability profiles given their existing models and existing physical assets. While the reinvention of models and replacement of assets is needed, it will require time and significant investments. Behaviorally informed tactics can help produce results now through soft measures that align business processes with realistic assumptions about the way people think and act.

The essence of being a behavior-smart company is to put the human being at the center of the business—the traveler, the entrepreneur, the employee. A human-centered lens can help tourism entrepreneurs see beyond the needs of their own sector and benefit from the opportunity to show responsibility to society at large by addressing some of its most complex challenges. In that sense, behavior-smart sustainability for tourism companies would mean placing the human being at the center of business thinking and balancing the three aspects of sustainability, natural environment, sociocultural environmental, and economics, with human well-being.

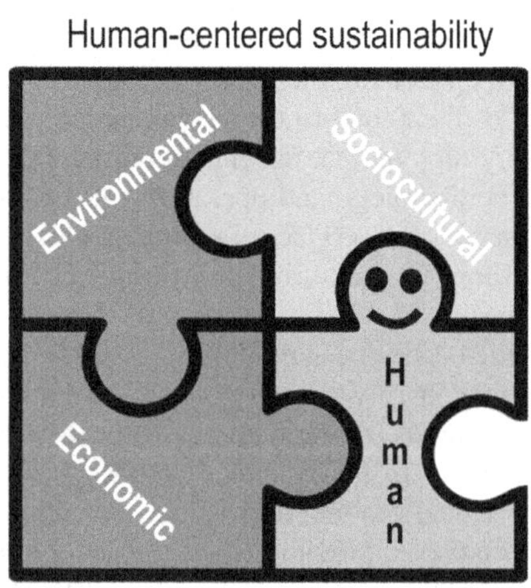

References

Aggarwal, P., & Vaidyanathan, R. (2003). Use it or lose it: Purchase acceleration effects of time-limited promotions. *Journal of Consumer Behaviour, 2*(4), 393–403. Available from https://doi.org/10.1002/cb.116.

Ariely, D. (2009). *Predictably irrational, revised and expanded edition: The hidden forces that shape our decisions*. London: HarperCollins Publishers.

Ariely, D. (2017). *Dollars and sense: How we misthink money and how to spend smarter*. HarperCollins.

Ariely, D., Kahneman, D., & Loewenstein, G. (2000). Joint comment on "When does duration matter in judgment and decision making?" (Ariely & Loewenstein, 2000). *Journal of Experimental Psychology: General, 129*(4), 524–529. Available from https://doi.org/10.1037/0096-3445.129.4.524.

Ariely, D., & Zauberman, G. (2003). Differential partitioning of extended experiences. *Organizational Behavior and Human Decision Processes, 91*(2), 128–139. Available from https://doi.org/10.1016/S0749-5978(03)00061-X.

Asenov, J. H., Lazarova, J., & Nikolova, M. S. (2016). *Focusing on the consumer value: Price and product presentation effects on online consumers' perceptions and decision making. 2016 winter marketing academic conference*. Las Vegas, NV: American Marketing Association.

Bagchi, R., & Davis, D. F. (2012). $29 for 70 items or 70 items for $29? How presentation order affects package perceptions. *Journal of Consumer Research, 39*(1), 62–73. Available from https://doi.org/10.1086/661893.

Becker, E. (2013). *Overbooked: The exploding business of travel and tourism*. New York: Simon & Schuster.

Biswas, A., Bhowmick, S., Guha, A., & Grewal, D. (2013). Consumer evaluations of sale prices: Role of the subtraction principle. *Journal of Marketing, 77*(4), 49–66. Available from https://doi.org/10.1509/jm.12.0052.

Burkel, E. (2019). *Hydrao shower heads* (personal communication).

Carmon, Z., & Ariely, D. (2000). Focusing on the forgone: How value can appear so different to buyers and sellers. *Journal of Consumer Research, 27*(December), 360–370. Retrieved from www.insead.fr/facultyresearch/marketing/.

Carù, A., & Cova, B. (2006). How to facilitate immersion in a consumption experience: Appropriation operations and service elements. *Journal of Consumer Behaviour, 5*(1), 4–14. Available from https://doi.org/10.1002/cb.30.

Cheng, L. L., & Monroe, K. B. (2013). An appraisal of behavioral price research (part 1): Price as a physical stimulus. *AMS Review, 3*(3), 103–129. Available from https://doi.org/10.1007/s13162-013-0041-1.

Cialdini, R. B. (2007). *Influence: The psychology of persuasion*. New York: Collins.

Cialdini, R. B., & Goldstein, N. J. (2004). Social influence: Compliance and conformity. *Annual Review of Psychology, 55*, 591–621. Available from https://doi.org/10.1146/annurev.psych.55.090902.142015.

Clawson, M., & Knetsch, J. L. (2011). Economics of outdoor recreation. In *Economics of outdoor recreation* (2nd ed.). Available from: https://doi.org/10.4324/9781315064215.

Coulter, K. S., Choi, P., & Monroe, K. B. (2012). Comma N' cents in pricing: The effects of auditory representation encoding on price magnitude perceptions. *Journal of Consumer Psychology, 22*(3), 395–407. Available from https://doi.org/10.1016/j.jcps.2011.11.005.

Cowley, E. (2007). How enjoyable was it? Remembering an affective reaction to a previous consumption experience. *Journal of Consumer Research, 34*(4), 494–505. Available from https://doi.org/10.1086/520072.

Dholakia, U. M. (2001). A motivational process model of product involvement and consumer risk perception. *European Journal of Marketing, 35*(11/12), 1340–1362. Available from https://doi.org/10.1108/eum0000000006479.

Epler Wood, M., Milstein, M., & Ahamed-Broadhurst, K. (2019). *Destinations at risk: The invisible burden of tourism*. Retrieved from www.thetravelfoundation.org.uk

Eriksson, J., Noble, R., Pattullo, P., & Barnett, T. (2009). *Putting tourism to rights: A challenge to human rights abuses in the tourism industry*. A report by Tourism Concern Written and researched by. Retrieved from www.lithosphere.co.uk.

Font, X., & Mccabe, S. (2017). Sustainability and marketing in tourism: Its contexts, paradoxes, approaches, challenges and potential. *Journal of Sustainable Tourism, 25*(7), 869–883. Available from https://doi.org/10.1080/09669582.2017.1301721org/10.1080/09669582.2017.1301721.

Fredrickson, B. L. (2000). Extracting meaning from past affective experiences: The importance of peaks, ends, and specific emotions. *Cognition and Emotion, 14*(4), 577–606. Available from https://doi.org/10.1080/026999300402808.

Greenleaf, E. A., Johnson, E. J., Morwitz, V. G., & Shalev, E. (2016). The price does not include additional taxes, fees, and surcharges: A review of research on partitioned pricing. *Journal of Consumer Psychology, 26*(1), 105–124. Available from https://doi.org/10.1016/j.jcps.2015.04.006.

Hansen, A. H., & Mossberg, L. (2017). Tour guides' performance and tourists' immersion: Facilitating consumer immersion by performing a guide plus role. *Scandinavian Journal of Hospitality and Tourism, 17*(3), 259–278. Available from https://doi.org/10.1080/15022250.2016.1162347.

Helliwell, J. F., Layard, R., & Sachs, J. D. (2019). *World happiness report 2019*. Retrieved from http://worldhappiness.report/.

Homburg, C., Totzek, D., & Krämer, M. (2014). How price complexity takes its toll: The neglected role of a simplicity bias and fairness in price evaluations. *Journal of Business Research, 67*(6), 1114–1122. Available from https://doi.org/10.1016/j.jbusres.2013.05.049.

Iyengar, S. (2010). *The art of choosing*. New York: Twelve.

Kahneman, D. (2011). *Thinking, fast and slow*. London: Penguin Books.

Kahneman, D., Wakker, P. P., & Sarin, R. (1997). Back to Bentham? Explorations of experienced utility. *The Quarterly Journal of Economics, 112*(2), 375–406. Available from https://doi.org/10.1162/003355397555235.

Karmarkar, U. R., Shiv, B., & Knutson, B. (2015). Cost conscious? The neural and behavioral impact of price primacy on decision making. *Journal of Marketing Research, 52*(4), 467–481. Available from https://doi.org/10.1509/jmr.13.0488.

Kay Smith, M., & Diekmann, A. (2017). Tourism and wellbeing. *Annals of Tourism Research, 66*, 1–13. Available from https://doi.org/10.1016/j.annals.2017.05.006.

Kleinsasser, S., & Wagner, U. (2011). Price endings and tourism consumers' price perceptions. *Journal of Retailing and Consumer Services, 18*(1), 58–63. Available from https://doi.org/10.1016/j.jretconser.2010.09.011.

Lee, T. H. (2011). How recreation involvement, place attachment and conservation commitment affect environmentally responsible behavior. *Journal of Sustainable Tourism, 19*(7), 895–915. Available from https://doi.org/10.1080/09669582.2011.570345.

Lowe, B., Barnes, B. R., & Rugimbana, R. (2012). Discounting in international markets and the face value effect: A double-edged sword? *Psychology & Marketing*, *29*(3 (March)), 144–156. Available from https://doi.org/10.1002/mar.

Lynch, J. G., & Ariely, D. (2000). Wine online: Search costs affect competition on price, quality, and distribution. *Marketing Science*, *19*(1), 83–103. Available from https://doi.org/10.1287/mksc.19.1.83.15183.

Meacci, L., & Liberatore, G. (2015). Towards a senses-based model for experimental tourism: The youtooscany.com case. *Proceedings 1st International Conference on Experiential Tourism*, *10*, 9–11.

Miller, P. (2010, April 20). *E.U.: Vacationing a human right*. Retrieved from http://harvardpolitics.com/world/e-u-vacationing-a-human-right/.

Miller, G., Rathouse, K., Scarles, C., Holmes, K., & Tribe, J. (2010). Public understanding of sustainable tourism. *Annals of Tourism Research*, *37*(3), 627–645. Available from https://doi.org/10.1016/j.annals.2009.12.002.

Mossberg, L. (2008). Extraordinary experiences through storytelling. *Scandinavian Journal of Hospitality and Tourism*, *8*(3), 195–210. Available from https://doi.org/10.1080/15022250802532443.

Nawijn, J. (2011). Determinants of daily happiness on vacation. *Journal of Travel Research*, *50*(5), 559–566. Available from https://doi.org/10.1177/0047287510379164.

Nikolova, M. S. (2009). *Brand effects on retrospective evaluations of past consumption experiences*. The George Washington University.

Nikolova, M. S., Asenov, J., & Lazarova, J. (2015). *From virtual goods to the real economy: Can psychological principles in the videogaming marketing increase sales in the new tourism market realities? TTRA-Europe Conference*. Innsbruck: TTRA.

Nikolova, M. S., & Hassan, S. S. (2013). Nation branding effects on retrospective global evaluation of past travel experiences. *Journal of Business Research*, *66*(6), 752–758. Available from https://doi.org/10.1016/j.jbusres.2011.09.014.

O'Dell, T. (2005). Experiencescapes: Blurring borders and testing connections. In T. O'Dell, & P. Billing (Eds.), *Experiencescapes: Tourism, culture, and economy* (pp. 11–33). Copenhagen, Koge, Denmark: Copenhagen Business School Press.

Pine, J. B., & Gilmore, J. H. (1998). Welcome to the experience economy. *Harvard Business Review*, *July–August*, 97–105.

Pine, J. B., & Gilmore, J. H. (1999). *The experience economy: Work is theatre & every business a stage*. Harvard Business Press.

Porter, M. E., & Kramer, M. R. (2011). Creating shared value how to reinvent capitalism-and unleash a wave of innovation and growth. *Harvard Business Review* (January–February), 2–17. Retrieved from http://www.nuovavista.com/SharedValuePorterHarvardBusinessReview.PDF.

Puccinelli, N. M., Chandrashekaran, R., Grewal, D., & Suri, R. (2013). Are men seduced by red? The effect of red versus black prices on price perceptions. *Journal of Retailing*, *89*(2), 115–125. Available from https://doi.org/10.1016/j.jretai.2013.01.002.

Romani, S. (2006). Price misleading advertising: Effects on trustworthiness toward the source of information and willingness to buy. *Journal of Product & Brand Management*, *15*(2), 130–138. https://doi.org/10.1108/10610420610658965.

Simon, H. A. (1990). Bounded rationality. In J. Eatwell, M. Milgate, & P. Newman (Eds.), Utility and probability ((pp. 161–176). London: The New Palgrave. Palgrave Macmillan.

Simonson, I., & Tversky, A. (1992). Choice in context: Tradeoff contrast and extremeness aversion. *Journal of Marketing Research*, *XXIX*(August), 281–295.

Stone, M. J., & Petrick, J. F. (2013). The educational benefits of travel experiences: A literature review. *Journal of Travel. Research*, *52*(6), 731–744. Available from https://doi.org/10.1177/0047287513500588.

Sunstein, C. R., & Thaler, R. H. (2003). Libertarian paternalism is not an oxymoron. *The University of Chicago Law Review*, *70*(4), 1159–1202. Retrieved from http://chicagounbound.uchicago.edu/cgi/viewcontent.cgi?article = 5228&context = uclrev.

Tasic, V., Staake, T., Stiefmeier, T., Tiefenbeck, V., Fleisch, E., & Tröster, G. (2012). Self-powered water meter for direct feedback. In Proceedings of the 2012 international conference on the internet of things, IOT 2012, October 24–30. https://doi.org/10.1109/IOT.2012.6402300.

Thaler, R. H. (1999). Mental accounting matters. *Journal of Behavioral Decision Making*, *12* (September 1998), 183.

Tost, H., Champagne, F. A., & Meyer-Lindenberg, A. (2015). Environmental influence in the brain, human welfare and mental health. *Nature Neuroscience*, *18*(10), 4121–4131. Available from https://doi.org/10.1038/nn.4108.

Tribe, J., & Mkono, M. (2017). Not such smart tourism? The concept of e-lienation. *Annals of Tourism Research*, *66*, 105–115. Available from https://doi.org/10.1016/j.annals.2017.07.001.

Tully, S., & Meyvis, T. (2016). Questioning the end effect: Endings are not inherently overweighted in retrospective evaluations of experiences. *Journal of Experimental Psychology: General*, *145*(5), 1–13. Available from https://doi.org/10.1037/xge0000155.

Uysal, M., Sirgy, M. J., Woo, E., & Kim, H. L. (2016). Quality of life (QOL) and well-being research in tourism. *Tourism Management*, *53*, 244–261. Available from https://doi.org/10.1016/j.tourman.2015.07.013.

Villarino, J., & Font, X. (2014). Sustainability marketing myopia: The lack of sustainability communication persuasiveness. *Journal of Vacation Marketing*, *21*(4), 326–335.

Voss, K. E., Spangenberg, E. R., & Grohmann, B. (2003). Measuring the hedonic and utilitarian dimensions of consumer attitude. *Journal of Marketing Research*, *40*(3), 310–320. Available from https://doi.org/10.1509/jmkr.40.3.310.19238.

Zeithaml, V. A. (1988). Consumer perceptions of price, quality, and value: A means. *Journal of Marketing*, *52*(3), 2. Retrieved from http://www.freepatentsonline.com/article/Academy-Marketing-Studies-Journal/166751762.html.

Chapter 6

Best practices and approaches using behavior-smart thinking in 10 tourism industry scenarios

Chapter outline

Introduction

Throughout the previous chapters, this book advances the idea that behavioral economics can enhance the thinking and practices in the growing travel economy. Many of the discussions in the text propose that behavior-smart thinking helps explain some of the failures in the contemporary tourism system and can be at the core of the solutions to address them. Chapter 3, Tourism of the (Near) Future: Growing, Faster, On-the-Go, reviewed some of the big picture trends in our societies and contemporary living that will deepen issues such as our relationship with technology, human impact on pristine areas, and the sustainability crisis. Chapter 4, Behavior-Smart Thinking for Destinations, zoomed into the contemporary realities of destination management and offered a behavioral read of why some of the challenges exist and how they can be fixed. Chapter 5, Behavior-Smart Thinking for Tourism Companies, applied a behavioral lens to the practices in the private sector and proposed that behavior-smart thinking can optimize commercial success and the footprint of businesses along the tourism value chain.

To build on that, this chapter offers a set of 10 different cases that demonstrate how behavior-smart thinking can work in reality. To enhance the conceptual propositions and discussions presented throughout the book, this collection of cases reveals already existing practices that can serve as a proof that there is a significant benefit in drawing on behavioral economics knowledge. Many of the projects and solutions that are presented in the cases are new and still under development, but they are producing results and lessons learned that can be of benefit to others willing to experiment.

The scale of the different examples collected here also differs. The first case explores a bold experiment conducted by Virgin Atlantic and offers an ambitious demonstration of how simple and low-cost behavioral interventions can produce

Behavioral Economics for Tourism. DOI: https://doi.org/10.1016/B978-0-12-813808-3.00006-X

significant reduction in the carbon footprint and profitability of the airline sector. With the growing attention on the climate crisis and the economic challenges that COVID-19 caused to the airline industry, this story is worth wider attention. The second case presents a recently developed technology-enabled tool for the restaurant industry that translates the complicated science of estimating the carbon footprint of different foods into a simple-to-understand system categorizing meals from low- to high-impact. The story talks about how this system influences customer choices and empowers chefs to optimize the carbon footprint of their entire menus.

The third case presents the 2030 tourism strategy of one of the innovation-oriented destinations, The Netherlands, and shows the benefits of using behavioral segmentation. Another destination-level case reveals the experience of Finland's capital, Helsinki, with the roll-out of a sustainability platform that uses behavior-smart thinking to simplify responsible choice-making for both residents and visitors. The fifth case focuses on an unusual resort located in the Bulgarian Rhodope mountains that use behavior-smart design to engage its guests in experiences and activities that are good for them and good for nature. Case 6 takes the reader to beautiful Iceland and discusses its experience with the Iceland Academy, an online platform using behavior-smart design to ensure that travelers arrive at the destination prepared for the unusual weather conditions, rugged terrains, and specific cultural norms. Another northern example comes from Fogo Island, which is the focus of the seventh case presenting the economic nutrition mark developed there and discussing why it is a brilliant solution to the behavioral barriers for responsible traveler behavior.

Case 8 presents Adventure Junky, a young but fast-growing tourism company from Australia that gamifies sustainable tourism experiences and rewards responsible choice making. The ninth case talks about the efforts of the food service industry in Norway to cut food waste and optimize failures along the food value chain. The discussion highlights tools and tactics that are at the core of the waste-cutting strategy and explains why they are effective in producing the desired behavioral change. The final case in the collection takes the reader to the Västmanland Region—a small but ambitious regional destination in Sweden. It tells the story of the bold experiment of the local tourism authority in applying behavior-smart thinking to support the achievement of its strategic goals and to enable local tourism businesses to apply behaviorally informed solutions to optimize profitability and sustainability efforts.

The diversity of the stories is a demonstration of the different scale and scope with which behavioral practices can be applied in the travel industry. They can be a good encouragement for individual entrepreneurs and business leaders, who are offered proof that companies can optimize their commercial practices and strengthen sustainability performance by adopting behavior-smart thinking. The real-world stories from destinations can hopefully inspire more tourism authorities and politicians to apply insights from behavioral economics and improve policy and management practices.

Case 1 Behavior-smart lowering of airline carbon emissions...Today

The challenge

One of the biggest sins of the travel industry is the carbon footprint of air travel. The fast growth of the tourism sector is accompanied by a fast increase in the number of flights that are taken internationally (8.4% increase in 2017) or domestically (7.1% increase in 2017) (ICAO, 2018). The aviation industry produces about 859 million tons of CO_2 annually, which constitutes 2% of the global emission generated by human activities (ATAG, 2018). Even though the industry is making progress in fuel efficiency technology and utilization of biofuels, this takes time and requires sizable investments.

The behavioral approach

An experiment conducted a few years ago by Virgin Atlantic and researchers from the University of Chicago, and the London School of Economics revealed that there might be great potential in applying behavior-smart tactics for the lowering of CO_2 emissions of planes with the existing technology and existing fuels. As one of the airlines that lead in efforts to do business in a responsible manner, Virgin Atlantic has a special Fuel Efficiency team, tasked with exploring ways in which CO_2 emissions can be lowered through optimization of the fuel efficiency of flights. The three most effective tactics established by the team require proactive efforts of the pilots and include (Gosnell, List, & Metcalfe, 2016):

1. Efficient fuel load, which means calculating and loading the precise amount of fuel needed for the respective flight to avoid unnecessary overload.
2. Efficient flight, which means benefitting from several in-flight behaviors that can impact fuel efficiency, including ensuring optimal speed and altitude based on information from air traffic control, monitoring and adjusting to en-route weather updates, and ensuring efficient aerodynamic arrangements with respect to flap settings, takeoff, and landing gear.
3. Efficient taxi-in, which means turning off at least one engine during taxiing to the gate upon landing.

Despite the simplicity of the three approaches and their inclusion in the standard operating procedures in pilot manuals (Virgin Atlantic, 2017), most pilots did not automatically adopt them.

To encourage the proactive use of these fuel efficiency tactics, the team leading the experiment applied a series of behavioral interventions that aimed to influence the motivation of pilot teams. About 335 captains were randomly assigned to four groups: three experimental and one control group (Metcalfe, Gosnell, & List, 2016):

- The *feedback group*: pilots in this group started receiving a monthly report of their fuel efficiency flight performance, which included comparing the percentage of flights in which they applied the three fuel-saving tactics to the percentage from the prior month.

- The *targets group*: captains in this experimental group also received a monthly report of their fuel efficiency flight performance, but it was complemented by a personalized monthly performance target that was 25% above their preexperiment baseline performance. For example, if the preexperiment performance was 5%, the target for the following month was set at 30%.
- The *prosocial incentives group*: pilots in this experimental group received the monthly performance report, as well as targets and were also informed that if they achieve their personalized targets, a £10 donation will be made on their behalf to the charity of choice.
- The control group: pilots in this group continued operating as usual but were aware of the ongoing experiment.

The experiment was executed over an 8-month period covering over 42,000 flights.

The results of this unique trial reveal that soft behavioral interventions produce significant optimization of fuel efficiency leading to lowering of CO_2 emissions and significant cost savings. The researcher team estimated that over the course of the study, the modified behavior of pilots produced 6.8 million kilograms of fuel saved for the airline translating to cost savings of $5.37 million and CO_2 reduction of 21 million kilograms. These savings translate to the impressive cost of emission reduction of negative $250 per ton of CO_2 given that at the time of the experiment, efficient residential lighting is the lowest cost technology for reducing carbon emissions performing at about $180 per metric ton of CO abatement (Gosnell et al., 2016; Metcalfe et al., 2016).

Discussion

This experiment is probably the most significant effort to apply behavioral knowledge toward more sustainable operations in the travel industry. The effective behavioral change among captains is triggered mainly by the so-called *Hawthorne effect* or the awareness of being monitored. The mere fact that fuel efficiency behavior is monitored and tracked makes captains much more likely to apply the three fuel-saving tactics. This is observed across all groups, including the control group in the experiment. The personalized performance reports and especially personalized targets are very powerful in fueling pilots' motivation to engage in fuel-efficient flying. The prosocial incentive did not strengthen the likelihood that captains will apply the tactics beyond the levels achieved by the personalized targets but increased their job satisfaction. An important finding was that the experiment triggered long-term changes in pilot behavior sustained long after the end of the project.

The results of this experiment hold several important lessons for the airline industry and the travel sector at large. First, while investment in new clean technologies, energy efficiency, and cleaner fuel mixes should not slow down, there seem to be opportunities for behavioral optimization of company operations that can produce significant savings and lowering of footprint. A widespread adoption of the same soft behavioral measures by all airlines can immediately produce significant reduction of CO_2 emissions and generate substantial fuel and cost savings for the companies. If Virgin Atlantic achieved CO_2 reduction of 21 million kilograms and saved 6.8

million kilograms of fuel over 42,000 flights, imagine the magnitude of CO_2 reduction and fuel optimization that can be achieved by the 41.9 million scheduled flights that were executed globally in 2017 (ATAG, 2018).

Second, companies in the sector, especially large ones such as airlines, transport operators, large hospitality groups, big tour operators, attraction operators, and others, hold tremendous power for triggering responsible behavior among their employees and producing significant improvement in sustainability performance across the sector. If more companies made their staff aware that, for example, energy efficiency, fuel efficiency, or social impact behavior are priorities, and therefore relevant employee behavior is monitored and reported on regular basis, they can produce major effects. The fact that the behavioral measures are relatively simple and inexpensive further reinforces the importance of exploring this potential on a sector-wide level.

References

ATAG. (2018). *Aviation: Benefits without borders*. Geneva. Retrieved from <https://aviationbenefits.org/media/166344/abbb18_full-report_web.pdf>.

Gosnell, G.K., List, J.A., & Metcalfe, R. (2016). *A new approach to an age-old problem: Solving externalities by incenting workers directly* (NBER Working Paper Series No. 22316). Retrieved from <http://www.nber.org/papers/w22316>.

ICAO. (2018). *ICAO Annual Report 2017*.

Metcalfe, R., Gosnell, G., & List, J. (2016). *Virgin Atlantic tested 3 ways to change employee behavior. Harvard Business Review, August*.

Virgin Atlantic. (2017). *Virgin Atlantic Sustainability Report 2016*. London. Retrieved from <https://www.virginatlantic.com/content/dam/vaa/documents/footer/sustainability/Virgin_Atlantic_Full_Sustainability_Report_2016.pdf>.

Case 2 Making climate footprint a factor in food choice

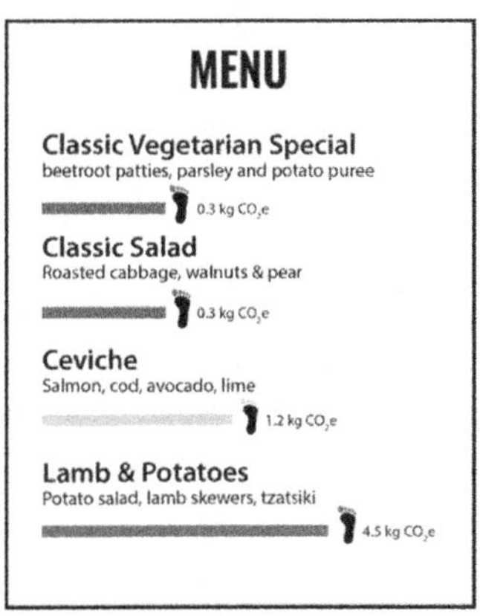

The challenge

The food system on global level is responsible for the production of a quarter of greenhouse gas emissions. The livestock sector alone generates the equivalent of 7.1 gigatonnes of CO_2e emissions per year, which represents 80% of the emissions produced by the food system and more than 14% of all human-induced greenhouse gas emissions (FAO, 2017). The majority of the harmful emissions come from beef and cattle milk production, which respectively contribute 41% and 20% of what the entire sector generates. Pork accounts for about 9% followed by poultry and egg production, which contribute 8% to the emissions of the sector (Gerber et al., 2013).

While many other harmful activities that contribute to climate change and degradation of the natural environment can be limited or prevented, food is a basic human need. The food products provided by the livestock sector are fundamental to diets in many cultures around the world. That means that there is a need to explore ways in which food habits can be adapted to sustain healthy nutrition while at the same time lowering negative impacts on global warming.

One of the beliefs that shape contemporary thinking about food and climate change is that moving to a menu with more plant-based foods and meats from animals with little enteric fermentation can lead to lower emissions from the food system (Bryngelsson, Wirsenius, Hedenus, & Sonesson, 2016; Carlsson-Kanyama & Gonzalez, 2009). Emphasis on local produce can also have an impact as long-haul transportation can increase the emission footprint of foods that are imported from distant source markets even if they are climate-friendly when produced locally (Carlsson-Kanyama & Gonzalez, 2009). In that sense beans or rice that are generally characterized with lower footprint than fresh chicken, might end up being less climate-friendly than chicken if imported from a producer from another continent.

The main challenge with prompting a change in eating behavior that accounts for climate footprint of different foods is complexity. First, climate change is a complicated issue that people effectively ignore in everyday life (Marshall, 2015). Second, the science that underlies the footprint of different foods is not easily accessible to everyone. Third, making an effort to track food and adjust eating behavior based on climate footprint is nearly impossible for the average contemporary person who is not equipped with scientific tools that make it possible to calculate the CO_2 emissions of every food on their daily menu and whose attention is drowning into many other tasks with much more immediate consequences.

The behavioral solution

A brilliant solution to the complexity of tracking the climate footprint of foods is *CarbonAte*—a carbon footprint calculator that enables restaurants to add climate labels to menus. Powered by extensive scientific knowledge, the web-based system provides an easy to use menu-planning tool for restaurants and generates easy to understand carbon footprint labels for their guests. On the back end, the system enables restaurant owners and chefs to plan and ensure smooth management of purchasing processes. To power the climate footprint calculator the platform prompts chefs to enter detailed information about the ingredients that go into each meal. Based on that *CarbonAte* produces a climate footprint value for every item on the restaurant menu. Depending on the estimated value meals are marked as green if their climate footprint value is low, yellow if the value is average, and red if the footprint value is comparatively high. The color code system simplifies the processing of the value and makes it easy for customers to understand whether a meal is more or less climate-friendly.

Discussion

Food choice is one of the contexts in which present bias or the inclination to put more focus on immediate gains rather than likely gains in the future is most powerful. Usually when restaurant guests decide what meals to choose they are motivated by the need to satisfy the hunger they feel at the respective moment and less so by the importance of tackling climate change. In general, it has been established that food choice is usually more heuristic-driven rather than fueled by rational weighting of options (Scheibehenne, Miesler, & Todd, 2007).

The *CarbonAte* food label makes it possible to include climate footprint as a factor, albeit secondary, in the decision-making process. After guests see the menu, they usually bring their choices down to two to three options that align most with their taste and try to make a decision between them. At this stage the carbon footprint value can be a factor considered by the guest and can become the reason for choosing one meal versus another from the narrowed choice set. Initial experiments with *CarbonAte*'s labeling system confirmed its effectiveness in influencing consumer behavior by increasing the likelihood of choosing a green-labeled meal and lowering the likelihood of going with a red-labeled option (Brunner, Kurz, Bryngelsson, & Hedenus, 2018). Further applications across different contexts confirmed that labeled menus produce emission reductions from existing users of up to 25%–30% (Bryngelsson, 2018).

An interesting side effect of the introduction of the *CarbonAte* solution is modification in the behavior of head chefs in restaurants using the system. Empowered by the climate labels, the chefs in many of the participating restaurants felt motivation to make adjustments to meal recipes in effort to lower their carbon footprint and strengthen the overall climate profile of the menu (Bryngelsson, 2018).

Changing diets and nudging people to make food choices that are more climate-friendly can lead to significant optimization of the footprint of the food system but also improve the well-being of consumers. It is important to realize that climate footprint might not be the factor that leads to the decision-making of most guests or consumers (Peattie & Collins, 2009) but the salience of the footprint information makes it possible to include climate-friendliness as a factor in general. A visible and easy to understand classification enables guests to easily process and compare climate-related information, and include it as factor in the decision-making. Consumers will not make the effort to figure out climate footprint of foods and meals in a restaurant or at home but once it is available and easy to understand, they readily take that into account.

References

Brunner, F., Kurz, V., Bryngelsson, D., & Hedenus, F. (2018). Carbon label at a university restaurant–label implementation and evaluation. *Ecological Economics*, *146*(April), 658–667.

Bryngelsson, D. (2018). Personal communication 15 June 2018.

Bryngelsson, D., Wirsenius, S., Hedenus, F., & Sonesson, U. (2016). How can the EU climate targets be met? A combined analysis of technological and demand-side changes in food and agriculture. *Food Policy*, *59*, 152–164. Available from https://doi.org/10.1016/J.FOODPOL.2015.12.012.

Carlsson-Kanyama, A., & Gonzalez, A. D. (2009). Potential contributions of food consumption patterns to climate change 1–4. *The American Journal of Clinical Nutrition*, *89*(5), 1704S–1709S. Available from https://doi.org/10.3945/ajcn.2009.26736AA.

FAO. (2017). *FAO Strategy on Climate Change*. Rome.

Gerber, P.J., Steinfeld, H., Henderson, B., Mottet, A., Opio, C., Dijkman, J., ... Tempio, G. (2013). *Tackling climate change through livestock – A global assessment of emissions and mitigation opportunities*. Rome. Retrieved from www.fao.org/publications.

Marshall, G. (2015). *Don't even think about it: Why our brains are wired to ignore climate change*. Bloomsbury Publishing.

Peattie, K., & Collins, A. (2009). Guest editorial: Perspectives on sustainable consumption. *International Journal of Consumer Studies*, *33*(2), 107–112. Available from https://doi.org/10.1111/j.1470-6431.2009.00758.x.

Scheibehenne, B., Miesler, L., & Todd, P. M. (2007). Fast and frugal food choices: Uncovering individual decision heuristics. *Appetite*, *49*(3), 578–589. Available from https://doi.org/10.1016/j.appet.2007.03.224.

Case 3 Behavioral segmentation for destination Netherlands 2030

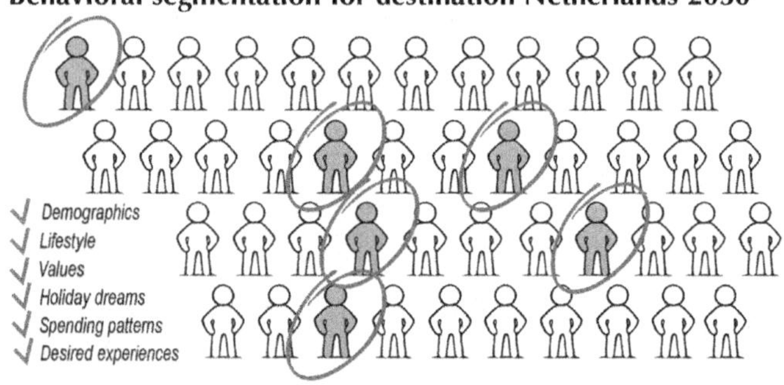

The challenge

An essential component of marketing strategies is segmentation. This is the step of breaking down the total market into groups of consumers that are united by similar characteristics. Once segments are defined, companies or destinations can select the ones that they would like to target as part of their strategy.

Even though marketing textbooks have long ago rejected the effectiveness of using basic demographic characteristics as basis for formulating segments, many tourism destinations continue to do so. The main identifier that is used by destination authorities to characterize segments is nationality or source destination. This means that numerous national and regional tourism strategies are grounded on the goal of targeting visitors from Germany, France, or the United States rather than visitors who travel in a certain way. While this approach is simple and easy to manage, it is not optimal in terms of defining who is really the desired customer and what will be the impact their travel behavior will have on the destination. Nationality alone cannot be an effective differentiator because two families living on the same street in a city in say, Germany might have radically different travel styles and holiday expectations. One family might be the classical sun-and-sand resort goers interested in all-inclusive holidays with everything taken care of and little possibility for surprise. Their next-door neighbor family might love adventure and have interest in places where they can experience interesting cultures and have fun out in nature while hiking or biking. The different holiday preferences of these two families require different tourism offerings, different services, and different physical infrastructure. On the other side, their travel styles produce different impacts on the destination and the local service providers. In that sense their nationality does not reveal much except the starting point of their trip.

The behavioral approach

As discussed in earlier chapters of this book, there is much more meaning in using travel behavior as basis for segmentation and identification of desired traveler profiles for targeting. For years many leading destinations have been using personas or traveler profiles to identify desired consumer audiences based on their value systems, travel curiosity, and holiday habits. A great example among them is the Netherlands with its Perspective 2030 strategy, which identifies a careful selection of targeted traveler profiles as a key step toward its goal of making tourism beneficial for all Dutch citizens (NBTC, 2019e). It states: "*In order to amalgamate tourism with the everyday society as optimally as possible, to optimise the benefits for Dutch people and the economy and to minimise overload trouble, we aim to attract visitors who will contribute to the Netherlands as a future-proof destination. These visitors will add value and will not cause trouble.*"

In order to identify the desired visitors who could be attracted to the Netherlands and will make positive impact on its economy, the Dutch tourism board (NBTC) produced five excellent personas with details about their specific lifestyles and holiday preferences. They include:

Achiever Michael—a young professional in his mid-30s with strong orientation toward status, materialism, and career. Still unmarried and with higher than average income, Michael is eager to spend on experiences that involve thrill, physical activity, and entertainment (NBTC, 2019a).

Upper-class Paul—an established and successful professional in his 50s who cares about tradition, family, and etiquette. With grown-up kids and a successful career, Paul is health- and environment-conscious making him interested in experiences that offer opportunity to share interesting experiences with family, be active, and feel rejuvenation away from crowds and close to nature (NBTC, 2019d).

Traditional Mary—a family-oriented part-time professional with strong preference in predictable and well-planed life. With grown-up kids and grandchildren, Mary lives away from the city and is comfortable with traditional norms, order, and discipline. She is interested in holiday experiences that are outside of the main season and include quiet, somewhat active and relaxing activities (NBTC, 2019c).

Postmodern Nora—a young freelancer in her mid-30s with one child and an open-minded, immaterial, and tolerant outlook to the world. Nora is an urban creature and fan of yoga, photography, and travel adventures with friends. An enjoyable holiday for her means an open itinerary, which includes some socializing and bar hopping, shopping, and enjoyment of local lifestyle (NBTC, 2019b).

Mainstream Peter—a traditionalist in his early 40s with a wife and two children, Peter seeks to balance between his older-school thinking and the recognition that the contemporary realities bring new norms and values. He likes spending time with the family but loves socializing too. An ideal holiday for him includes some classics such as taking a beach vacation, staying at an all-inclusive resort, and visiting amusement parks.

The NBTC personas are a fantastic illustration of the value of a behavioral deep dive in desired market segments. To offer a realistic sense of who is the traveler that is to be invited to the Netherlands the profiles offer a glimpse at the persona's daily calendar and work life, as well as personal lifestyle specifics such as favorite magazines and music, hobbies, and typical leisure activities. A fun and exciting element of these personas is the look in their hand luggage revealing further details about them. For example, in his small black bag Achiever Michael carries an iPad and noise-isolating headphone, a sports magazine, mints, sunglasses, a high-quality sports watch, and a male cosmetic set. On the other hand, Postmodern Nora carries a casual beige personal bag with a couple of magazines such as Psychology Today, a Lonely Planet guide, purple sunglasses, a bag of dried basil, a classical photo camera, a black Moleskine notebook, and a pencil.

Based on all lifestyle details the personas include specifics about the attitude toward the Netherlands and the characteristics of a potential holiday in the destination. For example, we find out that Upper-class Paul associates the Netherlands with cycling, Amsterdam, beautiful landscapes, cheese, and friendly locals. He finds it an attractive destination for a short holiday. He would visit with his family during shoulder season, stay at a nice hotel in Amsterdam, and mix cultural experiences with culinary adventures and shopping. The likely holiday of Traditional Peter is also short and not his main family vacation for the year. His visit style, however, is very different from Paul's. He is likely to stay at a holiday home rather than a hotel and be in Duirell rather than Amsterdam where the family can go to the local amusement park, spend some time at the nearby beach, and enjoy some Dutch pancakes.

Discussion

The use of behavioral segmentation that groups travelers on the basis of how they travel and consume the visited destination, is the most effective way of understanding potential audiences and targeting the ones that are a good fit. It ensures a great level of focus that matters for two reasons. First, a deep behavioral dive helps ensure the best match between the offerings of the destination and the visit style of the guests. If a small region is predominantly rural and has well-preserved traditional villages with little infrastructure, it makes sense to target travelers who are curious about local traditions, comfortable in rural setting, and do not mind hiking or biking. Targeting a wider audience risks inviting guests who are uncomfortable with the travel style that the destination requires and whose unmet expectations will lead to great dissatisfaction. The second reason is that in the era of overtourism casting a wide net of targeting entire nations is not sensible because it stimulates overdemand that is damaging. To balance between the opportunity to extract socioeconomic benefits from tourism and the threat of being overwhelmed with too many visitors requires careful selection of targeted audiences. Behavior-smart targeting is also the best way to ensure optimal balance between visible and invisible tourism impacts.

There is one more significant benefit in the use of behavioral segmentation and personas. The development of personas that are realistic and easy to imagine is powerful for local businesses. They can easily relate to them and build natural familiarity with the potential guests, which makes them more successful in meeting their needs.

Contemporary destinations should no longer use source destination as a generalizing characteristic that is basis for segmenting the market. In order to identify the travelers whose behavior will best fit with the local social norms and align with economic goals, tourism boards should place traveler behavior at the heart of their segmentation and targeting strategy.

References

NBTC. (2019a). Passport Achiever Michael. In *Motivaction & NBTC Holland Marketing*. Available online https://doi.org/10.1017/CBO9781107415324.004.

NBTC. (2019b). Passport Postmodern Nora. In *Motivaction & NBTC Holland Marketing*. Amsterdam.

NBTC. (2019c). Passport Traditional Mary. In *Motivaction & NBTC Holland Marketing*. Available online https://doi.org/10.1017/CBO9781107415324.004.

NBTC. (2019d). Passport Upper-Class Paul. In *Motivaction & NBTC Holland Marketing*. Available online https://doi.org/10.1017/CBO9781107415324.004.

NBTC. (2019e). *Perspective 2030 - Destination the Netherlands*.

Case 4 Using behaviorally-friendly design to encourage loan payoff[1]

The challenge

According to data from the Federal Reserve Bank of New York as of December 31, 2016, total household indebtedness of US households was $12.58 trillion, marking a 1.8% increase from the third quarter of 2016 and 12.8% from the second quarter of 2013. As of December 31, 2016, 4.8% of US household outstanding debt ($607 billion) was in some stage of delinquency and 3.3% ($412 billion) was seriously delinquent (at least 90 days late or "severely derogatory") (Federal Reserve Bank of New York, 2017).

1. This case is based on the *Pay off Loans Faster (EarnUp)* project story published in the Common Cents Lab End of Year 2016 Report, and has been supplemented with additional research and data.

A large share of household debt is associated with mortgages. In 2014 the total number of households using more than 30% of their income for housing increased to 40 million, with almost 20% of households using more than 50% of their income to pay for housing costs (Common Cents Lab, 2016). Long payoff periods generate additional debt burden due to interest, higher risk of default, and lack of savings.

To respond to this need, fintech startup *APASave* developed a smart software-based service that intelligently syncs household income and expenses to enable faster mortgage payoff and thus an increased savings rate. Even though the opportunity offered by the young company is easy to use and translates to obvious benefits such as decrease in loan term by over 5 years and faster building of net worth through saving money, consumers are very hesitant to enroll and benefit from this opportunity.

Assumptions that fuel the problem

According to traditional thinking, debt repayment decisions are a tradeoff between the desire to minimize current and future total costs over the life of the loan. If this reflects typical consumer behavior, most debtors would base their repayments on a calculated amount that offers optimal balance between minimizing current costs and total costs depending on the household's income. However, behavioral scientists have established that due to a strong anchoring effect, minimum required payments strongly determine the decision for what amount the consumer will pay (Navarro-Martinez et al., 2011). Making information about future cost of the debt salient has also proved to influence debt repayment behavior, suggesting that under regular circumstances, consumers do not consider future cost and do not seek to optimize against their current ability to pay.

Another traditional assumption, which seems to be violated here, is that consumers optimize when choosing between different options available to them. If that was the case, making debtors aware of the APASave service should be sufficient to motivate them to choose the service, as it provides a favorable optimization between current costs and long-term wealth accumulation.

The behavioral explanation for why the problem exists

Previous research in the area of behavioral finance has revealed that average consumers seek to simplify financial decisions and often use heuristics. Biases, such as anchoring, have powerful influence on the decisions that consumers make, including when deciding on what payment amounts to make on their debts (Navarro-Martinez et al., 2011).

One common heuristic used by consumers to simplify debt payment decisions is rounding. According to Wang and Keys (2014), two-thirds of the consumers who stick to minimum rate payments when repaying their credit cards round up within $50 of the required amount. Analysis of mortgage repayment data conducted by the Common Cents Lab and *APASave* also revealed that many people are paying more than required due to rounding of payment amounts to the nearest $5 or $10. This suggests that the voluntary inclination of debtors to make higher payments is part of a decision simplification tactic rather than rational effort to optimize current and future costs.

Resistance to switching to the more favorable *APASave* service could be explained by two effects. One is inertia or status quo bias, which has been shown to have strong influence on consumers' financial decisions, preventing them from benefiting from apparently superior options (Madrian & Shea, 2000). The second effect is associated with the perception of savings as loss (seeing earned money as money that cannot be spent).

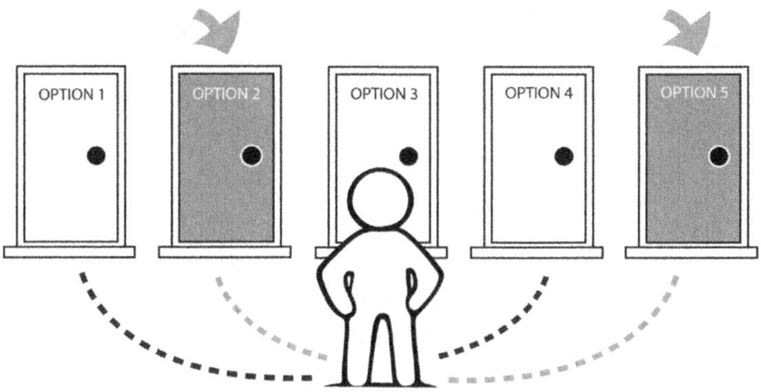

The behavioral solution

To respond to the challenge, *Common Cents Lab* and *APASave* took a behaviorally-informed approach. First, to suppress the association between savings and loss, communication messages promoting the company's services were reframed around earning money back rather than saving. The value proposition of the service was changed from "save money on a mortgage" to "earn money back from a mortgage." As part of that intervention, the name of the company was also changed from *APASave* to *EarnUp* (Common Cents Lab, 2016).

The second intervention revolved around battling the anchoring effect of minimum payment rates. To overcome the inertia of choosing to make a monthly payment that equals the required minimum, *EarnUp* proactively prompted consumers to overpay by explaining the advantage of increasing monthly payments by even a small amount. Given that the average mortgage amount for a new loan in the United States is $312,700 at a 30-year-fixed interest rate of 3.76%, adding just an extra $25 a month to the repayment amount will translate to savings of over $7,000 and early full repayment by a whole year (Common Cents Lab, 2016). Using knowledge about rounding up as heuristic, the team tested two prompt designs: (1) prompt to overpay by rounding up and (2) prompt to overpay without a suggestion for rounding up.

Results and benefits of using the behavioral solution

The emphasis on earning versus saving in the value proposition and in the name of the company translated to a sharp increase of the interest among consumers exposed to advertisement. The new framing of the marketing messages led to an increase of click-through rates on online advertisements by 59%.

Direct prompts for overpaying provided rationale and also led to change in repayment behavior. Both conditions (prompt to overpay and prompt to overpay by rounding up) increased individual monthly payments, but the rate observed for the roundup group was higher (13% compared to 10% for the general overpay prompted group). In both conditions, the average amount by which consumers decided to overpay was $60, which translated to about $8,000 of savings over the life of a loan and a total of $1,300,000 in interest saved for *EarnUp* users who agreed to pay more than their minimum payment. A full 86% of the people who agreed to overpay declared that they had never before done that with any other loan (Common Cents Lab, 2016).

Based on insights on financial behavior, *EarnUp* continues to successfully grow its business of integrating loans and optimizing their repayment. Using heuristics-based design in messaging and service, the startup simplifies financial decision-making and optimizes repayment and saving in a way that is favorable for debtors and profitable for the company.

References

Common Cents Lab. (2016). *Common Cents Lab End of Year 2016 Report.* Retrieved from https://advanced-hindsight.com/wp-content/uploads/2017/01/Using-Psychologically-Satisfying-Numbers-to-Pay-Off-Loans-Faster-EarnUp.pdf.

Federal Reserve Bank of New York. (2017). *Quarterly Report on Household Debt and Credit.* New York. Retrieved from https://www.newyorkfed.org/medialibrary/interactives/householdcredit/data/pdf/HHDC_2016Q4.pdf.

Madrian, B.C., & Shea, D.F. (2000). *The power of suggestion: Inertia in 401(k) participation and savings behavior the power of suggestion: Inertia in 401(k) participation and savings behavior* (No. Working Paper 7682). Cambridge. Retrieved from http://www.nber.org/papers/w7682.

Navarro-Martinez, D., Salisbury, L. C., Lemon, K. N., Stewart, N., Matthews, W. J., & Harris, A. J. L. (2011). Minimum required payment and supplemental information disclosure effects on consumer debt repayment decisions. *Journal of Marketing Research, XLVIII*(Special Issue 2011), S60–S77. Retrieved from https://www2.bc.edu/linda-salisbury/Navarro-Martinez_Salisbury_etal_2011.pdf.

Wang, J., & Keys, B. J. (2014). *Perverse nudges: Minimum payments and debt paydown in consumer credit cards.* Penn Wharton Public Policy Initiative No. Book 25. Retrieved from http://repository.upenn.edu/pennwhartonppi.

Case 5 Factory Food-N-Dance: designing the experience with what is good for the traveler in the mind

The challenge

The principles of healthy and happy living are well known—eating high-quality, fresh and carefully prepared food; spending more time outside in nature; being physically active and exercising; and spending time with close ones (Helliwell, Layard, & Sachs, 2019). Because contemporary daily life has evolved in a way that makes all of these principles difficult to adhere to, they often remain plans for the future when there is more time and energy, maybe during the next holiday.

In reality, however, holiday is rarely a time when travelers get the chance to eat healthier or be more physically active than their day-to-day life. The design of most holiday resorts also does not help and creates favorable environment for people to do what they "normally" do in day-to-day life both in terms of food or activity. In most recent years technology has exacerbated that. Whether it is television or mobile devices, they absorb the attention of family members and take away from social interaction and relationships (Ayeh, 2018). Devices also alienate guests from the space around them and the place of their holiday (Tribe & Mkono, 2017). In that sense, even if they are at a resort in a destination with fantastic nature, guests can easily miss the opportunity to engage with it. For children who do not experience nature in day-to-day life being outdoors during a holiday can be an opportunity to establish an important link to nature and learn about it (Bruni, Winter, Schultz, Omoto, & Tabanico, 2017).

What if the holiday is designed in a way that includes all the "right" elements making guests do what is best for them but in a way that is effortless and enjoyable? There are already examples of resorts that nudge travelers to stay away from technology (by limiting access to Wi-Fi), to eat healthy (by offering only healthy items on the menu), or to stay active (by offering different sports activities as part of the holiday package). In most cases, however, these are specialized places that guests book because they intentionally want to get away from unhealthy dynamics in daily realities. And what about the rest who might know "what is right" but who do not have the time or means to go on such a holiday.

The behavioral approach

An example of how the traveler experience can be designed to gently nudge the guest to do what is good for them comes from *Factory Food-N-Dance,* a small outdoors resort for families located in a mountainous village in the Rhodope Mountains in Bulgaria. The resort was found by a young couple who early in life realized that the stressful lifestyle of the busy professionals in the big city cannot be a healthy setting for a family. They decided to find a life model that allows them to live outdoors and raise their children in a way that keeps them connected to nature and ensures healthy living. This led the couple to the idea to open a resort that was designed to offer a back-to-nature experience for families.

The design of the complex is such that it keeps guests mostly outside engaging them in a variety of family adventures. The accommodation space is simple and relatively small, which makes it less likely for people to stay in, except when they are sleeping. There are no TV sets anywhere in the resort and no internet connection beyond the mobile 4G, which is spotty. The outdoors area is large and green with plenty of attractive facilities and exciting things to do. In addition to a natural water pool with boats, there is a dry pool (a large pool with small balls offering children an alternative when weather makes swimming less attractive), hot tubs, sauna, steam room, a Himalayan salt room, an extra-long tube slide, trampoline, giant Lego corner, large jumping airbag, bike track, electric bikes, foam making machines, as well as snow-sliding donuts for the winter. All of these amenities make up a family paradise, which attracts parents and children for a holiday of fun.

What makes the Factory Food-N-Dance extraordinary, however, goes beyond its physical features. The all-inclusive format of the resort actually engages guests in a mindfully designed sequence of nature-based and healthy recreational activities. From the delicious all-natural meals with mostly local ingredients to the craft workshops for children and parents, guests are invited into a behavioral routine that is good for their bodies, their minds, and their relationships. The daily program starts with a healthy breakfast, during which children can make their own pancakes or waffles. In the afternoon children take part in bread-making or home pizza making workshops, which teach them how to prepare their own food and how to be creative with it. Every morning and every afternoon there are hikes in the surrounding mountains, offering a wide variety of routes with nature observations spots, small rivers, waterfalls, diverse landscapes and a rich biodiversity. Hikes are usually led by the Factory's founder who enriches the experience with different stories and local legends.

Every day there are some craft workshops engaging children and parents in learning how to work with leather and wood or how to knit and paint. In the evenings, children also learn how to make home-made chocolate candy or other healthy desserts. The end of the day for young guests is in the Himalayan salt room where the Factory's owner tells them interesting stories or plays music for some dancing fun. At the same time parents can enjoy some social fun with a cup of local herbal tea or a glass of wine around the fire in a large outdoors tent.

Discussion

The 360-degree experience offered at the Factory is a great example of how behavior-smart thinking can lead to the design of holidays that are both exciting and good for the traveler. Families do not really come to this resort for a wellness holiday. Their primary motivation is the attractive design of the space and the richness of things to do for the kids. It is the mindfully crafted routine combined with the attractive space that leads to the powerful combination of offering an enjoyable and healthy vacation.

Both the physical space and the intangible routine influence the behavior of resort guests. The physical space is designed in a way that nudges everyone to be outdoors. The many exciting attractions for children naturally keep them physically active and outside, away from devices and screens. The workshops and food preparation sessions give them a break from physical movement, and engage their hands and minds thus developing their creativity, sense of independence, and facility. The excitement of preparing their own meals also makes them more likely to eat them. The availability of fruits and only freshly squeezed seasonal fruit juices means that children do not have an alternative to healthy food and drink. The fun activities planned for the evening in the Himalayan salt room are also inspired by behavior-smart thinking. It is healthy and calming for children to spend time in a salt room but making that a requirement would not work well. Therefore by organizing fun things to do in the salt room, the focus is placed on the fun and not on the salt therapy itself.

The resort routine hides wellness nudges for parents too. The plenty of nice ways to spend time outside by the pool, the hot tubs, sauna, steam bath, and the fun workshops engage them in activities that do not involve technology and that offer opportunity for interacting with family, friends, and other guests. The regular daily hikes trigger a social conformity effect gently attracting guests who would not typically be interested in walking in nature. The interesting stories and interpretation make the hike enjoyable and educational as guests learn about plants, animals, and often enjoy picking some seasonal wild fruits. Available yoga and CrossFit classes also present an opportunity for many who have not done that before, to try and experience. The social space around the fire encourages guests to spend evening time together and interact while being outside even in the dark.

A key factor in the success of the Factory model is the all-inclusive format. The only way that guests can come to this attractive family resort is by paying for everything in a package. Namely because the price includes everything, including workshops, activities, and classes, they actually engage in them. If the Factory gave guests the opportunity to pay only for accommodation and food, and then asked them to pay extra for everything else, many would not take part in the workshops, the hikes or the classes. The all-inclusive model eliminates a barrier for trying something new so the mix of social conformity and curiosity actually nudges guests to do so. For many nature walks or yoga classes become something pleasant that potentially finds place in their live after the holiday.

Factory Food-N-Dance is a great example that illustrates how behavior-smart thinking can influence the design of both physical space and the leisure experience in ways that can facilitate exciting and restorative holidays. With reverse responsibility in mind, this is an illustration that more suppliers in the industry can find ways to combine good and fun in the design of offerings that do not trade off wellness for excitement.

References

Ayeh, J. K. (2018). Distracted gaze: Problematic use of mobile technologies in vacation contexts. *Tourism Management Perspectives*, *26*(February), 31–38. Available from https://doi.org/10.1016/j.tmp.2018.01.002.

Bruni, C. M., Winter, P. L., Schultz, P. W., Omoto, A. M., & Tabanico, J. J. (2017). Getting to know nature: evaluating the effects of the Get to Know Program on children's connectedness with nature. *Environmental Education Research*, *23*(1), 43–62. Available from https://doi.org/10.1080/13504622.2015.1074659.

Helliwell, J.F., Layard, R., & Sachs, J.D. (2019). *World Happiness Report 2019*. Retrieved from http://worldhappiness.report/.

Tribe, J., & Mkono, M. (2017). Not such smart tourism? The concept of e-lienation. *Annals of Tourism Research*, *66*, 105–115. Available from https://doi.org/10.1016/j.annals.2017.07.001.

Case 6 Iceland academy: traveler education for better experience and proper behavior

The challenge

As this book argues in earlier chapters, overtourism does not have to be caused by overwhelming volumes of visitors; it can be caused by an overwhelming mismatch between local behavioral customs and traveler behavior. This mismatch can relate to two areas. First, it can concern local social dynamics and cultural norms, in which case it produces irritation among host residents who perceive guests as disrespectful or disruptive. Second, it can concern interaction with local surroundings and the local environment, in which case it demonstrates lack of preparedness for local lifestyle, nature, or weather conditions.

With the fast rise of tourism and the increasing accessibility of even remote spots around the world, many destinations are facing the undesired effects of the mismatch between local behavioral norms and traveler behavior. And while lack of awareness about local customs or lifestyle can merely lead to unpleasant situations or awkward experiences for guests and hosts (Sharpley, 2014), lack of preparedness for local weather conditions and interaction with the specific local surroundings can produce life-threatening situations (Kaltenborn, Haaland, & Sandell, 2001).

With the constantly increasing number of trips taken internationally and domestically (before the COVID-19 crisis imposed a global pause of the tourism sector) professional and academic discussions often emphasize local perceptions of well-being and quality of life as the indicators that truly measure the balance between desired growth and undesired impacts. They suggest that negative attitudes toward tourism and visitors are fueled by the sense that public resources, natural attractions, cultural heritage, and urban public spaces do not feel the same way because they are used by tourists in ways that modify them (Jóhannesson & Lund, 2019). Iceland, which has been referred to as a posterchild of the fast growth of contemporary tourism (Sheivachman, 2016), has been focus of especially interesting analyses about whether it is facing a problem with the pure volume of visitors or a challenge with the way they behave in local cultural and environmental realities (Anna & Hall, 2020), and the extent to which public spaces need to cater to visitors rather than residents (Jóhannesson & Lund, 2019).

The behavioral approach

The Nordics are one of the regions enjoying growing appeal among tourists from different regions around the world. It is also an area where the behavioral aspects of the mismatch between resident lifestyle and the acts of the growing numbers of tourists has been very visible. A growing number of publications in general media and academia have been discussing the effects of the growing tourism economy across Norway, Sweden, and Iceland emphasizing as a problem both dimensions of the resident-visitor behavior mismatch—disrespect to local social dynamics and cultural norms, and lack of preparedness for the local environment and weather conditions (Becker, 2018; Jóhannesson & Lund, 2019; Sheivachman, 2016). It has translated in multiple issues such as sudden increase of waste in natural areas, which until recently did not need to be cleaned because being out in nature with no trace is part of everyday culture in the Nordics. The growing number of foreign guests who engage in outdoor activities, however, come with different habits, including leaving waste behind. Another challenge has been safety and preparedness for being out in nature and understanding the dynamics of Nordic weather. Along with increase in international arrivals countries in the region have experienced a sharp rise in rescue operations assisting tourists who were caught outdoors by severe weather or who suffered injuries due to lack of proper gear and physical fitness. Understanding weather patterns and recognizing signs of approaching weather changes is part of the advanced outdoors culture of residents in the Nordics who know when it is wise to turn around or not go to the mountains at all. For the less-experienced tourists, a sunny start of the day can easily trick them into starting a long hike without the needed gear and without even suspecting that the weather might drastically change. Another frequent problem is undermining the risks of going off trails, walking on rocks, approaching powerful waters, walking on moss or plants, etc. Knowing how to stay safe and respect nature is part of common sense in the Nordics so locals like outdoor spaces natural without significant visitor infrastructure except perhaps markings. They do not need safety railings or signs to take care when they are close to steep rocks or near turbulent sea shores and rivers; they know not to walk outside of trails and avoid stepping on moss or plants. For visitors, however, the lack of paved trails, manmade steps in steep areas, safety or support infrastructure, warning and information signs is unexpected and produces challenges, and occasionally even high-risk situations.

While different countries and regions in the Nordics have launched a variety of interesting initiatives seeking to close the preparedness gap for visitors in the region, this case will put the spotlight on one particular program called Iceland Academy initiated in 2016 by the national tourism promotion body *Inspired By Iceland*. Iceland Academy is an initiative that seeks to close the cultural gap between residents and visitors by shedding light on local customs related to everyday behaviors, culturally-specific activities and safe interaction with the local natural environment.

The program includes six short brief video courses that cover the following safety and etiquette topics:

Course	What does it teach?
Responsible traveling in Iceland	Iceland is one of the most awe-inspiring places on Earth. This course shows how visitors can respect and be in harmony with nature while enjoying their travels. Topics include stepping or walking on moss, proper camping etiquette, and rules for setting a tent.
How to drive in Iceland	Driving in Iceland involves passing through rugged terrains so this course warns guests that they should be prepared for both paved and unpaved roads, narrow paths and one-lane bridges. Specific guidance is given for stopping to take pictures of nature while being on the road and for understanding specific road signs.
Avoiding hot-tub awkwardness	Taking a hot tub is one of the most treasured customs for Icelanders and naturally a desired activity for visitors. This course prepares guests for the proper hygiene steps that they need to take to avoid unpleasant situations and awkwardness.
A guide to safe selfies	As we know selfies are now part of the routine of visiting interesting spots. In a rugged terrain, severe weather and proximity to powerful natural forces, that can be dangerous. This course reminds travelers of the risks they may mistakenly take while looking to make the perfect selfie. It points to specific dangers such as slippery areas, powerful waters and high water temperature around hot springs.
Staying safe in Iceland	Icelandic nature is beautiful but also harsh. This course invites visitors to take safety seriously and to prepare for safe exploration of Iceland's natural treasures. It offers guidance on proper equipment, reminds guests to charge their phones and using location beeper when venturing out in nature. It also offers tips for using extra gear for specific activities such as going on glaciers.
Pack warm	Iceland is home to stunning nature but parts of it has been shaped by hard weather, which presents risks, especially for guests who have not visited the Nordics before. This course advises travelers to expect dynamic weather conditions and dress in layers allowing them to adjust to changes that can sometimes happen within minutes.

The style in which the Academy content presented is well thought out. It uses humor but without undermining important messaging. The topics focus on very specific issues that are observed to be at the heart of unpleasant encounters, damaging behavior or high-risk situations involving international visitors. Because it has been established that in many cases these problematic situations are caused by lack of preparedness rather than anything else, the courses target this gap with information that is understandable and fun to consume. For example, in most instances guests walk on the beautiful moss because they are unaware that while it looks sturdy it is in fact fragile and takes decades to recover; or visitors embark on exploring Iceland by car without expecting that they will have to drive on unpaved roads and follow well-established protocol for driving through narrow bridges and icy paths.

The course leaders delivering the content are with interesting and relevant profiles too. They are experts in the respective fields they cover and are perceived as reliable sources of the presented guidelines. For example, safety topics are delivered by Jónas Guðmundsson who is a project manager for accident prevention in tourism in Iceland. Stinga Bang who is a tour guide by professional is another instructor covering topics such as responsible travel in Iceland and safe taking of selfies.

A neat detail is that guests are invited to complete the full set of courses and to receive a certificate of completion from the Iceland Academy.

Discussion

Researchers in the area of cultural differences have long known that cultural gaps between hosts and guests impact psychological needs and the experiences, and require preliminary awareness and education (Reisinger & Turner, 2002). This is especially valid when the gap between the sociocultural background of the guests and the sociocultural make of the destination differ greatly. In the example of Iceland, which attracts with its unusual nature and rugged terrains, the potential for safety issues is higher so the gap between local norms and tourism behavior can produce dangerous situations that go beyond cultural misunderstandings (Kaltenborn et al., 2001). Residents of Iceland grow up with strong connection to nature and with advanced outdoors culture that nurtures appropriate skills for enjoying and surviving in the natural environment. This translates into advanced ability to mitigate the risks of extreme weather and rugged landscapes, as well as to preparedness to enjoy nature without leaving a footprint.

For foreign visitors coming from destinations where outdoors culture is significantly different, proper behavior out in nature is not automatic. With the rising numbers of guests visiting Iceland from regions with various attitudes, weather and relationship with nature, it is not hard to understand that most of the acts of undesired tourist behavior are due to lack of awareness rather than malicious intentions. Therefore with its focus and style, the Iceland Academy is a behavior-smart solution that precisely addresses gaps in traveler understanding of local etiquette and the specifics of interacting with Nordic natural environment. The typical Icelandic style of presenting the content and the employment of humor increase the appeal of the program and the likelihood that the content will be consumed in ways that will have a real impact. Researchers have proven that safety guidelines presented with humor are more likely to be processed and remembered than similar information presented in serious manner (Seneviratne & Molesworth, 2015).

Iceland's awareness raising program for international guests is a good example for destinations that seek to be more proactive in declaring and encouraging desired norms of behavior. As it was argued earlier in this book, as part of their strategic management efforts, destinations should be much more proactive in identifying targeted segments based on their behavioral profiles and in setting norms about what behavior is in line with local culture and expectations. An effective way of doing this is by being proactive in making the traveler aware before or upon arrival about what are the fundamental rules and principles of behavior they are expected to abide by. In that aspect, Iceland Academy is a best practice that could serve as example for others.

The big challenge with such programs is how to design them in order to increase their reach and ideally ensure that every future visitor has been exposed to them. In this specific the initiative is executed by the promotional body of Iceland and is available on the main website that most potential visitors are likely to explore when planning their trip. This increases the likelihood for exposure and impact. The incorporation of a reward mechanism, a certificate of completion, gamifies the experience and increases the likelihood that visitors will really benefit. Its voluntary nature, however, still leaves the opportunity for many to miss or skip the program and come for their Iceland adventure unprepared. It remains to be seen whether in the future destinations will find it useful to move to formats that require visitors to complete such programs as part of the entry procedures or as part of a pledge they sign upon arrival.

References

Anna, D., & Hall, C. M. (2020). From boiling to frozen? The rise and fall of international tourism to Iceland in the era of overtourism. *Environments*, *7*(59), 1–19.

Becker, E. (2018). Arctic crush: The friendly residents of one of the most remote parts of Norway have begun to organize to combat overtourism. *Travel Weekly*. Available from https://www.travelweekly.com/Europe-Travel/Arctic-crush-Norway-combats-overtourism.

Jóhannesson, G. T., & Lund, K. A. (2019). Beyond overtourism: Studying the entanglements of society and tourism in Iceland. In C. Milano, J. M. Cheer, & M. Novelli (Eds.), *Overtourism; Excesses, discontents and measures in travel and tourism* (pp. 91–106). CABI Publishing.

Kaltenborn, B. P., Haaland, H., & Sandell, K. (2001). The public right of access – Some challenges to sustainable tourism development in scandinavia? *Journal of Sustainable Tourism*, *9*(5), 417–433. Available from https://doi.org/10.1080/09669580108667412.

Reisinger, Y., & Turner, L. W. (2002). Cultural differences between Asian tourist. *Differences*, *40*(February 2002), 295–315. Available from https://doi.org/10.1177/0047287502040004004.

Seneviratne, D., & Molesworth, R. C. B. (2015). Employing humour and celebrities to manipulate passengers' attention to pre-flight safety briefing videos in commercial aviation. *Safety Science*, *75*, 130–135. Available from https://www.sciencedirect.com/science/article/pii/S0925753515000077.

Sharpley, R. (2014). Host perceptions of tourism: A review of the research. *Tourism Management*, *42*, 37–49. Available from https://doi.org/10.1016/j.tourman.2013.10.007.

Sheivachman, A. (2016, August). Iceland and the Trials of the 21st Century Tourism. *SKift*.

Case 7 Economic nutrition: making economic impact of spending salient

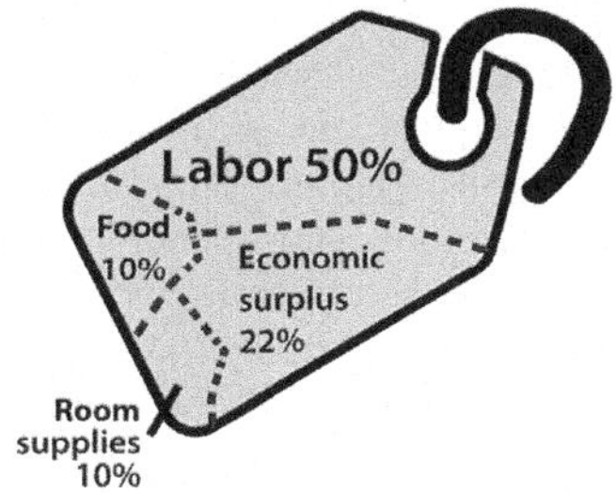

The challenge

While tracking economic impact of tourism activity in its full has been recognized to be challenging, it is known that its main driver is the monetary contribution to the local economy, respectively the well-being of the residents of the visited area (Frechtling, 1994). There is also sufficient understanding that different activities and different modes of travel leave different shares of the tourism revenue in the local economy (LENS, 2017; Nikolova, Fernandes, & Shahidsaless, 2015) but there is also understanding that the default principles for many large players in the industry is optimization of profit rather than local contribution (Ambrosie, 2015).

Among the biggest challenges in encouraging travelers to be sustainable in their choices are the complexity and invisibility of the impacts of tourism activity and their choices (Epler Wood, Milstein, & Ahamed-Broadhurst, 2019). Tracking the social impacts of a tourism operation, let alone an entire destination industry network, is complicated. This reflects on the behavior of both suppliers and buyers. While many suppliers of tourism and hospitality services are motivated to operate as responsible enterprises (Garay & Font, 2012) they often cannot observe or quantify the impact breakdown and therefore do not have basis for improvement.

For the customer lack of understanding and information make the idea for responsible consumption vague. Every visitor has the freedom to apply their own understanding, values and motivation in choosing how to travel and whether to consider impact as a factor in their consumer choices. Even if they proactively seek to make responsible choices and achieve higher positive impact with their spend, they have no way of knowing whether they have been successful.

The behavioral approach

Fogo Island is recognized as one of the pioneering and inspiring illustrations of sustainable development in the contemporary tourism industry. Even if on small scale, it illustrates how a tourism industry ecosystem can be shaped around the principles of place enhancement and community betterment. In many ways, it is a real-life example of how the shared value principle introduced by Porter and Kramer (Porter & Kramer, 2011) looks in the context of the contemporary travel economy.

The Fogo Island story is inspiring in all its aspects: from how old traditions can be given new life through contemporary art and storytelling, how local architecture can coexist with futuristic design, to how tourism can inspire a whole array of new local businesses that reinvent the island's economy (Lewis, 2012). A particularly interesting element of the story, which is the focus of the current case, is the pioneering of a tool for recognizing and stimulating positive local impact of the tourism economy—the economic nutrition mark. Developed by the local charity organization Shorefast, the economic nutrition certification mark is intended to serve as "a means to help increase buyer awareness of the economic impact of their purchasing decisions while also spotlighting seller accountability" (Shorefast, n.d.).

So what is the economic nutrition label? It mimics nutrition labels, which reveal the type and quantity of the different ingredients that have been used to prepare a food product. In a similar format it breaks down the price tag that customers are asked to pay and identifies the different items that form the price along with their respective shares. For example, the economic nutrition label for a one-night stay in Fogo Island Inn reveals the following breakdown (Fogo Island Inn, n.d.):

Item	Share (%)
Labor	49%
Food, room supplies	12%
Commission, fees	5%
Operations, admin	18%
Sales, marketing	4%
Surplus (reinvested in the community of Fogo Island)	12%

Even more importantly that that, the economic nutrition label offers an easy look at where the generated revenue goes specifying the share that stays in the island's economy, the share that goes in the broader economies of Newfoundland and Canada. For example, the Fogo Island Inn guests learn from their receipts that the money they have paid for their stay leaves 65% of their spend in the local economy of Fogo Island, 13%—in Newfoundland, 19% in the economy of Canada, and 3%—elsewhere in the world.

The mark is designed to be used by tourism businesses to track and demonstrate the makeup of their prices, and to make customers aware of their impact at the point of the purchase. It is also hope that it can serve as an example for others in the industry "looking to build a new economic system that offers a better balance between the return on economic capital and the health of diminishing sacred capital (natural, cultural, social, human, and physical capital)" (The Woodshop on Fogo Island, n.d.).

Discussion

The reason Fogo Island's economic nutrition mark is a behavioral best practice is that in a brilliantly simple way it overcomes two psychological barriers that currently complicate responsible traveler behavior. First, it overcomes the complexity behind tourism and hospitality services, which makes it impossible for the traveler to understand what it takes to deliver accommodation service or a tour for example, and how that impacts the local economy. Because it is complex and because they are on holiday guests cannot be expected to make an effort to understand the details of how their experience is organized and delivered. The economic nutrition label makes it very easy to understand the exact makeup of the accommodation experience or the elements that go into the production of a piece of local craft.

The second behavioral barrier that the economic nutrition label overcomes is invisibility or the fact that a traveler often does not think about where the money they spend during a holiday goes and who it might benefit. By presenting in simple terms the share of the spend that stays in the local economy and goes for local salaries or local purchasing the label makes the local economic impact of traveler choices visible and easy to understand. While it cannot reflect the full complexity of the socioeconomic impacts associated with tourism activity, it focuses on the main factor—share of the spending that stays in the local economy, which is easy to understand and relate to.

As discussed in a previous case study in this book, saliency tools such as the economic nutrition label (similar to CarbonAte and carbon footprint) influence not only the behavior of customer but that of suppliers too. This reverse effect is a fact because the label can nudge operators to constantly improve their "balance" of impacts and increase the desired local impact. In the case of Fogo Island enterprises are set up to maximize local sourcing from the start (The Woodshop on Fogo Island, n.d.) but for tourism businesses that might decide to adopt the tool in other destinations, the ability to track and improve local impact could be an expected side effect.

It is worth noting that from a behavioral point of view the economic nutrition mark complements an overall behavior-smart approach that is at the heart of the Fogo Island tourism model—the fact that the sustainability decisions are premade by the host and are not left to the visitor. As this book argues, it makes much more sense for destinations and host businesses to take control of sustainability by choosing and setting the norms and principles that define tourism on their territory. For example, by default all Fogo Island businesses are social businesses and the local tourism ecosystem is set up to revitalize the local economy and make it resilient in the new socioeconomic realities (CBC News, 2020). This means that the decision about maximizing the impact of the traveler spending is premade for the traveler and not left up to them. In this sense the economic nutrition mark is a tool for transparency and awareness rather than a nudge to choose a responsible option. It is also a trigger for consumer pride and satisfaction because even when customers do not make the proactive decision to spend responsibly, they enjoy the recognition that they have done good.

In any case, just like many other aspects of the Fogo Island experience can serve as inspiration for bettering of the contemporary tourism model, the economic nutrition mark is a brilliant best practice that can be shared by businesses and destinations around the world. It is a tool that holds the behavioral power to nudge operators to pursue better and better makeup of their price tag with stronger economic impact. It is also a brilliant way to demonstrate to travelers how their exciting holiday experiences can be personally enriching but can also deliver well-being for host places and their residents.

References

Ambrosie, L. M. (2015). *Sun & sea tourism: Fantasy and finance of the all-inclusive industry*. Cambridge Scholars Publishing.

CBC News. (2020, January 5). Entrepreneur Zita Cobb 's social conscience lands her in the Business Hall of Fame Everything starts with believing. *CBC News*, 1–6.

Epler Wood, M., Milstein, M., & Ahamed-Broadhurst, K. (2019). *Destinations at risk: The invisible burden of tourism*. < www.thetravelfoundation.org.uk > .

Fogo Island Inn. (n.d.). *Fogo Island Inn: Economic nutrition certification mark*. Fogo Island Inn Website. < https://fogoislandinn.ca/in-between/economic-nutrition/ > .

Frechtling, D. C. (1994). Assessing the economic impacts of travel and tourism—Introduction to travel economic impact estimation. *Travel, Tourism and Hospitality Research*, 27.

Garay, L., & Font, X. (2012). Doing good to do well? Corporate social responsibility reasons, practices and impacts in small and medium accommodation enterprises. *International Journal of Hospitality Management*, *31*(2), 329–337. Available from https://doi.org/10.1016/j.ijhm.2011.04.013.

LENS, U. (2017). *Assessment of the mountaineering sector in Jordan, Amman*.

Lewis, J. (2012). The possibility of an island. *The New York Times Style Magazine*, 29–32. Available from https://doi.org/10.7767/9783205202271-007.

Nikolova, M., Fernandes, E., & Shahidsaless, R. (2015). *Strengthening tourism competitiveness in the OECS countries: Market analysis* (OECS Competitiveness Project (P152117)).

Porter, M. E., & Kramer, M. R. (2011). Creating shared value how to reinvent capitalism-and unleash a wave of innovation and growth. *Harvard Business Review*, 2–17. *January-February*. < http://www.nuovavista.com/SharedValuePorterHarvardBusinessReview.PDF > .

Shorefast. (n.d.). *Economic nutrition certification mark*. Shorefast Foundation Website. < https://www.shorefast.org/what-you-can-do/#economic-nutrition-certification-mark > .

The Woodshop on Fogo Island. (n.d.). *The woodshop on Fogo Island: Economic nutrition mark*. The Woodshop on Fogo Island Website.

Case 8 Gamifying responsible travel: Adventure Junky

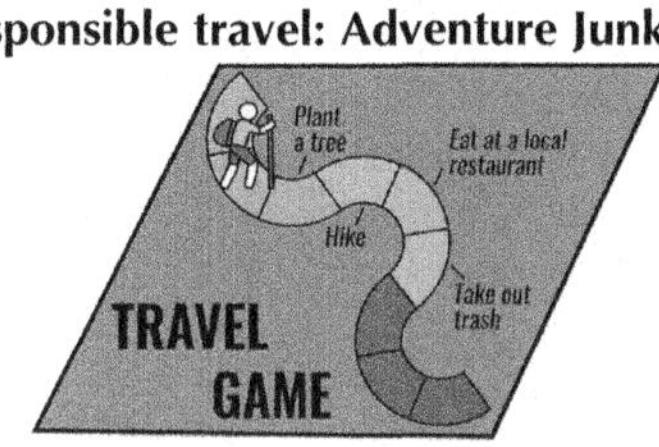

The challenge

The classical approach to influencing traveler behavior toward more responsible choices during holiday relies on awareness and education. There are two major problems with it. The first is associated with the mere volume of travelers, international and domestic, that trot across the globe. Educating all of them would take monumental efforts and resources. The second major problem is that we know that even when people have the information they make poor decisions regarding their own health (Loewenstein, Asch, & Volpp, 2013), let alone the health of a place that they are vising for a short period of time or the planet, which is a vague and difficult-to-imagine concept anyway.

Growing media coverage of overtourism and tourism's impact on the climate have triggered growing awareness among travelers on the need to be mindful of their impact during holidays. Despite that, there are two significant behavioral barriers that people face in changing the way they travel. The first is lack of understanding of what it means to be sustainable and lack of idea where to start. Even if more and more people have genuine desire to make the right choices, they do not know how to translate sustainability principles into specific decisions that they make during travels.

The second behavioral barrier is associated with the natural inclination of people to release of control during holidays. When they are away from home and daily routines, travelers seek to free themselves of worries, including about daunting issues such as sustainability or the climate. Therefore they are not only not likely to behave more responsibly than at home but are quite likely to deviate from sustainability routines or habits that are part of their everyday behavior (Miller, Rathouse, Scarles, Holmes, & Tribe, 2010). For example, even if one is religiously strict with separate waste collection and efforts to recycle as much as possible at home, they might spare themselves the effort to keep waste separate during holidays, especially if there are no easily accessible bins for separate collection.

Given that awareness raising and education is not likely to produce fast and impactful change of traveler behavior, there is need for other more effective solutions.

The behavioral solution

While people are on holiday, they should enjoy themselves. And what better way to do that than to have fun and do good at the same time. An exciting contemporary solution that activates responsible traveler behavior in a guilt-free way is Adventure Junky, a platform gamifying sustainable travel (Sims & Malone, 2019). How does it work? Adventure Junky connects subscribed travelers to its constantly growing collection of carefully curated exciting adventures from around the world. As they engage in different travel experiences subscribers collect points and badges that are automatically added to their profile. Every adventure comes with a points score and badges that are added to the profile of anyone who has experienced it. Points and badges are the basis for a global ranking of Adventure Junky travelers called the Leaderboard, which fuels serious competition for who will collect more and climb to a higher spot. The essential key here is that the score is generated by an algorithm designed around solid sustainability principles. For example, a high-score adventure would be one that is delivered by a B Corp certified travel operator, that is carbon neutral, includes no single use plastics, offers only locally-sourced food options, includes multiple-nature-friendly low-impact activities and engages a local guide.

The list of sustainability criteria that are the core of Adventure Junky's scoring algorithm includes: biodiversity, biosphere reserve, buying local, carbon offsetting, community development, conservation, eco-lodge, energy efficiency, homestay, indigenous, leave no trace, research, rewilding, and world heritage site. For illustration about 80% of all adventures on the platform include a conservation element, more than 75% incorporate buying locally, over 60% have positive impact on community development, over 55% are designed around leave-no-trace-behind principles, and over 20% include carbon offset.

Discussion

Despite growing concerns about the impact of travel, people's desire to explore and visit new places around the world will not vanish. Nor it should, because travel is associated with great benefits for the traveler, as well as the host. At the same time the sustainability crisis in tourism requires a drastic change in tourist behavior and new social norms that guide it. As explained earlier, the classical approach of educating tourists and hoping that they will automatically improve their impact, is not optimal.

The Adventure Junky way is actually to flip the process and first shape behavior along the desired norms while weaving education for the phase when responsible consumption is already a fact. Traveler motivation is shifted away from the daunting "save the earth," which is more likely to suppress desire to act (Thaler & Sunstein, 2009) and which is in conflict with the natural inclination of travelers to release control. The motivation with Adventure Junky is the fun and the competition. Travelers join the game to engage in exciting experiences and to compete against other players. A major draw is also the fact that the platform promises predesigned adventures that are curated and that cover a wide range of preferences. That eliminates the need to think about where to go next and to have to design every trip on one's own. It also eliminates the need to consider sustainability as all trips on the platform are designed responsibly. In other words, while subscribers join for the fun and the exciting competition with peers, they automatically become sustainable travelers because sustainability is a non-negotiable element in the Adventure Junky model.

An important aspect of the platform is the mentioned earlier flipped approach to educating travelers. The points system and the badges are tied to established sustainability principles so as users seek to increase their performance in the Leaderboard, they begin identifying the trip characteristics that give them points and continue to seek to pursue them. Along the way the platform offers brief and easy to understand explanations for why staying with locals or visiting a national park are acts of responsibility, not only points generators. This bitesize gradual education along with the learning that users do by seeking out high-score adventures, produce much more effective and sustainable behavioral change than classical approaches. In the words of one of the Adventure Junky travelers: *"What started off as a game, which is what grabbed my attention, has turned into something completely different. ...now I'm looking for experiences like meeting the locals, supporting the community, learning about the cultures and places I visit."*

References

Loewenstein, G., Asch, D. A., & Volpp, K. G. (2013). Analysis & commentary behavioral economics holds potential to deliver better results for patients, insurers, and employers. *Health Affairs*, *32*(7), 1244–1250. Available from https://doi.org/10.1377/hlthaff.2012.1163.

Miller, G., Rathouse, K., Scarles, C., Holmes, K., & Tribe, J. (2010). Public understanding of sustainable tourism. *Annals of Tourism Research*, *37*(3), 627–645. Available from https://doi.org/10.1038/372486b0.

Sims, F.C., & Malone, N. (2019). *Personal communication with Fuchsia Claire Sims and Nigel Malone (Adventure Junky founders).*

Thaler, R. H., & Sunstein, C. R. (2009). *Nudge: Improving decsions about health, wealth and happiness.* London: Penguin Books.

Case 9 Cut Food Waste 2020: an integrated effort to cut food waste

The challenge

According to the United Nations Environment Program (UNEP), one-third of food around the world is not consumed and is wasted due to inefficiencies in the global food system (UNEP, 2016). The gaps in the food chain that lead to such dramatic losses are numerous—from failures in production, processing, and packaging protocols through inadequate storage and transportation facilities (FAO, 2016). And while physical infrastructure and amenities play a major role, processes and practices at restaurants, catering operators and hotels (as well as private households) are a major contributor to the loss of food too.

The throwing away of usable food is a two-fold problem. First, it means that the global food system wastes products that are fit for consumption while large shares of the global population (13% of the population in developing regions) do not have access to sufficient food (UNEP, 2016). Second, food waste contributes to climate change as when it ends up in landfills it emits methane, which is a potent greenhouse gas (World Wildlife Fund & American Hotels & Lodging Association, 2017).

The processes and protocols at food service operators are complex and influenced by numerous considerations such as health, safety, and profitability. A lot of the inefficiencies leading to the loss of eatable products are due to the behavior of the suppliers (owners and workers) at the food establishments on one side and the behavior of clients on the other side. Restaurant, catering and hotel staff contribute to food loss by failing to use products or ingredients that are good enough for use, by not making an effort to donate remaining good food and divert it from reaching landfills (World Wildlife Fund & American Hotels & Lodging Association, 2017). On the customer end the behaviors that contribute to food loss include ordering or taking from the buffet more food than can realistically be consumed, trying out foods or meals as experiment or as experiencing something different (especially when visiting a different country with different culinary traditions) (Juvan, Grün, & Dolnicar, 2018). Both, for suppliers and customers, these damaging behaviors are due to the fact that motivation is shaped by other considerations and food waste is not a forefront concern that impacts decisions.

The behavioral approach

As result of proactive awareness raising by major international organizations and charities, there is increased sensitivity toward the need to minimize food waste at different points of the global food system. And while there are many fruitful practices that come from different players around the world, there are few instances of integrated industry efforts on country level. This case tells the story of Norway's national-level program designed to unify and integrate industry-wide efforts to cut waste using behavior-smart techniques.

Norway's concentrated effort to cut food waste especially by changing food management practices at hotels, restaurants, supermarkets and other food establishments was launched in 2017. The *Cut Food Waste 2020* program was initiated and has been led by *Matvett* ("food sense")—an entity set up by the food and service industry especially to coordinate efforts to reduce and prevent food waste. The common goal was to cut food waste by 20% by 2030 and to engage at least 50% of the industry in this effort (Ministry of Climate & Environment, 2017).

The initial analysis of the food waste problem identified the factors that fueled it and that needed to be addressed to achieve the ambitious goal. It revealed that a lot had to do with operational practices in the kitchen, kitchen workers perceptions about food waste and lack of prioritization of avoiding waste (Schrøder, 2019). On the consumer side the main contributing factors seemed to be mainly lack of awareness about the scale of the problem and the tactics that could help avoid food waste.

Armed with clarity on the awareness and behavioral factors that fueled food waste in the food and service industry the *Cut Food Waste 2020* program developed solutions to address them. The first challenge that needed to be solved was salience. Both kitchen workers and consumers needed to be made aware of the scale of the food waste problem in a way that is easy to understand so the program developed an impactful awareness raising campaign. It was based on visual posters and display cards that illustrated in simple terms the scale of the challenge. For example, they would include an image of a fresh fish or a deliciously looking plated meal with a line cutting through one-third of it to visually show how much of the product or meal is likely to end in the waste bin. The awareness raising visuals were placed in kitchen areas to target workers in the sector as well as in consumer halls, buffet and shopping areas to increase the sensitivity of clients.

Awareness alone was not going to be sufficient so the approach of the *Cut Food Waste 2020* program naturally included a second level—designing tools for action that would facilitate behavioral change. On the consumer side participating food service providers used a set of tactics that seek to influence the decision at the moment of ordering food (at a-la-carte facilities) or picking up food (at buffets). First, wherever possible, they transitioned to using smaller plate sizes, which is a proven technique for cutting food consumption and respectively waste, especially at entities with a buffet format (Kallbekken & Sælen, 2013). In addition to this nudge customers were openly encouraged to make conscious efforts to minimize food waste through postcards and stand cards that sought the influence the social norm and the sense of acceptability of returning to the buffet and picking up food multiple times rather than seeking to pile large amounts at once. This addressed the established concern among consumers that returning to the buffet tables multiple times is not perceived favorably (Schrøder, 2019).

The Matvett toolset targeting professionals in the industry was two-step. The first step was to perform proper measurement of food waste and incorporate that in the kitchen processes. This is important for two reasons. First, it quantifies the wasted volume and offers a clear picture of what products and ingredients are lost at what point of the preparation journey. Second, it allows staff and entities to monitor the effect of applied tactics and to track their progress toward the end goal. The rolling out of regular measurement as a permanent step in kitchen processes is challenging so the role of the toolset was to offer the specific steps facilitating behavioral change and to ensure the measurement practices are consistent across the industry.

The second step of the Matvett approach was focused on equipping the industry professionals with specific tactics for cutting food waste. This included the development and distribution of specific solutions for canteen and buffet design, as well as for the safe reuse of left-over ingredients or product parts. The know-how was delivered and disseminated through hands-on manuals and different forms of training that were available for workers at participating operations.

Discussion

The *Cut Food Waste 2020* program continues to grow in its influence every year and has already triggered significant change in the practices and behavior of employees and hotel guests throughout the food service industry in Norway. Recent data published by the program reveals that in 2020 many of the participating entities have achieved the goal of reducing food waste by 20%, including 42% of the hotels, 63% of the canteens, and 46% of the restaurants. The main success factor has been identified to be the transition to smaller servings and plate sizes (Matvett, 2020).

The *Cut Food Waste 2020* program is a great illustration of how behavior-smart thinking can enhance large-scale initiatives that seek to correct fundamental sustainability challenges in hospitality, tourism, and other sectors. Its approach is based on mapping the behavioral factors that contribute to the food waste problem and targeting them directly. The two-phase solution involves awareness raising—making the problem visible and impossible to ignore for both sides of the market (the service supplier and the consumer). As simple as this sounds, this is extremely important because until a problem is clearly visible and quantified, it is psychologically easy to ignore. In addition, decisions on the side of the consumer and the supplier are driven by more immediate factors than battling food loss. For service providers these are profitability, competition with other players on the market and hygiene requirements. As these are more forefront concerns, they take lead in shaping processes and behaviors of businesses in the sector. Similarly, for consumers food waste is a vague and distant issue, and their decision-making at the point of purchase/ food selection is shaped by factors such as food taste, interest in experimentation and sometimes the fear of missing out prompting people to put more food on the plate. In that sense the simple but impactful communication campaign using posters and cards visualizing the problem at the point of preparation and selection is an effective way of making food waste salient at the right moment when it can impact choice.

The second phase of the program approach is equipping both consumers and professionals with tactics enabling them to act. Experience shows that even when people are alert and generally concerned about a problem such as the environment or poverty, they often do not act on it because they feel they are not empowered or do not know what to do (Datta et al., 2015). Consumers are empowered to contribute to cutting food waste through very simple tactics, including optimization of available foods, smaller servings, and smaller plates. This is supplemented with gentle nudges such as reminders that buffet customers are invited to come back and serve themselves a second time rather than take everything at once or as the possibility to top up dips and side dishes. Increased awareness in combination with these tactics influence social norms and change the desirability of acts that minimize food loss.

Suppliers are empowered to act through practical solutions that target the moments when food waste is most likely to occur: during the preparation of meals, and after meals (or parts of them) are prepared but not consumed. The first major focus that is addressed is measurement. By providing the steps and tools to execute careful measurement the program enables service providers to quantify and monitor food waste, and to map the moments when food waste is most likely to occur. Feedback from food and beverage professionals reveals that the ability to measure alone has powerful awareness effect on staff members who suddenly really understand the scale of the problem and begin to proactively contribute with ideas. Measurement leads to salience of food waste as success indicator on the job as well and this makes it impossible to ignore (Metcalfe, Gosnell, & List, 2016). The ability to track which kind of ingredients or products were left unused or unconsumed empowers decision makers to optimize by reengineering menus and redesigning buffets. Through the program they were equipped with safe tactics for efficient use of products. For example, slight adjustments of menus could ensure that parts of a tomato are used for a fresh salad and the left overs are cooked into a sauce for a main course rather than thrown away.

Measurement offers a systematic look into the problem allowing participating businesses to optimize food processes beyond the tactics provided by the program. For example, the ability to track the food that is least consumed at a buffet leads to the easy decision to eliminate it from the menu. In fact, service providers relying on a buffet format report cutting food waste by more than 30% by merely cutting the quantities and the number of items they serve, and by focusing on foods that are favored and rarely left. Optimizing the size of servings without really limiting the amount of food available to the customer emerges as an effective solution for a-la-carte restaurants. The volume of wasted side dishes or dips prompts service providers to move to smaller portions but to offer customers free top-ups if they desire them (Matvett, 2020). This measure alone leads to tremendous cuts in lost food.

The entire process of buying, storing and preparing meals can be optimized once there is specific measurement revealing which foods are most likely to remain unconsumed, on which week day and at what time of the day. Tracking the food journey also gives companies the opportunity to organize food donation or programs such as "Too Good To Go," which are adopted by many entities participating in *Cut Food Waste 2020.*

In conclusion, it is important to mention that the integrated effort to equip the food service industry with tools that facilitate behavior change incorporates new norms in the design of the sector. The integration of measurement and food waste elimination tactics in daily protocols ensures sustainable transition to new behavioral models for the entire professional community. This is of great importance because the industry often relies on young, untrained and temporary workers who cannot be expected to learn everything about food waste as part of their standard training but who will adhere to the already existing norms that make the loss of food undesirable and easy to avoid.

References

Datta, S., Miranda, J.J., Zoratto, L., Calvo-González, O., Darling, M., & Lorenzana, K. (2015). *A behavioral approach to water conservation: Evidence from Costa Rica* (No. 7283; Policy Research Working Paper). <https://openknowledge.worldbank.org/bitstream/handle/10986/22156/A0behavioral0a0ence0from0Costa0Rica.pdf?sequence = 1&isAllowed = y>.

FAO. (2016). *Food loss & waste*. <http://www.fao.org/platform-food-loss-waste/en/>.

Juvan, E., Grün, B., & Dolnicar, S. (2018). Biting off more than they can chew: Food waste at hotel breakfast buffets. *Journal of Travel Research, 57*(2), 232–242. Available from https://doi.org/10.1177/0047287516688321.

Kallbekken, S., & Sælen, H. (2013). "Nudging" hotel guests to reduce food waste as a win-win environmental measure. *Economics Letters, 119*(3), 325–327. Available from https://doi.org/10.1016/j.econlet.2013.03.019.

Matvett. (2020). *Cut Food Waste 2020.* KuttMatsvinn2020.

Metcalfe, R., Gosnell, G., & List, J. (2016). *Virgin Atlantic tested 3 ways to change employee behavior. Harvard Business Review, August.*

Ministry of Climate and Environment. (2017). *Industry agreement on reduction of food waste between the authorities of Norway and the food industry.*

Schrøder, A.M. (2019). *Personal communication with Anne Marie Schrøder on 12 September 2019.*

UNEP. (2016). *Why do we need to change our food system?* United Nations Environment Program. Available from https://youtu.be/VcL3BQeteCc.

World Wildlife Fund, & American Hotels and Lodging Association. (2017). Fighting food waste in hotels. In *World Wildlife Fund.*

Case 10 Piloting behavior-smart thinking on destination level (Västmanland Region, Sweden)

The challenge

As the texts throughout this book argue, the advancing knowledge about human behavior offers a wealth of insights that can help destinations improve current approaches to planning and management. Tourism is complex and involves the operationalization of orchestrated coordination among multiple small and large, public- and private-sector players. Behavioral insights can add value at multiple levels—from optimizing the design and operations of the individual business to the strategic models and processes that shape destination management. At the individual company level behavior-smart thinking can inform decisions that guide the training and management of staff, sustainability efforts, marketing tactics, pricing strategies and the design of offerings in ways that guarantees that the hearts and minds of travelers will be captured. At the destination level behaviorally-informed solutions can address strategic marketing, including segmentation and the setting of norms for the behavior of visitors. It can also influence the collaboration between the different players in the local industry network and the coordinated efforts to optimize the balance between desired and undesired impacts of tourism.

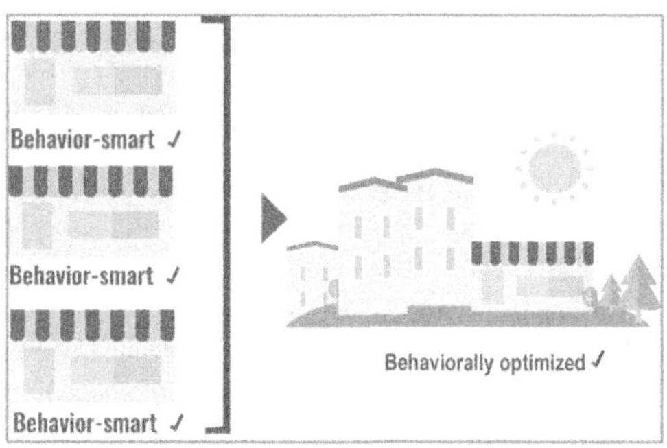

To the best of the knowledge of the author of this book, at the time of writing, no destination, except the one featured in this case, has made an effort to experiment with behavior-smart thinking as a way of accelerating the achieving of its strategic market and sustainability goals. As the rest of the cases included in this book reveal, there are already examples of behaviorally-informed solutions at individual company level or at the level of a specific solution.

The behavioral approach

Västmanland, a small regional destination in Sweden, is the first to experiment with behavior-smart thinking as vehicle for optimizing commercial and sustainability practices among local tourism businesses. The project "Applying behavioral economics thinking to tourism in Västmanland region" is executed in 2018–19 by the local tourism board Västmanland Tourism. It is initiated with the aim to benefit from the advances in behavioral sciences and use them to support local service providers in improving their marketing tactics such as messaging, pricing, online presence, etc., as well as their sustainability efforts (Stanaway & Wernersson, 2018b). The hope is that by helping companies throughout the destination adopt behavior-smart tactics, the region will benefit from the cumulative effects of stronger commercial success and optimized footprint of the tourism sector.

Because of the innovative nature of the project and the lack of previous experience with behaviorally-informed solutions, the program design included a strong experimentation component to help arrive at the specific measures that would be developed and shared with the entire business community in the region. It involved working with a small set of innovation-prone pilot companies interested in experimenting with behavior-smart tactics to confirm their validity for the local context. The following table summarizes the key steps and milestones in the project.

Key project activities and milestones.

Activity	Purpose	Why?
Project ideation phase	Create the design and plan the activities that guarantee meeting of objectives	This is a specific project, which in itself represents an experiment with a lot of unknowns. It was important to design a unique process that accounted for the uncertainties but guaranteed maximum likelihood for success.
Project kick-off and pilot companies	Introduce the project and behavior-smart thinking to the local industry to raise awareness and invite pilot participants	Behavior-smart thinking is relatively new for the travel industry and not many businesses have structured knowledge about it. This kick-off activity was designed to provide the framework and explain the benefits of using insights from behavioral sciences to optimize business and destination success. It also served as the basis to identify companies, which were interested and motivated to serve as pilot host of the experimentation activities.
Agreement on tactics	Select a set of meaningful tactics that would be tested and applied to the industry throughout the region	It was important to arrive at a set of solutions to be tested that are both relevant to the larger business community but attractive enough for the participating pilot companies because they are the ones investing time and resources at this phase of the project.

Testing and analysis	Execution of the testing action plans for the selected tactics; analysis of the results and synthesis of the findings	The results of the solution tests was essential in ensuring that they work in the specific context and that they can be easily executed by a large number of operators throughout the region. The testing also offered very convincing and directly relevant data that motivated the interest of more businesses to roll these solutions out.
Hands-on manual	Synthesis of the practical steps to apply behavior-smart solutions in a manual for businesses	In order to reach the entire business community throughout the region, the knowledge about the tested behavior-smart solutions needed to be distributed in a format that is easily digestible and available in a flexible format. Västmanland Tourism decided that the best approach was to develop a hands-on manual with specific step-by-step guidance on how to plan, test and execute behavioral solutions.
Workshops and consultations	Destination-wide roll-out workshops and consultations	In order to activate interest and engage companies in exploring and applying the available and tested behavior-smart solutions Västmanland Tourism initiated a series of workshops with private sector companies throughout the destination. Their purpose was to introduce the manual, engage entrepreneurs in using the tactics it presents and offer advisory assistance to ensure that they receive all necessary support to succeed.

Västmanland Tourism identified three pilot companies to test the behavior-smart tactics and offer insights as to how they can be applied to the rest of the business community. They three offered a good mix representing different segments of the industry. The first participant representing attractions was *Kokpunkten Actionbad*—an indoors water park with a wide variety of slides and water-based attractions for adults, young adults and children. The water park is one of the main attractions in the region geared toward residents of the area and visitors coming for a short holiday or on a day trip. The second participant in the project representing food service providers was *Saluhallen Slakteriet*—an indoors food market featuring different restaurants, small shops, and small event venues emphasizing local and sustainable food. While the outfits in the food complex offer food from around the world, there is strong emphasis on local sourcing and the promotion of nearby farms, herbs and locally produced ingredients. The final participant, *Schenströmska Herrgården*, represented the accommodation and event sector in the region. Schenströmska Herrgården is a stylish mansion away from the city and surrounded by nature. It attracts leisure guests who stay for short holidays or long weekends, and hosts private and business events (from weddings to corporate celebrations and retreats).

Once the pilots were confirmed each of them was engaged in a process of identification of relevant tactics that will be tested by them. The factors that influenced the selection were (Stanaway & Wernersson, 2018a):

1. Ensuring that the tactics relate to existing and relevant issues that will produce direct benefits for the participating business
2. Ensuring that the solutions can realistically be tested within the timeline of the project
3. Ensuring that the testing of the tactics is not resource-intensive
4. Ensuring that each of the pilots tests at least one commercial and one sustainability practice
5. Ensuring that the tested solutions are relevant to a wide share of the local industry community

The table below summarizes the tactics that were tested with the participating pilot companies.

Summary of selected behavior-smart solutions.

Pilot company	Category	Commercial tactics	Footprint tactics
Kokpunkten Actionbad	Attraction	Menu design and presenting information on products/services	Saving energy
Saluhallen Slakteriet	Food service provider	Optimizing menu design/offering presentation	Encouraging local buying
Schenströmska Herrgården	Accommodation and events venue	Presenting price for tailored offers	Minimizing cleaning and energy use

The results from the pilot projects were the basis for the synthesis of a set of behavior-smart tactics to be used by all tourism businesses operating in Västmanland region. They were presented in a special hands-on manual that offered brief overview of the principles of behavior-smart thinking followed by a step-by-step guide on how to execute each presented solution. The guiding document offers all tools, such as a short evaluation, or a measurement plan, that an entrepreneur needs to apply the solution. The document was tested with business audiences to ensure that the language and content are indeed practical and relevant (Nikolova, 2019).

The final step in the project was the roll out of the manual with a series of workshops and advisory services for companies (Stanaway & Wernersson, 2019). The events involved presenting the manual in details and engaging companies in selecting and starting to work with tactics that seem relevant to their businesses. The available advisory support ensured that any professionals will receive support at any stage of the execution.

Discussion

Västmanland Tourism is one of the smallest regional destination in Sweden but despite that, it was the first to experiment with behavior-smart thinking on destination level. From a behavioral perspective the project "Applying behavioral economics thinking to tourism in Västmanland region" is a best practice for three reasons. First, it extracts relevant insights from behavioral sciences in order to optimize the commercial and sustainability practices of businesses operating on the territory of the region. There is unlimited potential in using insights about human behavior and decision-making in the optimization of marketing content, pricing strategies, or experience design for travel companies.

The second aspect is the very design of the project, which aimed to operationalize the solutions and ensure that they are adopted by a maximum number of companies in the destination. The experimental nature of the program made it natural to include a pilot test element, which not only allowed the testing of specific tactics in the local context but provided local evidence. This secures an important psychological effect as the rest of the business community is much likelier to engage with new solutions if they have been tested locally with peers.

The third important success factor was the writing of the manual and the roll out with hands-on workshops. Preparing a document that will reach all companies in the region made a lot of sense because it becomes a resource that can reach the local industry network and that offers entrepreneurs the flexibility to use it when they have the time and resources. To make sure the tone of voice and context are completely aligned with the needs of the business, a small group of companies were asked to review and provide feedback on the tactics and the offered guidelines. The downside of a passive document is that it can be read and remain as a resource on the shelf. The decision of Västmanland Tourism to roll out the manual with a series of activation workshops and available advisory services minimized this risk. By educating companies how to best benefit from the resource and by helping them launch some of the solutions the workshops increase the likelihood that more companies will adopt behavior-smart thinking and that the destination will enjoy cumulative effects with behaviorally-optimized commercial and sustainability practices.

References

Nikolova, M.S. (2019). *Smart ways: A manual with behavior-smart solutions for increased profitability and sustainability in the tourism industry*. Västmanland Turism.

Stanaway, Å., & Wernersson, A. (2018a). *Personal communication with Åsa Stanaway and Angelika Wernersson on 17 April 2018*.

Stanaway, Å., & Wernersson, A. (2018b). *Personal communication with Åsa Stanaway and Angelika Wernersson on 2 February 2018*. Västmanland Tourism.

Stanaway, Å., & Wernersson, A. (2019). *Personal communication with Åsa Stanaway and Angelika Wernersson on 25 July 2019*.

Conclusion

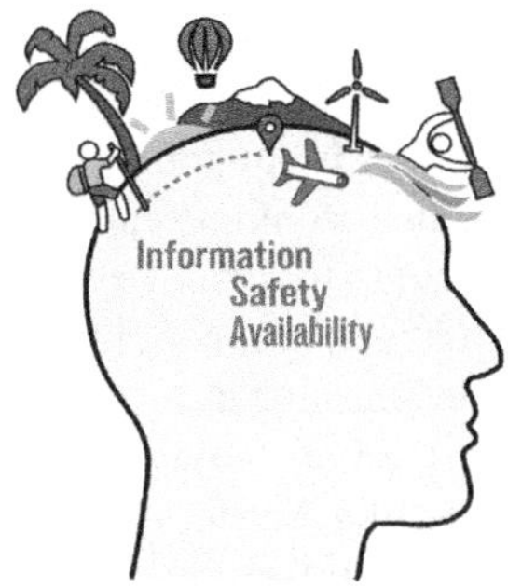

The tourism industry is facing the need to reinvent itself and move toward behavior-smart systems thinking. Overwhelming challenges such as overtourism, the climate crisis, and unsustainable development require a combination of solutions, many of which are complicated, technology intensive, and expensive. While they need to be invested in and worked on, they will require time and resources. Meanwhile, there is an opportunity to achieve a lot with soft measures influencing the behavior of travelers, hosts, destination managers, and politicians. Nudges and modifications in decision or consumption journeys can begin producing much needed changes today.

Behavior-smart thinking can help understand, adjust, and reshape the ecosystem

Behavior-smart thinking can help in three directions: understand the issues better, adjust existing systems, and reshape future systems.

First, behavioral thinking can help diagnose negative forces in the travel sector. Breaking down complicated dynamics around overtourism or sustainability into behavioral acts that fuel them, helps to identify the incentives or barriers that determine human actions triggering undesired effects. In its introduction this book started with three anecdotes that illustrate how many of the mistakes in the travel system are made because the respective incentives are not well thought out. Politicians such as Mr. Smith introduce inappropriately designed volume-based subsidies because the quality of their work is measured only on the basis of the tourism arrival numbers. If their performance was evaluated on the basis of the satisfaction of local residents with tourism, Mr. Smith and the likes would be incentivized to design policies that shape the local tourism economy in ways that are desired by host communities. Similarly service providers such as Mrs. Jones misreport numbers and hide part of their business motivated by the wrongful but immediate benefit of saving on taxes. If Mrs. Jones was to receive some financial incentives or special status because she manages to grow her business well, then she will want to report everything to be recognized as successful business leader and be eligible for rewards. So a behavioral lens can help identify incorrectly placed incentives and barriers across different challenging contexts, and identify the needs to make changes. Such misplaced incentives and barriers are what contributes and in some cases fuels some of the biggest challenges in the tourism industry.

Second, behaviorally informed thinking can lead to solutions that adjust decision or consumption patterns to achieve behavioral optimization. As illustrated throughout the book, sometimes simple adjustments in the way information is presented or the framing in a description can really influence behavioral outcomes. Behavior-smart solutions apply this knowledge by incorporating nudges or eliminating barriers to encourage desired behavior. A great example for behavioral optimization where behavioral tactics help to address an overtourism challenge is the discussed in Chapter 4, Palau Pledge. The core of the pledge is the integration of many behavioral solutions across the visitor journey that make travelers more likely to be mindful of the impact they have on the local destination. The required in-flight movie shown to all arriving tourists and the pledge stamp placed in every passport upon border entry raise awareness and trigger sense of responsibility. Carefully planned signage around the destination systematically reminds guests of the different commitments they have made as part of the pledge. The key is that the signs appear in places where travelers are likely to engage in irresponsible acts: for example, signs around beach areas remind travelers that they should not be picking up shells or pebbles, and that they should not disturb marine life. Behavior-smart thinking offers a wide variety of tools and tactics that used individually or in combination can help address a lot of significant challenges within the existing system design.

Third, behavioral economics has helped recognize that many of the existing systems in our societies, including in tourism, are designed around incorrect assumptions about human behavior. While behavioral optimization is pursued in existing systems and already designed spaces, there is an opportunity to begin designing future systems with behavior in mind. As the story about the Factory Food-n-Dance in the case collection in Chapter 6 reveals, the smart combination of physical design of a leisure space and design of the experience can influence the likelihood that people engage in desired holiday behavior. This means that in the future destinations might design public space and recreational areas in ways that increase the likelihood that residents and visitors are healthier and happier, and that they generate zero litter and have net-positive impact on the natural environment. Hotels, restaurants, and other service providers can benefit from behavior-smart design to increase the quality of the experience while nudging employees and guests to behave in ways that minimize the negative footprint of operations. Behaviorally informed itineraries can be designed in ways that make travelers happier and their impact on the destination net positive. So a behaviorally optimized future would mean considering decision and behavior patterns in advance to shape physical and intangible elements in the tourism ecosystem in ways that make it sustainable and human centered.

Where to start with behavioral optimization?

The collection of cases in the final chapter of this book presents a set of examples illustrating behavior-smart solutions applied across the tourism supply chain. Behavioral thinking can optimize commercial and sustainability aspects of different scale at different levels. First, behavioral thinking can help individual entrepreneurs and companies to optimize commercial aspects such as pricing, promotional content, service and product design, staff training, and management. It can also help optimize sustainability aspects such as energy and water consumption, elimination of single-use plastics, waste generation, and management, social impact. While at first the optimization effect of individual operators might seem small, the cumulative impact generated by many behavior-smart service providers can be quite significant.

A lot can be achieved if some of the largest players in the industry pursue behavioral optimization for sustainability. Large digital platforms apply behaviorally informed tactics when it comes to pricing, promotion, and upselling. What if they also started applying similar tactics to encourage their customers to be more responsible when they visit the place they have just booked? What if they used nudges to encourage travelers to bring a reusable water bottle, to buy locally or to be mindful of a local water shortage problem? Similarly, what if some of the large map service providers incorporate nudges that incentivize responsible travel? What if they allowed users to choose whether they want the fastest and shortest route from point A to point B, or the happiest, most beautiful or most carbon neutral? Perhaps some bold innovation-smart destinations will revolutionize relationships with such large players and experiment with such redesigns.

Second, behavior-smart thinking can optimize destination management efforts by activating behavioral thinking across the different strategic areas of destination leadership, including promotional efforts. As many tourism authorities already realize, managing tourism growth requires reshaping of existing institutional models that place much more focus on marketing without having any influence over all aspects of the destination ecosystem. Behavioral economics can be source of new perspectives and solutions that inform new destination management techniques, including behaviorally informed promotion. Behavior-smart destinations are most likely to start reforming management practices by redefining success and identifying new performance indicators to move away from volume-based ones (see illustration on the Faroe Islands in Chapter 4).

Success measures can incentivize decision makers to focus on increasing arrivals regardless of whether they create any value or to focus on increasing local spending of tourists.

Behavioral thinking can optimize destination marketing too. In addition to informing smart promotion and presentation of destination information, it can transform segmentation. As illustrated in the case with the new tourism strategy of the Netherlands, behavioral segmentation is the best vehicle for identifying and pursuing the target groups that are most appropriate for the destination and its strategic goals. In the pursuit for more focused and selective marketing efforts destinations can be most precise if they identify their future guests based on the consumption behavior they would like to see. This is a significantly different approach from the one that continues to prevail in the industry—geographic segmentation, which targets potential guests solely on the basis of the country or region in which they reside.

The third level at which behavioral thinking can secure optimized performance is destination-level footprint management. The rising importance of proactive management of tourism growth creates the need for proactive setting of desired behavioral norms for both travelers and locally operating service providers. Just like hosts set the protocol for guests coming into their house, destination communities should set the norms for guests coming on their territory. These norms should seek not only to impact the behavior of travelers but also that of all local tourism service providers. For example, if the destination community is interested in protecting a sensitive natural areal located nearby, then no local business should offer services that enable tourists to visit that place. Similarly if it is established that local stakeholders are interested in eliminating single-use plastics from the destination, then all service providers should adjust their offerings to minimize the use of plastics.

Fourth, proactive tourism management requires relevant policies so behavior-smart thinking can inform regulatory adjustments facilitating transition toward desired behavioral norms. Based on careful analysis of where adjustment of incentives and barriers can produce desired impacts destination authorities can seek to formalize rules that shape desired behavioral patterns. Leaning on the earlier example of destination willingness to eliminate single-use plastics, authorities may wish to support voluntary actions by local stakeholders with regulations that, for example, prohibit all local hotels operating in the destination from offering toiletries in small single-use plastic containers. Similarly a public grant or tax incentive program can support local cafes and restaurants to install accessible tap water fountains that minimize the need for buying bottled water and generating plastic waste. There are already some destinations that have declared the ambition to go plastics free and such policies can accelerate the process.

Fifth, as stated earlier in the conclusion, behavior-smart thinking can actually inform the design to new projects for physical infrastructure or intangible solutions. The behavioral perspective can be weaved in from early ideation stage throughout the execution cycle of future projects that lead to investment in physical infrastructure or intangible elements such as technology or skills that enable a high-quality experience. In a human-centered future, destination ecosystems will grow based on behavior-smart perspectives that optimize the interaction between people (travelers and host), physical space, and technology.

Behavior-smart thinking and ethics

Understanding decision making models along with mechanisms that influence behavior comes with new levels of responsibility. Unfortunately, the marketplace offers many examples of companies that use behavioral insights for unethical promotional or pricing practices. With the increasing sensitivity toward behavioral thinking and behavior-smart solutions, such ethical failures will become more evident and easily recognizable by customers and business partners.

Today's industry realities suggest the need to rethink the common take on sustainability. As discussed throughout the book, the reasons why sustainability has not become nonnegotiable are to a large extend behavioral. First, sustainability is not new as a principle but since the beginning it was framed incorrectly as a niche or simply one of the possible ways of doing tourism. In reality sustainability is the only way of doing tourism if industry players want to continue having the business and consumers want to continue traveling. So the behavior-smart approach to sustainability is to reframe it as a nonnegotiable principle of doing tourism that can only encourage desired innovations to move away from tourism with a negative footprint and find ways to make it net-positive.

Second, a sustainable future, whether of tourism or society at large, cannot ignore human happiness. The well-being crisis is largely connected to the sustainability crisis. The broken link between people and nature is just as relevant to environmental health as it is relevant to human health. Tourism has the power to restore it and thus increase the likelihood that people will benefit from nature's recreational services and nature will benefit from increased care.

In this context it may make sense to add to the ingredients that form sustainability the human factor. Perhaps the behavior-smart definition of sustainability suggests the need to balance environmental, social, and economic aspects with the human happiness aspect.

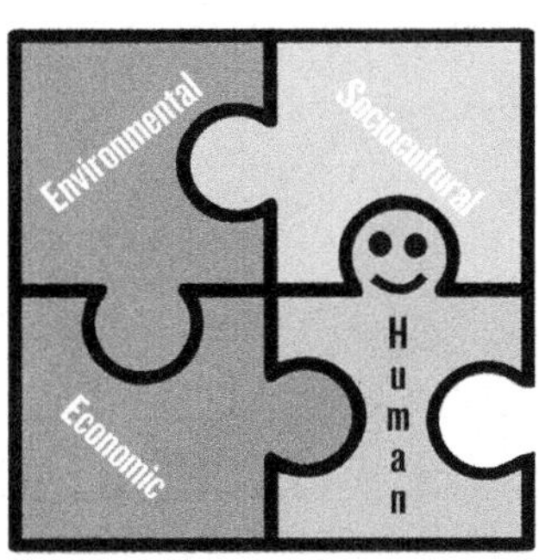

Index

Note: Page numbers followed by "*b*" and "*t*" refer to boxes and tables, respectively.

I

K

L

M

N

O

P

R

S

Made in the USA
Middletown, DE
03 December 2021

54089583R00157